MAGGIE SMITH

Michael Coveney is the theatre critic of the *Observer*. Born in East London in 1948, he was educated at St Ignatius College in North London and Worcester College, Oxford. He worked as a script reader for the Royal Court Theatre before joining the *Financial Times* arts page and subsequently the theatrical monthly *Plays and Players*. He was editor of *Plays and Players* from 1975 to 1978, and theatre critic and deputy arts editor of the *Financial Times* from 1981 to 1989. He has written for many publications, including the *New York Times*. His first book, *The Citz*, a study of Glasgow's famous Citizens' Theatre, received high praise on publication in 1990.

MAGGIE SMITH

A Bright Particular Star

Michael Coveney

VICTOR GOLLANCZ

LONDON

First published in Great Britain 1992
by Victor Gollancz Ltd

First Gollancz Paperback edition published 1993
by Victor Gollancz
A Cassell imprint
Villiers House, 41/47 Strand, London WC2N 5JE

A catalogue record for this book
is available from the British Library

ISBN 0 575 05626 6

Photoset by Rowland Phototypesetting Ltd
Bury St Edmunds, Suffolk
Printed and bound in Great Britain by
Cox and Wyman Ltd, Reading, Berkshire

For my parents and Marie
and
in memory of Nathaniel Smith (1902–1991)

'Of those whose business it is to imitate humanity in general and who do it sometimes admirably, sometimes abominably, some record is due to the world; but the player's art is one that perishes with him, and leaves no traces of itself but in the faint descriptions of the pen.'

WILLIAM HAZLITT

'You have to have been desperately unhappy before you can play comedy, so that nothing can frighten you any more. And you can't do tragedy before you know absolute happiness, because having known that you are safe.'

EDITH EVANS

Contents

Advance Billing

'I saw that Mary Smith in *Maggie Maggie* . . .' The play was really called *Mary Mary*, and Maggie Smith liked the chance, overheard remark because it jumbled up her identity with that of a character who never existed.

Actors use and subsume their personalities in the identities of figments. They want both to hide and to show off. By moulding imaginary characters to their own physical reality, they unwittingly reveal themselves.

And yet, in spite of forty years of revelations, Maggie Smith remains a mystery. She is, in the first place, very funny. But, like the greatest of vaudevillians, she believes that she only properly exists in the spotlight. What she thinks of the world – ghastly and depressing, on the whole – she believes is of no interest to anyone else. One of her chief qualities is her modesty. She is brilliant, and she can be 'difficult'. But she is not grand, and she is not boring. At work, she is obsessive.

She looks at all people, all vanities and all enterprises with a mocking sense of disquiet and disbelief. Her fear and astonishment at the world, allied to her instinctive technical talent, have made her a great stage actress in both comedy and tragedy, and an international film star.

This biography is an attempt not to pin her down, but to catch her on the wing before she flies into the fifth decade of an extraordinary career. She has gone from revue to West End stardom, from the Old Vic before the advent of the National Theatre, to distinction as a founder member of Sir Laurence Olivier's first National Theatre company.

She has won two Hollywood Oscars, four *Evening Standard* Best Actress awards and countless other distinctions. She was married for eight years to Robert Stephens and bore two sons by him. She disappeared from Britain for five years to lead the classical company at Stratford, Ontario, and to make films in Los Angeles.

Her background is ordinary, her talent anything but. Maggie Smith, even to those who know her best, is not only a mystery, but also an enigma. Her inner life is the source of her acting and out of bounds to everyone else. But in setting out to write primarily about acting, I discovered the footmarks of a fascinating and rather unusual personal journey. These are the signs of one Maggie's real existence. The other Maggie's *really* real existence lies in make-believe. Two Maggies, then, as the punter remarked, private and public, inner and outer, off stage and on, both demonic, each dependent on the other and finally indivisible.

I have seen most of Maggie's stage work in London since I first saw her in *The Recruiting Officer* in 1964. The work in Stratford, Ontario, I have seen only on that theatre's excellent video library collection. This was no substitute for the performances in the flesh, but it helped a lot. I have watched, in many cases watched again, every film she has made. And I have tracked down the few television plays that remain extant. I am not the first to complain of the ignominious disposal of much of our acting and writing heritage on television before the video age.

My greatest debt is to Beverley Cross, Maggie's husband, who provided information, contacts and encouragement with business-like precision, good grace and humour.

Maggie's father, the late Nathaniel Smith, lovingly maintained a comprehensive archive in his Oxford home from the minute his daughter first stepped onto a stage. This record goes far beyond being a proud parent's scrapbook. In five bulging volumes it documents a remarkably rich career in all its colour and variety, its ups and downs, its good reviews and stinkers.

Nat (although to me he was always 'Mr Smith') wanted his archive to be used as the database for a book, and in this respect my work has been the fulfilment of an extremely agreeable obligation to him. He became weak and extremely fragile after a fall in March 1991. He was found to be suffering from bone cancer and died a month later in King Edward VII Hospital in Midhurst. In the short time I knew him, Nat was a courteous and willing source of crucial family history and reminiscence.

Ian Smith, Maggie's brother in New York, was equally helpful and punctilious in supplying photographs, memories and, above all, an honest, sometimes painfully honest, appraisal of the family background.

The London Library, as ever, was an essential oasis of reference and research. Other source material, documents, photographs, recordings and viewing facilities were generously loaned or provided by Brian Baxter and Lorraine Dance at BBC Television; Lisa Brant, Ellen Cole and Keith Courtney at the Stratford Festival, Ontario; Steve Bryant, Elaine Burrows, Wayne Drew and Jackie Morris at the British Film Institute; Simon Callow, who supplemented a precious interview with a brilliant, unpublished account of how and why he snared Maggie in Cocteau; Ian Dowling at Redbridge Central Library in Ilford; Keith Jeffery (Shakespeare Prize); John Keble at ITC Entertainment; Alastair Macaulay; Peter Matthews at Filmbank Distributors Ltd; Mrs Elizabeth Sloan, librarian of the Oxford High School for Girls; Kathleen Tynan (estate of the late Kenneth Tynan); Video Palace in Chalk Farm Road, London; Sandy Wilson; and B. A. Young.

I am particularly grateful to David Pelizzari of the Citadel

Theatre in Edmonton, Alberta, who skilfully conducted an important interview on my behalf with Robin Phillips, and to Robin Phillips himself, who took immense trouble over the resultant forty-page document while travelling between Edmonton, New York and Toronto.

The following spared time to be interviewed and in many cases dispensed good cheer and hospitality: Dorothy Bartholomew, Brian Bedford, Isabel van Beers (whose injunction, when I found her in Oxford – 'Well, dear, I'm nearly eighty, I've had a heart attack and three strokes, so you'd better be quick!' – spurred me on), Alan Bennett, Michael Blakemore, Diana Boddington, Margaret Bonfiglioli (née Slater), Ronald Bryden (whose letters, suggestions and warm welcome in Toronto were especially appreciated), Jack Clayton, Michael Codron, Bridget Davidson (née Senior), Dame Judi Dench, Zoë Dominic, Christopher Downes, Patrick Dromgoole, Verrall and Peter Dunlop, Angela Fox, William Gaskill, Sir Peter Hall, Derek Jacobi, Bernard Levin, Kenneth Lintott, Alec McCowen, Joseph Maher, Miriam Margolyes, Patricia Millbourn, John Moffatt, Richard Monette, Riggs O'Hara, Michael Palin, Nicholas Pennell, Stephen Poliakoff, Anthony Powell, Lynn Redgrave, Kate Reid, Peter Shaffer, Ned Sherrin, Shān Smith, Christine Stotesbury (née Miller), Judith Stott, Gary Thomas of the Stratford Festival, Margaret Tyzack and Peter Wood.

Robert Stephens eagerly and inimitably shared his memories of glorious and difficult times while up to his neck in a demanding RSC season at Stratford-upon-Avon. Christopher and Toby, his and Maggie's sons, were illuminatingly proud of both parents, and of Beverley Cross.

I benefited from correspondence and telephone conversations with John Beary; Michael Caine; Ruth Clarke (née Ayers); Bamber Gascoigne; Jeremy Geidt; Alice Ghostley; Sir John Gielgud; Shirley Halstead (née Jenkins); Verena Johnston (née Hunt); Joan Plowright (Lady Olivier); Mrs V. M. Ridgman (estate of the late Pamela Brown); and Tom Stoppard.

Advice, kindness, criticism and good leads were proffered by Michael Billington; Frances Carey; my brother, Martin Coveney; the late Theo Cowan; Ernie Eban; Robert Fox; Tyler Gatchell in New York; Sidney Glazier in New York; my tolerant wife, Sue Hyman; Caradoc King at A. P. Watt Ltd; Janet Macklam; Helen Montagu; Sheridan Morley; Rivka Nachoma in New York; Toby Rowland; my inspiring and enthusiastic editor at Gollancz, Richard Wigmore; and Matt Wolf. My thanks, too, are due to the editor of the *Observer*, Donald Trelford, and to my arts editor, Gillian Widdicombe.

Michael Coveney
London, March 1992

Maggie Smith: Career at a Glance

BORN Ilford, Essex, 28 December 1934; moved with family to Cowley, Oxford, August 1939; Oxford High School for Girls, 1947–51; Oxford Playhouse School, 1951–53; marries Robert Stephens 1967; son Christopher born 19 June 1967; second son Toby born 21 April 1969; divorces Robert Stephens April 1975; marries Beverley Cross 23 August 1975.

NOTE: *F indicates film or movie, ITV, the Independent Television network and dir the director (where known). Maggie's Old Vic performances from 1963 are with the National Theatre, and most of them stayed in the repertoire for at least two or three years after the première. Stratford is always the Canadian version – Maggie has never appeared at Stratford-upon-Avon, England, except once on tour with the NT in* **Much Ado About Nothing**. *1989 was spent recuperating from illness.*

1951
Annaliese in *Children in Uniform* by Christa Winsloe, Cherwell Players in Cowley Road Congregational Church, dir Eva Maria Lorm-Schaffer; Jean in *The Pick-Up Girl* by Elsa Shelley, Oxford Playhouse

1952
Viola in *Twelfth Night* by Shakespeare, OUDS in Mansfield College Gardens, Oxford, dir Alistair McIntosh; Consuela in

He Who Gets Slapped by Andreyev, Clarendon Press Institute, Oxford, dir Peter Bailey; Court Page in *Cinderella*, Oxford Playhouse, dir John Gordon Ash and Frank Shelley

1953
Poppy Dickey in *Rookery Nook* by Ben Travers, Oxford Playhouse, dir Frank Shelley; Button Farringdon in *The Housemaster* by Ian Hay, Oxford Playhouse, dir Frank Shelley; *Cakes and Ale*, OTG Revue at Edinburgh Festival, dir Christopher Bell and Adrian Vale; Charity Gala, Carfax Assembly Rooms, Oxford, dir Ned Sherrin; Mme Frappot in *The Love of Four Colonels* by Peter Ustinov, Oxford Playhouse

1954
Gertrud in *The Ortolan* by Michael Meyer, Marston Hall, Oxford, dir Casper Wrede; Henriette in *Don't Listen, Ladies* by Stephen Powys and Guy Bolton, Oxford Playhouse; School Superintendent's Wife in *The Government Inspector* by Gogol, Oxford Playhouse, dir Peter Hall; Chinese servant in *The Letter* by Somerset Maugham, Oxford Playhouse; Maria in *A Man About the House* by Francis Brett Young, Oxford Playhouse; *On the Mile*, OTG Revue at Edinburgh Festival, dir Christopher Bell and Adrian Vale; *Oxford Accents* (BBC TV) dir Anthony Craxton; *Oxford Accents*, New Watergate, London, dir Ned Sherrin and Jeremy Bullmore; *Theatre 1900*, Oxford Playhouse, dir Peter Hall; West Wind in *Listen to the Wind* by Vivian Ellis and Angela Ainley Jeans, Oxford Playhouse, dir Peter Hall

1955
Beatie Tomlinson in *The Magistrate* by Pinero, Oxford Playhouse, dir Peter Wood; Maria in *The School for Scandal* by Sheridan, Oxford Playhouse, dir Peter Wood; *Oxford Eight*, New Watergate, dir Gareth Wigan and Don Erikson

1956
New Faces, Ethel Barrymore, New York, dir David Thimar and Paul Lynde

1957
Susie in *Boy Meets Girl* by Bella and Sam Spewack (ITV) dir Silvio Narizzano; Orange in *Share My Lettuce* by Bamber Gascoigne, Keith Statham and Patrick Gowers, Lyric Hammersmith, dir Eleanor Fazan

1958
Bridget Howard in *Nowhere to Go* (F) dir Seth Holt; Juliet Denise in *The Widower* by Cyril Campion (ITV) dir Wilfrid Eades; Fairy in *The Curious Savage* by John Patrick (ITV) dir Henry Kaplan; *Sunday out of Season* by Peter Draper (ITV) dir Peter Wood; Vere Dane in *The Stepmother* by Warren Chetham-Strode, St Martin's, London, dir Henry Kaplan

1959
Doto in *A Phoenix Too Frequent* by Christopher Fry (ITV); Lois in *For Services Rendered* by Somerset Maugham (ITV) dir Henry Kaplan; Lady Plyant in *The Double Dealer* by Congreve, Edinburgh Festival and Old Vic, London, dir Michael Benthall; Celia in *As You Like It* by Shakespeare, Old Vic, dir Wendy Toye; Queen in *Richard II* by Shakespeare, Old Vic, dir Val May; Mistress Ford in *The Merry Wives of Windsor* by Shakespeare, Old Vic, dir John Hale

1960
Anna Carnot in *Guardian Angel* by Guy Bolton (ITV) dir Jack Dixon; Maggie Wylie in *What Every Woman Knows* by J. M. Barrie, Old Vic, dir Peter Potter; Jackie Coryton in *Hay Fever* by Coward (ITV) dir Casper Wrede; Daisy in *Rhinoceros* by Ionesco, Strand, London, dir Orson Welles; Penelope in *Penelope* by Somerset Maugham (ITV) dir Mario Prizek; Kathy

Dawson in *Strip the Willow* by Beverley Cross on British tour, dir Val May

1961
Rose in *The Savages* by Peter Draper (ITV) dir Peter Potter; Lucile in *The Rehearsal* by Anouilh, Bristol Old Vic and Globe Theatre, London, dir John Hale

1962
Chantal in *Go to Blazes* (F) dir Michael Truman; Doreen/Belinda in *The Private Ear* and *The Public Eye* by Peter Shaffer, Globe, dir Peter Wood

1963
Mary McKellaway in *Mary Mary* by Jean Kerr, Queen's Theatre, London, dir Joseph Anthony; Miss Mead in *The VIPs* (F) dir Anthony Asquith; Silvia in *The Recruiting Officer* by Farquhar, Old Vic, dir William Gaskill

1964
Desdemona in *Othello* by Shakespeare, Old Vic, dir John Dexter; Hilde Wangel in *The Master Builder* by Ibsen, Old Vic, dir Peter Wood; Philpot in *The Pumpkin Eater* (F) dir Jack Clayton; Myra Arundel in *Hay Fever* by Coward, Old Vic, dir Noël Coward

1965
Nora Creena in *Young Cassidy* (F) dir John Ford and Jack Cardiff; Beatrice in *Much Ado About Nothing* by Shakespeare, Old Vic, dir Franco Zeffirelli; Julie in *Miss Julie* by Strindberg, Chichester Festival Theatre and Old Vic, dir Michael Elliott; Clea in *Black Comedy* by Peter Shaffer, Chichester and Old Vic, dir John Dexter; Desdemona in *Othello* (F), dir Stuart Burge

1966
Marcela in *A Bond Honoured* by John Osborne, Old Vic, dir

John Dexter; Avonia Bunn in *Trelawny of the Wells*, Old Vic, dir Desmond O'Donovan

1967
Beatrice in *Much Ado About Nothing* (BBC TV) dir Alan Cooke; Sarah Watkins in *The Honeypot* (F) dir Joseph Mankiewicz; Victoria in *Home and Beauty* by Maugham (ITV) dir Christopher Hodson

1968
Mrs Wislack in *On Approval* by Lonsdale (ITV) dir Peter Moffatt; Ann Whitefield in *Man and Superman* by Shaw (BBC TV) dir James MacTaggart; Patty Perwilliger in *Hot Millions* (F) dir Eric Till

1969
Jean Brodie in *The Prime of Miss Jean Brodie* (F) dir Ronald Neame; Variety singer in *Oh What A Lovely War!* (F) dir Richard Attenborough; Margery Pinchwife in *The Country Wife* by Wycherley, Chichester, dir Robert Chetwyn

1970
Mrs Sullen in *The Beaux' Stratagem* by Farquhar, Ahmanson Theater, Los Angeles, and Old Vic, dir William Gaskill; Masha in *Three Sisters*, Ahmanson, dir Laurence Olivier; Hedda in *Hedda Gabler* by Ibsen, Cambridge Theatre, London, dir Ingmar Bergman

1971
Gilda in *Design for Living* by Coward, Ahmanson, LA, dir Peter Wood

1972
Portia in *The Merchant of Venice* (BBC TV) dir Cedric Messina; Epifania Fitzfassen in *The Millionairess* by Shaw (BBC TV) dir William Slater; Amanda Prynne in *Private Lives* by Coward, Queen's Theatre, London, dir John Gielgud

1973
Aunt Augusta in *Travels With My Aunt* (F) dir George Cukor; Lila Fisher in *Love and Pain and the Whole Damn Thing* (F) dir Alan J. Pakula; Peter Pan in *Peter Pan*, London Coliseum, dir Robert Helpmann

1974/5
Connie Hudson in *Snap* by Charles Laurence, Vaudeville Theatre, London, dir William Gaskill; Amanda Prynne in *Private Lives* by Coward, Ahmanson, LA (and Chicago, Boston, Denver, Toronto and New York), dir John Gielgud

1976
Millamant in *The Way of the World* by Congreve, Stratford, dir Robin Phillips; Mistress Overdone in *Measure For Measure* by Shakespeare, Stratford, dir Phillips; Cleopatra in *Antony and Cleopatra* by Shakespeare, Stratford, dir Phillips; Dora Charleston in *Murder By Death* (F) dir Robert Moore; Masha in *Three Sisters* by Chekhov, Stratford, dir John Hirsch; The Actress in *The Guardsman* by Molnar, Ahmanson, LA (and Stratford, 1977) dir Phillips

1977
Hippolyta/Titania in *A Midsummer Night's Dream* by Shakespeare, Stratford, dir Phillips; Queen Elizabeth in *Richard III* by Shakespeare, Stratford, dir Phillips; Rosalind in *As You Like It* by Shakespeare, Stratford (and 1978), dir Phillips; Judith Bliss in *Hay Fever* by Coward, Stratford, dir Phillips

1978
Lady Macbeth in *Macbeth* by Shakespeare, Stratford, dir Phillips; Amanda Prynne in *Private Lives* by Coward, Stratford, dir Phillips; Miss Bowers in *Death on the Nile* (F) dir John Guillermin; Diana Barrie in *California Suite* (F) dir Herbert Ross

1979
Ruth Carson in *Night and Day* by Tom Stoppard, Phoenix Theatre, London, Kennedy Center, Washington, and ANTA Theater, New York, dir Peter Wood

1980
Virginia Woolf in *Virginia* by Edna O'Brien, Stratford and Haymarket Theatre, London (in 1981), dir Phillips; Beatrice in *Much Ado About Nothing* by Shakespeare, Stratford, dir Phillips; Arkadina in *The Seagull* by Chekhov, Stratford, dir Phillips

1981
Lois Heidler in *Quartet* (F) dir James Ivory; Thetis in *Clash of the Titans* (F) dir Desmond Davis

1982
Daphne Castle in *Evil Under the Sun* (F) dir Guy Hamilton; Anderson in *Better Late Than Never* (F) dir Bryan Forbes

1983
Lady Isobel Ames in *The Missionary* (F) dir Richard Loncraine; Florence Barlow in *Mrs Silly* by Bob Larbey (ITV) dir James Cellan Jones

1984
Lily Wynn in *Lily in Love* by Frank Cucci (BBC TV) dir Karoly Makk; Millamant in *The Way of the World* by Congreve, Chichester and Haymarket, London, dir William Gaskill; Joyce Chilvers in *A Private Function* (F) dir Malcolm Mowbray

1985
Nadia Ogilvy-Smith in *Interpreters* by Ronald Harwood, Queen's Theatre, London, dir Peter Yates

1986
Charlotte Bartlett in *A Room With A View* (F) dir James Ivory;

Jocasta in *The Infernal Machine* by Cocteau, Lyric Hammersmith, dir Simon Callow

1987/88
Halina Rodziewizowna in *Coming in to Land* by Stephen Poliakoff, National Theatre, dir Peter Hall; Lettice Douffet in *Lettice and Lovage* by Peter Shaffer, Globe, London, dir Michael Blakemore; Judith Hearne in *The Lonely Passion of Judith Hearne* (F) dir Jack Clayton; Susan in *Bed Among the Lentils* by Alan Bennett (BBC TV) dir Alan Bennett

1990
Lettice in *Lettice and Lovage*, Ethel Barrymore, New York

1991
Wendy in *Hook* (F) dir Steven Spielberg

1992
Mrs Pettigrew in *Memento Mori* by Muriel Spark (BBC TV) dir Jack Clayton; Mother Superior in *Sister Act* (F) dir Emile Ardolino

1993
Lady Bracknell in *The Importance of Being Earnest* by Oscar Wilde, Aldwych Theatre, dir Nicholas Hytner; Mrs Venable in *Suddenly Last Summer* by Tennessee Williams (BBC TV), dir Richard Eyre; Mrs Medlock in *The Secret Garden* (F), dir Agnieszka Holland

Overture in New York

IN November 1990, Dame Maggie Smith was coming towards the end of the Broadway run of Peter Shaffer's *Lettice and Lovage* at the Ethel Barrymore Theater. I wrote to her, saying that I was interested in writing a book about her, and that I happened to be coming to New York very soon; that, although we had never met, I wondered if she could spare me a few minutes to discuss the project; and that I had been raised in the place of her birth, Ilford in Essex, before removing, like her, but as an undergraduate, to the more amenable and civilising environment of Oxford.

I did not seriously enter the Ilford/Oxford connection as a qualification for my role as her critical biographer, but the idea of revisiting those respectively mean and pleasant streets in search of clues and details had not been without its appeal. I knew that her father was still alive in Oxford, and that he harboured an extensive archive of his daughter's career.

When I arrived in New York on 14 November, a calm and pleasant Wednesday evening, I checked into the Algonquin Hotel and, on an impulse, before I had even unpacked, wrote Dame Maggie a note announcing my arrival and apologising for pestering her. I remembered to add that if by any chance she had not received my first letter, this second communication would appear both puzzling and impertinent.

I walked three or four blocks across the theatre district to

the Ethel Barrymore Theater and found the stage door. I left
the note, which was passed in my presence to Dame Maggie's
dresser, and took once more to the night air. It was about
9.30 p.m. I now had second thoughts. The star was to be
confronted by a footling and no doubt unwelcome missive
from a London theatre critic. The last thing she needed.
Curses.

I returned to the Algonquin. I was deep in that strange and
enjoyable process of acclimatisation to a new hotel bedroom,
and was slowly unpacking my suitcase, when the telephone
rang. It was 10.45 p.m. and I expected the caller to be one of
three close New York friends whom I was hoping to see in the
next few days.

To my utter astonishment, it was Maggie Smith, who must
have literally just come off the stage (the play, shorter than in
London, was running at two hours, forty minutes, after an
8 p.m. curtain up). My heart was in my mouth, my underpants
in my hands.

The first letter? It had not arrived. This was not a deceptive
ruse. I later discovered it really had not yet filtered through her
secretary's careful grasp. I stumbled out something grotesquely
crass about writing a book. About you.

'Ooh, how absolutely ghastly. How absolutely awful. I can't
think of anything worse.'

The voice twanged and gurgled, rich with the strain of a
demanding performance. I thought of a glass of madeira. She
either sounded like one or needed to drink it. I said, truthfully,
that I could not conceive of anything I would rather write at
the moment than a book about her.

'Ooh, but there's nothing to write about.'

Your career.

'But I haven't done anything.'

Your art.

'I don't know what it is I do.'

While you are still in full flood.

'Surely that sort of thing is only done when you're dead.'

I was still hopelessly flummoxed and rapidly trying to arrange my thoughts into comprehensible utterance; they'd been scrambled by the transatlantic flight and impending slumber. Some banal comment leapt out, to the effect that she must be relieved she was coming to the end of an exhausting run, during which she had suffered the aftermath of a painful back injury and other assorted physical misfortunes.

'Six hundred performances is quite enough. I've told them I can't do the American tour next year. Vanessa's going to do it.'

Vanessa?

'Vanessa Redgrave.'

Of course. As opposed to all the other Vanessas, dumbo. Vanessa had been Miss Brodie on the London stage, but Dame Maggie played the role on the big screen. (Vanessa never did do the tour of *Lettice and Lovage*; she fell out with the management after remarks she made about American involvement in the Gulf War of 1991.)

The conversation suddenly, and alarmingly, became relaxed.

'How do you like the Algonquin?'

Very much, I said, except that I didn't think that they had dusted much since the last time I was here.

'Yes, Michael Blakemore [the director of *Lettice and Lovage*] said something like that.'

How is your hotel?

'Ooh, it's just like a glorified bed and breakfast really.'

It wasn't.

'I can't wait to get home.'

Was there any chance I could call backstage to see her between the shows on Saturday?

'No, I can't do that. Ring me on Friday morning at about eleven o'clock.'

Fine, but I had a ticket for the Saturday matinée.

'Ooh, no, you mustn't do that. It'll be awful at the matinée. Well, do come back. I only said not to because Joe Mankiewicz's maid – do you know Joe?'

I didn't, but knew that this distinguished Hollywood writer and director, creator of the best backstage movie ever, *All About Eve*, had directed her with Rex Harrison in the 1967 remake of Ben Jonson's *Volpone*, *The Honeypot*, and was now very, very old.

'. . . I spend the weekends here with Joe and his wife – their maid, Dolores, is coming to see the matinée. Do you mind sharing with a Spanish maid?'

Of course I didn't, but knew I could hardly raise the topic of my book in mixed company. Almost capriciously, she then added, 'But ring me anyway on Friday morning. I'd better go now because they're all giving me funny looks here.'

I put down the receiver, intrigued by the pictorial notion of Maggie Smith in her dressing room surrounded by a seething mass of disgruntled backstage staff pulling faces at her, wanting to go home. We had been talking for twenty minutes. I unpacked the rest of my clothes, took a shower and went to sleep.

On Thursday, during my perambulations around town, I left a second note at her hotel, suggesting that on Friday we might meet for a quiet coffee or drink, lunch even, at the Pierre or in the Plaza Hotel, somewhere hushed and discreet, as I felt I could not talk turkey in a crowded dressing room.

I rang at the appointed time on Friday morning and she answered instantly. If anything, she sounded even huskier than on Wednesday night. The glass of madeira would no longer suffice. It had to be port, or a fine old cognac. She was unable to meet today because of another meeting about an appointment she had on Monday. She had been thinking about my suggestion. I could hear myself tensing.

'I really don't think it's a very good idea. I still can't think of anything worse. But please come back after the matinée.'

I was now convinced she would have nothing to do with my project, but the more she protested, the more I was determined not to be too downcast. I was telephoning her from the office near the Plaza where I had been working on a feature for the *Observer*. We had another, though necessarily shorter, fairly buoyant conversation.

As its temperature rose, and I emitted several involuntary cackles of laughter, it was my turn to feel funny looks in the back of my neck. I now realised that you could not have a half-cocked, tentative conversation with Maggie Smith. It was all or nothing: usually, nothing. We finished. I should have felt gloomier, but I didn't.

I anticipated the matinée with relish. These were the best sort of days in New York: bright and sharp, sunny and cold. But on Saturday the weather turned foul and the heavens opened. The Ethel Barrymore was heaving with damp mink and fur. A well-heeled, vulgar quartet from Texas pondered the forthcoming entertainment in the bar, one of the men drooling over a semi-clad model in the Playbill programme's advertising pages: 'Too darned bad *she's* not in the show,' he cracked, pleased with himself.

Lettice and Lovage had opened in London in October 1987. Maggie Smith as Lettice Douffet and Margaret Tyzack as Lotte Schoen played at the Globe Theatre for just over a year. (They were succeeded by Geraldine McEwan and Sara Kestelman.) The production opened in New York in March 1990, presented by Robert Fox in partnership with Roger Berlind and the Shubert Organization. As in London, it was directed by Michael Blakemore and designed by Alan Tagg, but had new costumes for Maggie by Anthony Powell.

The delay had been caused by a serious shoulder injury Maggie suffered when she fell off a bicycle. She had also discovered while convalescing that, like Barbara Bush, the wife of the President of the United States, she was afflicted with a hyperthyroid condition known as Graves' disease, which was causing a slight but unflattering distension of the eyeballs. She underwent corrective surgery before coming to New York. As if that wasn't enough, she had had trouble with her teeth throughout the New York run and, towards the end of it, had undergone a root-canal operation.

Thus, while playing one of the longest and most demanding roles of her career – and one of the most successful – she had endured what you might describe as a pretty tough time. Her determination to recover, and the physical discipline required, I later discovered, had been considerable. Despite all these handicaps, New York had been conquered and, in June 1991, both British Maggies won Tony Awards – Smith for Best Actress, Tyzack for Best Supporting Actress.

Lettice Douffet is one of Maggie Smith's greatest triumphs, a role in which she combines bravura comic eccentricity with clear, sustained indications of private grief. The external signs of her extraordinary behaviour as a tourist guide stem from an inner need to dramatise. 'Enlarge! Enliven! Enlighten!' is her battle-cry, as she elaborates dull fact with colourful fiction in the drab hallway of Fustian Hall in Wiltshire.

The play opens with four revue-style snippets of Lettice in action, delivering an increasingly embroidered account of a royal visit and a noble intervention 'on these very stairs' for the benefit of a group of tourists. That group is joined first by an academic cynic. Bending her neck, like a disturbed swan, Smith addresses him sideways: 'Excuse me, but there is a hostility in your voice which implies that what I am saying is an untruth . . . *Smith pause and a deadly, sympathy-gaining inflection as far as the tourist group is concerned, who want to*

believe the unlikely . . . that it is lacking in veracity.' The last
word is laid out like a decorated corpse.

The second, more decisive intervention is made by Lotte
Schoen, a rather brusque and severe representative of the
personnel department in the Preservation (i.e., National)
Trust, who casts severely incredulous aspersions on the
historical information Lettice is feeding the tourists, especially
that story of John Fustian leaping upstairs to stuff fried
hedgehogs into Queen Elizabeth's mouth directly from his
fingers.

After a killingly long pause, Lettice counters with 'I'm sorry
– but I cannot myself get beyond your own behaviour.' This
lights the blue touch-paper, and the audience ignites with a
great, whooshing roar of laughter. They now know whose side
they are on.

Lettice is summoned to Miss Schoen's office in Westminster
to discuss her dismissal on the grounds of unacceptable
embroidery of the dull truth, the everyday, the 'mere' as pronounced by Smith in one of the most contemptuous inflections
in modern drama. She arrives in Westminster dressed in a
black cloak and beret 'like some medieval abbot'. It transpires
that her mother ran a Shakespearean touring company in
France. The inherited histrionic talent of Lettice is cruelly
suppressed by the loss of her job.

The women subsequently meet in Lettice's basement flat in
Earl's Court, where antagonism slowly thaws into friendship.
Their relationship matures through Lettice's enthusiasm for
historical charades, though this leads to an unfortunate accident on Mary Queen of Scots's execution block, and requires
the third act participation of a bemused lawyer called Mr Bardolph. Lettice is consoled throughout by the attentions of her
cat, Felina, Queen of Sorrows.

Maggie Smith exudes in this role a sense of theatre as an
aspect of personality. The performance seemed to me to have

expanded and deepened since the London run. Not a single inflection, glance or gesture was lost in a big house. And Lettice's self-absorption had become a source of magnificent self-defensiveness.

In the second act, Lettice lost her left hand momentarily in a big floppy sleeve. Smith inquisitively shook her wrist and stared at the absent manual appendage with an air of bafflement. A slight, ten-second piece of outrageous comic business was transformed into a wholly comprehensible and revelatory comment on the character's enraptured scattiness.

With a twinge of near-painful recognition, Lettice's defiance of the grey, the analytical, the *sensible*, corresponded for me with the actress's reluctance to be drawn into direct personal combat. Lettice starts with dismay whenever the telephone or the front doorbell rings.

And when Mr Bardolph seeks information for the impending court case on what exactly took place prior to the accident on the scaffold, Lettice gives the tape-recorder the most terrible stare, arching backwards from the contraption and responding frostily and monosyllabically – 'Correct!' – to the early questions. Interviews are not Lettice's forte, nor are they Maggie Smith's.

The performance was magnificent, and the audience thought so, too. They stood and cheered, a rare occurrence at a weekend matinée, even at a 'hit show' towards which any Broadway audience is automatically well disposed. I later learned that every single performance of this play on Broadway was similarly received. 'They're ovating again,' the star would breathe delightedly in the wings.

I went backstage as bidden, but when I was ushered into the dressing room, there was no sign of Dolores, the Spanish maid. Dame Maggie was wrapped in a grey dressing gown, shaking out her luxuriant ginger mane, having given it a quick wash, and sipping half a glass of something red. Perhaps, after all, it was madeira. The flowers I had sent in earlier were beautifully displayed in a large glass vase.

I stood awkwardly blurting out a few comments which she received graciously, curtsying deeply in a very Lettice-like mock-Elizabethan style, one hand clasping both woolly lapels over her chest, as I unleashed the more glutinous of my remarks. She was ticking off each performance and dying to get home.

I said she was certain to need a rest before the evening show as I backed towards the door. This tiny, frail and bird-like creature had to be popped back in its cage for a couple of hours. Had she thought any further on the book? She really did think it was a very bad idea.

Before she finally closed the door on me, should I not speak to her husband, the film and theatre writer Beverley Cross? She immediately wrote out the home telephone number in West Sussex and told me to ring him. She said that she would 'warn' him of my approaches. That was it, as far as she was concerned. And, I felt, as far as I was concerned. I left the Ethel Barrymore in the deepening gloom and swirling rain.

On returning to London from New York, I immediately rang Beverley Cross. I was absolutely astonished to learn that he was keen that I should proceed. He confirmed the existence of the archive in Oxford and promised that it would be made available to me. Other proposed studies of Dame Maggie – a *New Yorker* profile by Kenneth Tynan and authorised books by Penelope Gilliatt and B. A. Young – had all come to nought. It was high time a book was written, he said, and both he and Dame Maggie would extend their co-operation to me as far as was reasonably possible.

The Flight from Ilford

MAGGIE SMITH was born in Clayhall, a residential district in Ilford, Essex, on 28 December 1934. She moved with her family to Oxford in 1939, attended the Oxford High School for Girls from 1947 to 1951, spent two years as a student with the Oxford Playhouse Drama School, took part in countless University productions and made her London début in October 1954 at the New Watergate Theatre Club. In 1956 she went to New York and appeared on Broadway in Leonard Sillman's *New Faces* revue of 1956 at the Ethel Barrymore Theater where, over thirty years later, she appeared in *Lettice and Lovage*.

'One went to school, one wanted to act, one started to act and one's still acting.' That is how Dame Maggie Smith sums up her life. There's a little more to it than that.

Ilford, a bustling, featureless urban sprawl which is part of the great East London overspill, is not a place bursting with show-business connotations. Will Kempe, Shakespeare's clown, is said to have danced through Ilford in 1599 en route from London to Norwich in East Anglia. He stopped only long enough to refresh himself from 'the Great Spoon'.

Not a lot happened after that, give or take the odd murder behind a privet hedge, until Ilford was granted borough status in 1926. The great housing development programmes gathered steam. The process had started before the First World War, with the new Pooters and professional classes occupying the creeping network of solid Edwardian villas which began slowly to displace the Essex fields and meadows beyond Whitechapel and Shoreditch.

The population intensified with the coming of the railway and the access it gave to the City of London. Ilford and its abutting neighbourhoods of Woodford, Clayhall, Gants Hill, Seven Kings and Goodmayes became convenient and popular dormitory suburbs in the south west of Essex, ideal for the lower-middle-class white-collar clerical and professional workforce engaged in local light industry and the City itself.

The working-class rump was centred on the Becontree Estate in Dagenham. Started in 1921 and completed in 1932, the estate was one of the London County Council's first serious attempts to relieve the congested areas in the metropolis. Ilford and environs were solidly lower-middle class. The idea of aspiration was reflected in the naming of some roads as 'Gardens', to lend an air of gentrification.

As a schoolboy there myself in the 1950s, I have a dim memory of an incongruous nightclub called the Room at the Top, on the top floor of the department store, Harrison Gibson. David Frost, Tommy Cooper, Barry Humphries and many other big, but mostly smaller, names appeared there quite regularly during the 1960s. And the Ilford Palais, where Jimmy Savile and Noel Edmonds, long-serving BBC disc-jockeys, worked early in their careers, enjoyed a county-wide notoriety. Both showbiz venues survive today under different, garishly inappropriate monikers: the first as the Penthouse Suite, the second as Fifth Avenue. They'll be renaming Harrison Gibson the Trump Tower before too long.

You could hardly imagine a less likely cradle for the most stylishly dazzling and instinctively gifted comic actress of our day. But Ilford did not produce only Maggie Smith. Ian Holm, the incisive film and Shakespearean actor, and Ken Campbell, the remarkable stage raconteur and dabbler in alternative culture, are two of the best known sons of Ilford.

Dudley Moore, the composer and film star who made his name in the revue *Beyond the Fringe*, was born in Dagenham. And, skipping backwards, an actress whose transatlantic fame equalled, and in some ways anticipated, Maggie Smith's, Lynn Fontanne, later Mrs Alfred Lunt, was born in 1887 in Woodford Bridge, an altogether leafier and more exclusive district than Clayhall, but hardly a bus stop or two away.

Margaret Natalie Smith, the third child of Nathaniel, or Nat, Smith, and his wife, Meg, was born in 68 Northwood Gardens. Margaret – she became 'Maggie' only in 1956 before going to America – was a pretty and mischievous little girl who was not particularly welcomed by her two elder brothers. Alistair and Ian, identical twins, had been born six years earlier on 8 December 1928, and were quite content with each other's company.

The curious product of this Nat/Meg tree was a bundle of genealogical roots of ordinary working-class provenance but unusual vivacity. By the age of ten, Alistair and Ian had decided to become architects. Margaret cannot remember not wanting to be an actress. All three children did as they chose. But there was very little in their background to encourage them.

That background is essential to an understanding of Maggie Smith's personality. Her father, a medical laboratory technician, was a Geordie, from Newcastle. Her mother was a cold and dour Glaswegian. Both parents, like many working-class people, harboured ambitions for their children. They were strict, they were thrifty, they were sticklers for good manners and proper conduct, and they were church-goers. Nat was a devout Anglican, mainstream Church of England, Meg a Scottish Presbyterian.

In Ilford, and later in Oxford, Maggie lived in comfortable,

but cramped, surroundings. She is renowned today for the
stifled aside, the muttered barb, the slightly malicious crack.
You can see why. From an early age she developed two characteristics that are stamped through her professional life like the
lettering in a stick of seaside rock: a keen sense of irreverence
and a sharp instinct for privacy.

She was a lonely child, at odds with her parents, with her
school, with her brothers and even with herself. But her
instinct was not to rebel; it was to mock tartly from the sidelines
and to retain, by stealth, her own spirit and independence. A
quiet life in a semi-detached house in Cowley, the Oxford
suburb to which the family moved in 1939, was not for her.
Cowley, like Ilford, was sleepy, respectable and slightly dull.
The front box-bedroom she was obliged to inhabit through her
teenage years and early adulthood measured scarcely twenty
square feet.

Maggie's parents, too, had made telling adjustments to
family expectations. Her father, born in 1902, was the seventh
of nine children. Of just about average height and slim build,
he was a delicate, chirpy fellow, rather bird-like, with surprisingly elegant wrists and fingers. Maggie's 'wrist work' and
elegantly tapering digits are two of her hallmarks.

Nat had bright orange hair as a youngster and was nicknamed 'Carrot-head'. His father, a keen gambler and a hard-
ened drinker, was a minor post office official who travelled for
years on business between Newcastle and Birmingham. Ian,
Maggie's surviving twin brother (Alistair died suddenly of a
heart attack in 1981) remembers the occasional family holiday
in Scotland; but neither Nat nor his young family ever went
back to Newcastle. Nat had been glad to get away.

Nat's family was religious, in spite of his father's faults, and
young Nat was a dedicated church-goer and choirboy. Though
their domestic circumstances were penurious, Jesmond, the
Newcastle suburb where they lived, had a touch of class. Nat

particularly liked the ecclesiastical garb of surplices and cass-
ocks which was provided by a rich shipowner in the parish
church; underneath, he wore his ordinary clothes, unlike the
other boys, who all wore Eton suits. In later life, Nat could
preach and he could lecture and he always enjoyed the cere-
monies of the church. A performing instinct of some kind was
in his genes.

He had, in fact, been named after an actor, his uncle Nathaniel Gregory who, aged about twenty, had, in Nat's words,
'shown a tendency towards the artistic life.' This Uncle Nat had
consequently fallen out with his father, and had joined the army
as an entertainer during the Boer War at the turn of the century.
His repertoire consisted of music-hall monologues, chiefly
those of Bransby Williams. He later lived in Australia.

This dramatic relation figured only once in Nat's memory.
As a boy of twelve or thirteen, he remembers a middle-aged
Uncle Nat paying a call, appearing over the brow of a Jesmond
slope in a tight black coat with an astrakhan collar, wielding
a malacca cane with a silver knob. There was no question,
said Nat, of him not being an actor. 'He was pedantic of speech
and quoted Shakespeare all the time, which staggered the
household.'

Shortly afterwards, Uncle Nat, who was appearing at the
Newcastle Hippodrome, cycled to Whitley Bay to visit Doris
Rogers, the girl he was planning to marry. He suffered a heart
attack, fell off his bike and died on the spot.

A year or so later, in 1918, young Nat left school and began
menial work in the local medical college. He took a diploma
as a laboratory technician and learned so much about morbid
pathology that he was lecturing in the subject three years later,
at the age of nineteen. One of the Newcastle laboratory dem-
onstrators was appointed to a children's hospital in the East
End of London. He wanted a technician and offered Nat the
job; thus Nat moved south and started work in the Princess

Elizabeth Hospital next to the Meredith and Drew biscuit factory in Shadwell.

Meg, whom Nat had met in Newcastle, where she had lived for a while in digs, had already moved to London. Six years older than Nat, she was living in Russell Square and working as head cashier for the London office of Maxwell Hart in Victoria Street. The company designed and built municipal parks, tennis courts, bowling greens and golf courses. Meg had originally worked for them in Glasgow. She married Nat at the Presbyterian Church in Regent Square, Grays Inn Road, on 2 January 1928. She continued working, but not for long: Ian and Alistair were born at the end of the year.

Meg – christened Margaret Little Hutton – was of mixed Celtic extraction. Her grandmother was born in Newry, Northern Ireland. Her father was an illiterate Glaswegian shipyard worker who could do no more than make his mark on Meg's birth certificate. Meg left school in 1911 or 1912 to work in a laundry where, says Ian, 'the hard and degrading work instilled in her a life-long horror of such soul-destroying employment.'

She must have acquired secretarial skills at night school, because she subsequently worked in the offices of the Gleniffer Motor Company in Glasgow (and in Fraserburgh on the east coast of Scotland) which made marine engines. She then joined Maxwell Hart in 1918 or 1919. She was obviously highly valued by the company, and was appointed to the London office at some time in the early 1920s.

Meg had a natural flair for figures. Nat said she could add up three columns of pounds, shillings and pence simultaneously. She counted money carefully all her life. But Ian also recalls her flair for drawing, which both he and Alistair inherited. She was both practical and resourceful, and made all of Margaret's clothes when she was growing up.

Once married, Nat and Meg found a house in Barkingside,

Ilford. Over the ten years they spent in Ilford, they owned three houses, never selling one when they bought the next, but renting it out. Meg supervised the rent collection and all the family's finances. The boys were born in the second house, in Martley Drive, very near Northwood Gardens.

Young Margaret never got on particularly well with her mother; Ian recalls that Meg was not a woman capable of showing her children much affection, although she was fiercely protective of them. Her daughter would later draw almost callously upon this icy temperament and brusque organisational manner in her Oscar-winning performance in *The Prime of Miss Jean Brodie*.

Ironically, it was only at this advanced point in Maggie's career that her mother stopped trying to convince her that she should do something sensible, such as a secretarial course, as an insurance against the vagaries of the theatre.

She wanted the best for her children, and she believed in hard work. It was indicative of Meg's dominance on important household matters that, after she and Nat were married, they joined the Presbyterian, not the Anglican, congregation in Ilford. Ian remembers his father giving sermons as a lay Presbyterian preacher.

The house in Northwood Gardens was one of eighteen houses constructed in 1934 by the one builder. The neighbourhood was developed in batches as the farmland was sold off and the council gave approval.

Today, number 68 looks very much as it would have done then, and there have been no architectural alterations. It is in the middle of a terrace of four properties, built on two floors. Downstairs, there is a hallway, front sitting room with a bay window, a dining room and a kitchen; upstairs, three bedrooms, bathroom and lavatory; a small front garden and a longer back one of a hundred feet complete the facilities. The façade is half brickwork, half pebble dash.

Many of the local residents have lived here since the houses were built. It is a quiet, pleasant but unarguably bland environment. Ian remembers the 'terrible housing estates' going up around them. He found Ilford dreary beyond measure. One consolation was Clayhall Park, at the top of Northwood Gardens, a little oasis of flower-beds and greenery where perambulators could be pushed and fresh air taken.

And, a little further towards the centre of Ilford, on the other side of the London arterial road, there was Valentines Park, a sanctuary in olden times, which still exudes something of a holiday atmosphere with its pleasant walks, decrepit wishing-well, artificial lakes, cricket club, cedars and rhododendron dells.

There is no bard of Ilford, but the poet Kathleen Raine, who was born there in 1908, has evocatively described the provisional exile she experienced before being saved by her vocation and geographical removal. Her parentage is remarkably similar to Maggie's: her father, a teacher of Latin and English literature, was a Northumbrian miner's son and a zealous Methodist (who, like Nat, was a lay preacher in his place of worship, the Cranbrook Park Wesleyan Methodist Church), and her mother was a parsimonious Scotswoman from Edinburgh who took money very seriously.

In the first volume of her autobiography, Raine registers dismay at the invasion of the Essex countryside by the proliferating estates and their tidy little secret families of shopkeepers and commercial travellers with their well-weeded gardens and small ambitions: 'Ilford, considered as a spiritual state, is the place of those who do not wish to be (or who cannot be) fully conscious, because full consciousness would perhaps make life unendurable.'

Kathleen Raine escaped from Ilford, with her poetic soul intact, to live an early life in a Northumbrian hamlet where she was closer to nature and to the mysterious challenges of a more dramatic landscape. She became a writer. Maggie and her family carried the suburban blight of Ilford with them to Cowley, and although she could never articulate her resentment, it is clear that Maggie channelled her spiritual rebellion into an ambition to enter the theatre. She no more belonged in Ilford than did Kathleen Raine.

Maggie and her brothers were all christened on the same day in the summer of 1935. Ian is certain that the ceremony was performed in the Presbyterian Church on the Cranbrook Road, where it bifurcates into The Drive, almost directly adjacent to the boating lake in Valentines Park. This was Wycliffe Church, a fine 1907 listed building which ceased ecclesiastical operations in 1969, when it became a theatre, home for the town's amateur drama companies, most notably James Cooper's Renegades.

At her own blessing, therefore, you could say that the swaddled, infant Maggie blessed a theatre. Today, however, after several years of closure, the handsome façade conceals nothing more exciting than several floors of offices, two of them occupied by the Abbey National Building Society.

Ian and Alistair attended the Gearies primary school in Barkingside. In March 1939, they took the written examination, later called the eleven-plus, and won scholarships to Ilford County High School, one of the best grammar schools in Essex.

Significantly, Nat told me that his sons had won places at Bancroft's School, a minor public school in Chigwell. This slip of memory reveals the extent to which aspiration sometimes outstripped reality. Nat's entire professional life, worthy though it was, smacked a little of disappointment.

He was a lab technician whose only bar to professional distinction was his lack of qualifications, rather like the tramp in the Dudley Moore and Peter Cook sketch who shakes his head and says he could have been a High Court judge, 'but I didn't have the Latin.' And yet Nat's career was more than honourable. He took immense pride in his forensic medicine, and his complete absorption in it, as well as his dedication and ceaseless scavenging for detail, is surely reflected in his daughter's obsessive approach to her work.

Maggie Smith is renowned for never ceasing to dig and delve in her texts. In rehearsals, she will habitually withdraw from the company coffee break and be found poring over the script at the back of the room. Even on the last night of a run she will sit in her dressing room transfixed over her script, puzzling out what else it might contain. She does not, as an artist, deal in cloudy notions or broad concepts. She works on the line, on the word, and she does so with brutal, scientific precision and persistence.

In 1962, Nat made a list of the eleven items published in medical journals which he had either written or co-written. The first is dated November 1934, the month before Margaret was born, and is titled *Case of Acholuric Jaundice*. Other titles include *The Role of Muscle in Obesity* (1936), *The Bactericidal Action of Isoniazid, Streptomycin and Terramycin on Extracellular Tubercle Bacilli* (1953), and *Vole Bacillus Vaccination in Guinea Pigs: Comparison of Immunisation produced by Virulent and Attenuated Strains of Vole Bacillus* (1962).

Come again, what was it Nat did? Ilford may have been on the sleepy side, but armed with his basic knowledge of morbid pathology, Nat settled into work at Shadwell and, in his own words, 'saw life.' In this busy children's hospital, Nat acquired what amounted to a good grounding in practical medicine. He learned haematology, though very little was known in those days about diabetes and anaemia; bacteriology – the hospital was overrun with cases of scarlet fever, whooping cough, chicken pox and measles; dermatology; and biochemistry. His later work on tubercular vaccines belongs to his Oxford career.

The work in Shadwell was incessant. Nat remembered how

· he would arrive home on a Friday night, exhausted, 'and the phone would ring at four in the morning. There was a case of meningitis, say, needing a lumbar puncture, and I would have to get dressed and back to the hospital. I nearly went bonkers. On one occasion, when I'd had no sleep for two or three days, I broke down. And yet I loved every second of it.'

In 1938, Nat volunteered, in the event of war, for 'work of national importance'. When Neville Chamberlain returned to England with his little piece of white paper and the Munich Agreement, Ian recalls that the family spent the period of the crisis at a vicarage in Norfolk. Nat and a neighbour in Northwood Gardens had concluded that, if hostilities broke out, there would be an immediate holocaust in London. So the children were despatched to Hawkeden, near Bury St Edmunds, where young Margaret gave her ever-watchful mother cause for yet more distress by wandering blithely through a field full of beehives.

The minute war was declared on Germany in September 1939, Nat was posted to Oxford and instructed to report to the Dunn School of Pathology in South Parks Road. Thanks to neighbours in Ilford, he found digs in nearby Museum Road. At the end of the month, Meg and the children received the call from Nat to join him. They all stayed for a short while in Museum Road until a new family home was found. This was about two miles south east of the centre of Oxford, along the Iffley Road in Cowley.

As Europe went to war, the Smith family began a new life in 55 Church Hill Road. The house was very much like the one in Northwood Gardens, but with the advantage of being semi-detached. Nat's work became even more complex and interesting. The twins secured places at the City of Oxford High School. And little Margaret, nearly five, was enrolled at the neighbouring church school, St James's. She later moved to Greycotes, a fee-paying kindergarten and preparatory school on the Banbury Road.

Thanks to Adolf Hitler, the escape from Ilford was complete. Nat's collection of second-hand books, which he kept at Shadwell, was lost in a bombing attack. Meg sold all three Ilford houses, and the income, though not exorbitant, would help pay for the school fees at Greycotes and a new set of boys' school uniforms. Only the best, as far as Nat and Meg could afford it, would do.

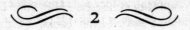

2

Oxford Accents

THE making of an actor is an odd, mostly incalculable, business. But Oxford definitely made Margaret Smith an actress. Her thespian development was part circumstantial, part temperamental. Although she has remained ambiguous on the subject of Oxford all her subsequent life, young Margaret found more room to manoeuvre and thrive than she would ever have done in Ilford.

The family became, in a quiet way, an integral part of the medical and intellectual life of the city. Cowley may have been on the suburban fringe, but Nat, as a technician at the Dunn School, was involved in a body of work on penicillin therapy that was, in the words of the *Encyclopaedia of Oxford*, 'among the most valuable undertaken in the whole history of medicine'. The work was led by Howard Walter Florey, later Lord Florey of Adelaide, who in 1945 shared the Nobel Prize for medicine with Sir Ernst Boris Chain and Sir Alexander Fleming, who had discovered penicillin in 1928.

The new house was built between the wars on an estate next to the vicarage of St James's Church, a High Anglican establishment where Margaret attended the infants' school and her brothers painted theatrical scenery for the social club. There was a modest garden, nearby fields and a cemetery where ghoulish games were played. Margaret claims to have been compelled by her brothers to eat deadly nightshade, though Ian has no memory of this.

Inevitably, 'the boys', as they were known to everyone, grew further apart from Margaret. Their back bedroom, cluttered with set squares, drawing equipment and two large elephant boards, was out of bounds to the little girl, who was nonetheless adept at making a nuisance of herself by stealing their pencils. There were hardly any toys in the house. It was a spartan, though certainly not deprived, childhood.

Years later, Alistair's widow, Shān Smith, recalled a striking detail: at Christmas, the children were never given presents, but ten shillings each, and were told to go and buy what they wanted. Shān, who came from a stable middle-class Welsh background, maintains that all three Smith children, partly because of a repressive childhood, suffered from black depressions and a sense of failure that would haunt them all their lives. Today, Maggie does not, on the whole, look on the bright side of life. Gaiety and good cheer tend to be reserved for her performances, or at least some of them.

The next-door neighbours, the Jenkins family at Number 53, were considered a slightly 'rackety' crowd. Margaret was allowed to be friends with Shirley Jenkins under some degree of sufferance from Meg. Shirley herself, just four months older than Margaret, married an American airman at the age of eighteen and left Oxford for the United States. She remembers Nat doing little magic tricks at children's tea-parties. Shirley used to play the piano loudly in order to gain Margaret's attention, and Margaret would bang on the wall with a poker to let Shirley know that she could hear the music. Meg used the same poker to bang on the wall as a signal to Margaret that it was time to come home.

'During the summers,' Shirley recalls, 'we would, along with other neighbourhood children, do "concerts" in our back gardens. Dancing and singing and dressing up. We did all the usual childhood things – hide and seek, hopscotch, skipping, rolling hoops, whips and tops, frozen statues . . . In the spring we would ride our bikes to Radley Woods and pick armfuls of bluebells.'

The apparent normality of this childhood was a mask for an unusually strict atmosphere in the home. Ian does not remember Margaret being naughty, but there was a marked antagonism between her and Meg: 'It never erupted into the open; it just sort of simmered.' But she was certainly the apple of Nat's eye.

The boys were allowed neither bikes nor roller-skates, and Meg forbade them to play rugby at school. If one of the children was scratched or bruised, bandages were efficiently applied, but the underlying parental attitude was 'What did you do that for?' as though, Ian says, one had done it deliberately.

Holidays were a rarity. And relatives were hardly ever made welcome. There was very little money – Nat was never well paid – and Meg watched every single penny. She had a job as an accounts secretary at the local Morris Motors car-manufacturing plant and was out every day. Margaret, cast as Cinderella from a very early age, did most of the ironing and cleaning around the house. She cannot recall her mother *not* going out to work.

Money was found for some things. While the boys settled into their new school and started on the long haul to fulfilling their ambition to become architects, Margaret moved from the little church school to Greycotes. One of her friends there was Graham Greene's daughter, Lucy, who was one year older but shared the same birthday. ·

There was a piano in the house for a time, and Margaret went across the road for lessons with Mrs Loxton. Margaret was no new Moura Lympany. Her skills were rudimentary, but useful in later professional life when she was obliged to act at the keyboard, as in *The Guardsman* on stage and A

Private Function on film. She also took ballet classes at the Vera Legge School of Dancing in a studio on the top floor of Taphouse's (now Debenham's) in Magdalen Street, equidistant by about fifty yards from both the Playhouse and the New Theatre.

No Oxford pantomime was complete in those days without a pirouetting band of Vera's pre-pubescent chorines, who were billed as 'Vera Legge's Juveniles'. There are photographs of the nine-year-old Margaret in her red satin blouse (with the initials 'VL' on the left breast), white pleated skirt and red ballet pumps, posing unpromisingly in the Church Hill Road back garden.

Ian remembers his sister tap-dancing on the top of the Morrison shelter, the big steel table which families jammed into their dining rooms during the war in case of a bomb attack. For most of the time they sat around it as a dining table, but could, if need be, crowd underneath and zip up the steel sides for protection against falling masonry. No such alarm was raised in Oxford. Ian's only dramatic memory of the Smiths' Morrison shelter was of Margaret dancing on it: 'She certainly gave a performance. I think she was pretty good. I was impressed.'

Though Margaret did not herself appear at the New Theatre in pantomime, the possibilities of performance as an escape from suffocating home life must have loomed invitingly, if not necessarily more powerfully than for any girl of Margaret's age.

She first 'went public', according to Nat, after one of her ballet lessons. Still attired in blouse, skirt and pumps, she was taken shopping by her mother. While Meg went inside to join a queue, Margaret stayed outside on the pavement to regale a small crowd with one of Arthur Askey's popular ditties: 'I'm a little fairy flower, growing wilder by the hour.'

There were few outings to theatre or cinema, though Maggie does remember seeing *The Shop at Sly Corner*, a popular thriller, at the Playhouse in the late 1940s and being so impressed by John Moffatt's performance that she asked for his autograph. She worked many times with Moffatt in later life. His was the only autograph she remembers ever collecting. She saw her first movie, *The Jolson Story*, in 1946. She didn't think much of it, and thought even less when Nat beat her for going to the cinema in the first place.

Otherwise, life was unexceptional after the war. Margaret continued at Greycotes through the freezing cold winter of 1946/47. Port Meadow froze over, and Maggie recalls her friend Lucy Greene's father, the distinguished novelist, materialising before them like a great tall bear in a huge grey coat. Nat says that Margaret was a delightful, happy creature through early adolescence, but Ian speaks of 'a very rigid, inflexible upbringing and a humourless childhood. That Maggie managed to break out of it as she did is all the more remarkable.'

The children were beaten for any minor transgression. Bottoms were bared and Nat would do his duty with a leather belt. This was nothing unusual in working and lower-middle-class families of the period. Neighbours, however, only saw an almost perfect small family, industrious and well-mannered, with two clever boys and a sweet little girl. A correspondent in the Cowley *Chronicle* of May 1970, Michael Clifford, painted a bright picture of Margaret aged twelve or thirteen:

'She could have been the inspiration for a Ronald Searle cartoon schoolgirl. Her red hair hung in a pair of long plaits, she had a freckled face and her teeth were rather agonisingly corrected from a Bugs Bunny aspect by a fierce metal brace which she parked on every possible occasion when her mother was not around. She was also as thin as a cocktail stick . . . Yet attractive she was even then. Her eyes were glorious and her delightful character sparkled through them. She was a born comedian and the actress showed in her brilliant recapitulation of things which had happened to her. Both my mother and I can remember our convulsions of mirth when Maggie recounted her efforts at making a white sauce in domestic science – a sauce which even the sink rejected as unpalatable.'

A charming little school essay at about this time, 1946, gives a clue to future obsessions. It concerns the 'Jimbies', no doubt an afterthought to Edward Lear's Jumblies, in a 'nonsensical essay and a deal of truth'. These jimbies, of no special shape, are like gremlins who get into the mechanics of a theatre and mess things up. Having isolated the problem, the young essayist outlines the steps to be taken: 'The only way to rid your theatre of them is to spray it regularly with DDT and spirit gum – and to drink as much tonic water and black coffee as possible.'

In the summer term of 1947, she went on an assisted place to Oxford High School for Girls, one of the best schools in Britain. Its list of old girls includes the former headmistress and moral scientist Dame Mary Warnock, the writer Rose Macaulay, the poet Elizabeth Jennings, the academic Helen Darbishire, and the young conductor – the first woman ever to wave the baton in the pit of the Royal Opera House, Covent Garden, and the new music director of English National Opera – Sian Edwards.

During her four years there, in spite of being remembered for the imagination she brought to English composition, Margaret made little academic impression and hardly any at all as an actress. Nonetheless, her school years had a considerable, if negative, influence in determining her future on the stage.

The boys went from strength to strength. On arrival from Ilford, Ian and Alistair had gone for interviews at the City of Oxford High School, just across the road from the New (now the Apollo) Theatre in George Street. Ian remembers that both he and Alistair had been struck by the story of Lawrence of Arabia, a fact that emerged in the course of the interview. The master said that T. E. Lawrence had been at the school at the turn of the century, and that therefore the twins had better be enrolled in Lawrence House.

The new world of physics and mathematics excited the boys very much, but they were even more impressed by their new surroundings. The school had been designed in the late 1870s by Sir Thomas Jackson (who had also designed the Examinations Schools in the High, and several other Oxford buildings, in the Early English Renaissance style), and they came to this architecturally meritorious haven after attending a primary school in Ilford of no architectural distinction whatsoever.

It was taken for granted that Ian and Alistair would become architects. They were precociously good draughtsmen and would go into the city in every spare moment to draw. When it came to the Schools Certificate, the teachers baulked at allowing them to take the architecture paper, chiefly because the school didn't teach it. But after pressing their case, they were allowed to sit the exam. At the age of fourteen, both gained distinctions.

Alistair, who was counted the brighter of two very bright boys, took his Higher Schools Certificate two years later in 1944, but Ian had already left, impatient to start studying at the School of Architecture within the Schools of Technology, Art and Commerce, now the Polytechnic in Headington.

A contemporary at the School of Architecture was Ronald Barker, later to become one of Britain's most popular television comedy actors. He, too, had grown up in Cowley and had been in the same class as the boys at the High School, where he was remembered as 'the fat boy who made everybody laugh'. He only studied architecture for one term. After a brief career as a bank clerk, the stage beckoned.

When Alistair joined Ian at the School, he caught up with him on the five-year course, compressing his studies into four, and both took the final examinations in 1949, aged twenty.

The minimum age for election to the Royal Institute of British Architects is twenty-one. Ian and Alistair kicked their heels for a time before leaving Church Hill Road, and Oxford, for good in 1950. They went to London and shared a flat in Peel Street, Kensington.

Margaret had no intention of competing with this sort of academic distinction. The trouble was that such a performance was expected from every girl at the High School. It still is today. An article on independent schools in the *Financial Times* in November 1990 revealed that forty-five per cent of the Advanced Levels achieved at the OHS were A grades.

In the summer of 1951, Margaret Smith was in the first batch of British girls to take the new General Certificate of Education at Ordinary Level. She managed to scrape four unimpressive passes, in English Language, English Literature (her best result: 54/100), French (by one mark) and art; she failed, quite badly, in history, geography and biology. She had not fitted in. One month before he died, Nat waxed more maudlin than usual on this subject:

'Even as a child, Margaret lived in a world where she was conscious of failure. She was a gorgeously happy child but one couldn't help but recognise that, beneath it all, there was a private world that Mother or Dad had no access to . . . She was very open as a girl, but I don't think she was entirely happy at the High School. The teacher in English was part of the cause, the one who stopped her acting in the play . . .'

That teacher was Dorothy Bartholomew, of whom more anon, and the play was *Twelfth Night* in which Margaret was cast as a page when she had set her heart on Viola or Feste. Ian saw this production: 'Her part was to come on between the acts and announce the scene changes by holding up a big piece of cardboard. She would then bow, and go off. There was no sign at all of this being the first step in an illustrious career!'

In a curious way, however, it was. The whole experience of the Oxford High School had the effect of concentrating Margaret's ambition elsewhere.

The school, founded in 1875, was the eighth of the great Girls' Public Day Schools Company. Its first prospectus declared its aim of receiving girls from all walks of life and of providing them with 'an education as thorough if not as extensive as that which their brothers are receiving at the public schools.' Its first home was the Judges' Lodgings in St Giles, but a new building was erected on the Banbury Road in 1880. Charles Dodgson, the mathematician of Christ Church better known as Lewis Carroll, the author of *Alice's Adventures in Wonderland*, delivered some lectures in logic at the school in 1887. The library still has several dedicated copies, in both English and German, of Carroll's most celebrated book.

Daughters of the University's intellectual élite, not surprisingly, dominated the school. Coincidentally, one of these privileged girls was a certain early twentieth century Maggie Smith, 'deliciously pretty' according to her contemporary, Lady Hilda Cash (née Napier), whose father, A. L. Smith, was a famous University activist, sportsman, educationalist and Master of Balliol. In Margaret Smith's time, one of the school's star pupils was Paquita Florey, daughter of the Professor of Pathology for whom Nat worked.

The building on Banbury Road was, like the boys' school, designed by Sir Thomas Jackson. Nowadays, No. 21 Banbury Road is the University's Department of Materials annexe, but it still boasts its distinctive cupola and terracotta façade-columns as the traffic roars past just a few yards from the front door. There were 240 girls on the school roll in 1888; by 1951, when Margaret left the same building, there were 468.

The first free place was claimed by a county council scholar in 1904, and in 1918, in exchange for a 'higher grant' from the Board of Education, the school trust allocated ten per cent of the annual intake to non-paying pupils. At the end of the war, in line with the great Education Act of 1944, the school had become a direct-grant institution, more related to the educational system of the whole country. Fees were paid on a sliding scale of what parents could afford, and there were more free places. In 1957, the OHS moved lock, stock and barrel a bit further out along the Banbury Road into spacious and blessedly airy new premises in Belbroughton Road.

In Margaret's day, the school's activities and dormitories (the school always had a proportion of boarders) spilled over into other more modest addresses in the vicinity. She must have thought at times that she was exchanging one cramped environment at home for another at school.

Other girls remember her walking into a classroom, bumping into a desk and raising a laugh. Much of Maggie Smith's physical comedy derives from her limbs seeming to extract themselves gracefully from tricky situations. It is tempting to suggest that her gesticulatory repertoire derives in part from being cabin'd, cribb'd and confined on all fronts in her childhood.

The school was renowned for its interest in acting. Apart from that early dynasty of Smith girls, there were also the Power sisters, one of whom, Elizabeth, became an eminent economic historian. Beryl Power was deemed magnificent as Flavius 'with a beard and a whip and a naturally powerful voice'. The plays were usually Shakespeare or Greek-in-translation. The aforementioned Hilda Napier played the lead in *Iphigenia in Tauris* in the translation later introduced to the London stage by Lillah McCarthy.

The most distinguished actress the OHS produced before Maggie Smith was Margaret Rawlings, who arrived from Japan in 1920 and was accepted 'because of worthy and scholarly letters' written by her clergyman father. Rawlings was an exemplary product of the school who, before gaining a reputation as an outstanding classical tragedienne, graduated from Lady Margaret Hall in the University.

Her best friend was one Leonora Corbett who also became an actress and played Elvira, the ghost-wife, throughout the New York run of Noël Coward's *Blithe Spirit*. Leonora, recalled Margaret Rawlings, used to arrive late each term and regularly confessed to her house mistress that she was plagued by 'carnal thoughts'. She was invariably consoled with cocoa and bourbon biscuits.

Another OHS actress of a more local provenance, and just a few years ahead of Maggie, was Judith Stott, whose family had a grocer's shop in Walton Street (her brother is a vintner and 'quality' grocer to this day, in Summertown). She remembers Maggie tap-dancing at a bus stop in Headington. Judith Stott's example must have been a spur to Maggie's ambition. After training, she became a prominent West End juvenile, playing the young girl in *The Chalk Garden* opposite Edith Evans in 1956.

Judith Stott appeared in countless plays wearing Clarks sandals and white ankle-socks. She crisscrossed with Maggie for many years subsequently, appearing with her (and Dame Edith) in a television version of *Hay Fever*; succeeding her in the Peter Shaffer double bill of 1962; and remaining friends throughout two decades, during which period she was married to the Irish comedian, Dave Allen: 'To me, she's just my Margaret. She's laughter and tears, and part of my life for so many years.'

Margaret Smith does not loom large in the school history and magazines. She played tennis once for her house, West Club. She earned 'special congratulation' as Puck in the lovers' quarrel scene from *A Midsummer Night's Dream* which her house performed in the Shakespeare Competition (East Club, with 'the pick of the acting', took the palm).

And a contributor to Violet Stack's 1963 school history, a

senior girl of the day, wrote in half-apologetic retrospection: 'Could one have attempted to keep in order the naughty little red-headed fourth former, even as far as we tried, if one had known that Maggie Smith would today be playing to packed houses in the West End?'

Miss Stack, who had taught at Holloway prison, had been headmistress since 1937. She had replaced Miss Gale, who was struck by lightning on holiday; the school magazine reported that 'although this terrible accident was fortunately neither fatal nor completely incapacitating, it made a return to work impossible.' The school's reputation for drama had dipped a little during the war, but that was put to rights by the advent of Dorothy Bartholomew.

Miss Bartholomew arrived at the OHS in 1948 and stayed for five years and one term. She was later headmistress of Norwich High School for twenty-two years and retired to a quaint little house in the cathedral close, where she still lives with her fat ginger cat, Fred, and mixed memories of Margaret Smith.

'Margaret was in the Upper Fourth when I arrived and they were very lively, both lots. I thought they were going to be my undoing. I remember her as a very private person. She was certainly naughty, but it was an attractive naughtiness, in a way. I think, looking back now, she already saw where she hoped to go, and maybe we missed out.'

Margaret certainly felt she missed out by not being cast as Viola, a fact she would sometimes bitterly refer to in later life. But although Miss Bartholomew saw the Viola Margaret eventually played with the Oxford University Dramatic Society in 1952, and admired it, she still harboured reservations: 'I think she had more the seed of a Beatrice than a Viola. She was very good at the pert parts; she's not really, or wasn't then, my idea of a Viola.

'When I joined Letty Stack, we hadn't done a Shakespeare

for about seven years. The old building was the last word in girls' schools when it was built, and it was still the last word. We had this one hall which had double-glazing – of necessity as the London brick lorries thundered past – and this is where we did the plays. Letty was keen we should do *Twelfth Night*. Margaret did, I am sure, understudy Tessa Collins as Feste, but Tessa was so healthy she was never likely to miss the performance. I think, in the end, Margaret could not sing very well, either.'

Miss Bartholomew was quite right. Although adept at 'putting across' a revue number, Maggie was never really happy with music on stage and was only too keen to escape from revue the moment she had made her mark in it.

Classroom contemporaries Margaret Bonfiglioli (née Slater) and Bridget Davidson (née Senior), who were later respectively head girl and deputy head girl, confirm that Margaret did rehearse as Feste, and was funny, though she was more renowned as a general wag and everyday comedienne than as a conscientious performer.

They deny that Miss Bartholomew had a down on Margaret, even though she was obviously a cantankerous handful in the classroom. But there remains a puzzle as to why she was not cast in the main school production when, according to Margaret Bonfiglioli, 'her real acting talent had become evident in her inspired and inspiring playing as the Porter in *Macbeth* in the Shakespeare Competition.'

Margaret's nickname was 'Woozler'. Everyone, says Bridget Davidson, called her that, but nobody, least of all Maggie herself, recalls why. Perhaps it was a result of some rustic mimicry, a precise evocation of the Banbury or Bidford inflections which the mature Maggie would later evoke so thoroughly as Margery Pinchwife in *The Country Wife*.

Of the two lots of the Upper Third in 1947, Margaret, testifies another contemporary, Ruth Clarke (née Ayers), was in 'the other form'; those girls were inferior except when it came to the Shakespeare Competition, whose trophy, the Power Shield, was named in honour of the Power sisters. In this one aspect of competitive school life, says Ruth Clarke, the 'other form' was formidable opposition indeed:

'Jean Wagstaff, who everyone knew wanted to be an actress, played the straight lead . . . If there was a comic part, it would be played by Margaret Smith. She made us laugh, but we never saw her having a possible future on the professional stage. It was a great surprise to us when Margaret Smith left school "early" to go to the Oxford Playhouse School with Jean Wagstaff. We received the coded message that Margaret was a "failure". Everybody was a failure if they didn't go to university. I was a failure because I went to London University, not to Oxbridge.'

Miriam Margolyes, who was at the school from 1945 to 1960, from the infants through to the sixth form, became a well-known actress, too. She felt uncomfortable at the school, even though she was 'a responsible form leader' and left with an Exhibition to Cambridge, where she emerged as a comedienne of a thousand voices. Her family was Jewish, her father a doctor, and definitely not part of the University milieu.

'It might be an absurd over-sensitivity, but I also felt a tinge of anti-semitism. Like Margaret, I was a bit of a clown. But I'm sure the school confirmed an air of snootiness that made her feel that she had to emerge in her own right, that she couldn't be part of this world and that she had to forge her own steel out of another factory.'

That factory would be the Oxford Playhouse. Another schoolfriend, Verena Johnston (née Hunt), who, like Ruth Clarke, lived in Cowley, went to the Smith home 'on at least two Saturday mornings' to play Monopoly with Margaret and her brothers. Her father, Tommy Hunt, was a theatre fanatic who collected playbills and programmes all his life, and used to take Verena and Margaret to both the New and the Playhouse.

Verena Hunt does not recall Margaret 'shining' at school, nor being aware of any class difference between herself and the other girls. But Margaret, she says, was adamant by the age of fifteen or sixteen that the stage was 'the only thing' for her. Tommy Hunt advised her of the many pitfalls. She should only go ahead, he said, if it was the only thing in the world she wanted to do. It was.

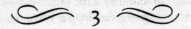

Clown of Town and Gown

MARGARET had decided she wanted to go to drama school in London. She had set her heart on RADA, the Royal Academy of Dramatic Art, but her parents said she could not leave home in Oxford. Meg wanted her to go to secretarial college and unhelpfully suggested that she could not hope to be an actress 'with a face like that'. Nat was torn between obeying his wife and pleasing his daughter.

Oxford High School had only fanned the flames of an ambition that was engendered outside. Margaret Smith was, and Maggie Smith is, a voracious reader. During her years at the High School, she devoured a popular fictional series by Pamela Brown, who wrote a children's novel about the theatre, *Swish of the Curtain*, in 1941. The book was written because its author, a fourteen-year-old wartime evacuee to Wales, wanted to sustain her playtime theatrical fantasies with her best friend in London.

By an extraordinary coincidence, the lodgings which Ian and Alistair had taken in Peel Street, Kensington, were in the house owned by this same Pamela Brown and her husband Donald Masters, a repertory actor. Margaret had read all of Pamela Brown's 'Blue Door' series, and she talked about them with the author when she visited her brothers. Pamela Brown had trained as an actress at RADA and had adopted the stage name of 'Mela Brown' in order not to be confused with the famous actress of the same name. She had then become a producer of plays for children on BBC television.

But even more extraordinary is the extent to which the books exactly reflected Margaret's developing situation. In *Swish of the Curtain*, a group of enthusiastic junior amateurs, the Blue Door Company, who have created their own theatre and presented a series of Shakespearean and vaudeville concerts, all progress from Fenchester (a country town of historic interest modelled on Colchester in Essex) to drama school in London; all, that is, except for young Maddy, the cheeky girl who becomes the heroine of the series.

In *Maddy Alone* (1945), Maddy's career takes off in spite of not going to London when she becomes embroiled in professional show business on her doorstep: a film is made for which there is a part for a local twelve-year-old. Later books, *Blue Door Venture* and *Maddy Again*, recount, respectively, the founding of a professional theatre company in Fenchester and the launching of Maddy's career in television. This last book appeared by popular request in 1956, just as Margaret Smith became Maggie and leapt from miscellaneous work in theatre and television to Broadway.

Pamela Brown died in 1989, shortly after several of her books had been reissued for a new young readership. If Margaret was ever stage-struck it was because of these stories. In 1972, she told the *Radio Times* that she did not like going out to the theatre: 'I get claustrophobic. And besides, I'm not at all stage-struck.' She was, though, when she read Pamela Brown. In later life, she often quoted with approval the other Pamela Brown, the actress who, like her namesake, trained at RADA and who played Ophelia to Robert Helpmann's Hamlet and Millamant to John Gielgud's Mirabell. This Pamela Brown said, 'It's the audience that's stage-struck, not me.'

In 1951, Margaret was unhappy at school and unhappy at not going to RADA. This tense situation was resolved by Nat going to see Isabel van Beers, a drama teacher who had a travelling brief among the Oxfordshire schools with a regular port of call at the High School. Margaret had responded to her, and Mrs van Beers had been a good deal more encouraging than Miss Bartholomew. Nat had heard she was starting a drama school based at the Playhouse in Beaumont Street.

Mrs van Beers, who had spotted Margaret's 'built-in timing', accepted her immediately as one of the first intake of the Oxford Playhouse School of Theatre. Thus she embarked on a two-year course which was to pitch her into the ferment of both the hard professional theatre and the softer, more glamorous whirlpool of University productions. Oxford made her. Over the next four years, she broke many hearts, played countless leads, became a fixture in University revues, a personality in her adopted city and a toast of the Edinburgh Festival.

The Playhouse School was her passport and Mrs van Beers her Svengali. Originally trained in ballet, the formidable and vastly experienced teacher had been sent to study acting in Oxford at the end of the 1920s. Like Margaret twenty years later, the budding actress had plenty of opportunity to rub shoulders with the best.

In 1932 and 1933, Isabel van Beers appeared, in a minor capacity, in two of the most renowned of all OUDS productions. The first was John Gielgud's version, designed by Motley, of *Romeo and Juliet*, a dry run for the Olivier/Gielgud 1935 production at the New Theatre in London. She was less than bewitched by Peggy Ashcroft's Juliet ('There was always a little bit of Miss West Kensington which left me cold'), and she partnered 'a rather superior' young reveller at the ball who was always telling her about the plays he was going to write. This was Terence Rattigan, who famously raised a hearty laugh in the wrong place each night with his delivery of the single line, 'Faith, we may put up our pipes and be gone.'

Her second OUDS blockbuster was an outdoor production

of *A Midsummer Night's Dream* on Headington Hill, directed by Max Reinhardt, who had already acquired a great European reputation but had just left Germany as Hitler came to power. Mrs van Beers played 'fairy number five hundred and four' alongside Joan Maude as a 'striking' Helena, Auriol Ross as Titania and Peter Glenville, later a notable West End director, as Puck.

She then married Stanley van Beers, a stage manager with Lilian Baylis at the Old Vic, and before the war worked in repertory in Leeds, Bradford and Coventry. The couple were divorced after the war, and Isabel took to teaching, basing herself in 28 Wellington Square, just off Beaumont Street and a stone's throw from the Playhouse.

The idea for the school at the Playhouse was hatched with Nevill Coghill, the Fellow of Exeter College who was at the heart of Oxford theatre for more than thirty years. Morning classes were held in a school hall in St Cross, and the Playhouse stage was made available, five afternoons a week, from 2.30 to 5. Most importantly, the school had an arrangement with Equity, the actors' union, to provide students for twelve small parts a year within the professional company.

Students were also encouraged, if invited, to take part in University and college productions. Thus the students could 'learn to handle their audiences', by listening to them, flushing them out and adjusting to their funny ways and habits. This was the most important skill, in Isabel van Beers's book, and one for which Maggie Smith would become justly renowned. The fees were twenty guineas a term. The reward was a certificate in acting from the Guildhall School of Music and Drama in London, of which Mrs van Beers was an honorary member.

Margaret had made a considerable impression on Mrs van Beers on one of her visits to the High School. The tutor gave her a speech of Helena's in *The Dream*. 'She sent it up! A child of fourteen. And I thought, oh my word, this is interesting. She had, even then, marvellous comedy timing, and she never made a mistake. By the time she came to the school it was obvious she was going to be something. She was on one track and her sights were at the top.'

Thus, in October 1951, Margaret Smith made her first appearance on the Playhouse stage as Jean in *The Pick-up Girl* by Elsa Shelley. A photograph shows her leaning over a banister in a silk shirt, mouth half-open, looking sultry. And in June 1952, as she completed her two-year course, she at last played Viola, in the OUDS *Twelfth Night*.

The President of the OUDS, John Wood, today's leading Royal Shakespeare Company actor, played Malvolio ('Looking as lean, lanky and statuesque as Don Quixote,' said the *Oxford Mail*), the future television executive Patrick Dromgoole was Sir Toby ('A dapper little man . . . [not the usual] gross-bellied understudy of Falstaff') and the founding director of the Royal Exchange Theatre in Manchester, the late Michael Elliott, who would one day direct Maggie as Miss Julie, was Antonio.

Margaret Smith – the unfamiliar name fooled the OUDS historian, Humphrey Carpenter – shivered in the gardens of Mansfield College every night, praying for rain. As Viola/Cesario she wore black tights, a white full-sleeved blouse and a sword, and she promptly collected her first rave review. The *Oxford Mail* was more than complimentary:

'Margaret Smith, whose loveliness has a boyish quality about it, made Olivia's infatuation for her seem quite natural . . . I was much struck by the simple sincerity of her acting. She approximates very nearly to the Viola of our dreams.'

In the summer vacation, the production toured to Clermont-Ferrand in France, and the Hebbel Theatre in Berlin as part of the Berliner Festwochen. Margaret was now fully immersed in the life of the University theatre, and its centre was the Playhouse, where the director of productions was Frank Shelley. She threw herself energetically into productions of both town and gown at a time when the Playhouse was a staging post for the leaders of tomorrow's theatre, and the OUDS full of ambitious undergraduates and future stage and television luminaries.

One such Oxford idol was Ned Sherrin, whose participation in the University revues was a crucial formative influence on Maggie. 'I think as she became older she became a little more extravagant, but I remember her as a quiet little thing, rather like one of Trollope's little brown girls. She obviously had tremendous talent, but she was not flamboyant.'

She did not, for Sherrin and his contemporaries, have the glamorously remote mystique of Zuleika Dobson: 'Our own Zuleika was a girl called Jennifer Weston who married a property tycoon, and of course Antonia Pakenham [later Lady Antonia Fraser] was up at the same time, floating around town on her bicycle. Margaret was simply considered to be one of the very best actresses.' But she did make some impression on Oxford fashion. Patrick Dromgoole says that in 1952 she was the first person he knew who bought a pair of jeans and sat in the bath water while wearing them, 'allowing them to dry to shape around her figure'.

Home was still 55 Church Hill Road, and Meg would despatch Nat to walk halfway into town if they thought Margaret was being detained at rehearsals beyond a proper hour. They were grudgingly reconciled to Margaret's ambition and may have been comforted by a perceptive progress report which Frank Shelley sent to Nat in January 1953:

'As raw material for the stage she is second to none in the school. But . . . I suspect that her very quickness and impatience to improve herself may at times get in her way, and make her her own "worst enemy". She *must* find patience towards her less gifted fellow pupils, and also towards the tutors at the school . . . Margaret has the essential stuff in her. It takes too long to try and define it; but some of us can recognise it.'

The *Oxford Mail* certainly had. Two months before Frank Shelley wrote his report, he had directed Margaret and Ronald Barker as two naughty children in *The Housemaster* by Ian Hay. The public-school farce also had Francis Matthews in the cast, but the *Mail* was more taken by the OUDS Viola transformed into 'Button' Farringdon:

'How John Betjeman would have approved of Margaret Smith, all legs and too brief "briefies", in which she hoarded hot sticky chocolate, destined in no time at all to become that great mountainous sports girl, Joan Hunter Dunn. She came as near to being a Great Dane puppy as any mortal, unhelped by Barrie, dare hope. I adored her.'

A note of besottedness is creeping in. But not everyone saw her potential. Ronald Barker, having renounced the clerical life, was a member of the Oxford Playhouse Company throughout Margaret's apprenticeship. Years later, at the height of his fame, Barker told a correspondent, B. A. Young, that all he remembered of young Margaret Smith was that he advised her to give up the profession 'as I didn't think she had the qualities or the talent necessary! How wrong I was.'

It is worth noting at this early stage that Margaret was as much in demand for serious drama as she was for revue. Either side of her final year at the Playhouse school, she appeared in T. S. Eliot's *Murder in the Cathedral* with the University Poetry Society (the poet Adrian Mitchell was the First Priest) in St Peter's in the East Church; with the University Players in Andreyev's *He Who Gets Slapped* (as Consuela, the doomed love object and bareback rider, to whom, said Frank Dibb in the *Oxford Times*, she brought 'both vernal freshness and a never self-conscious humour'); and with the OUDS again in February 1954 as Gertrud in Michael Meyer's first play, *The Ortolan*.

Meyer, the Ibsen biographer and translator, was then a tyro novelist and playwright, and his symbolic drama about a young poetess, the protégée of an older woman who cannot have children and seeks fulfilment in the girl's success, was favourably reviewed by four undergraduates nursing bright futures: Sherrin, Michael Elliott, Peter France (the television presenter) and Monty Haltrecht, the novelist.

Patrick Dromgoole, who appeared in the play and shared Oxford digs with Haltrecht, remembers his friend's description of Margaret in a minor role: 'frail as an opalescent moth'. She was, says Dromgoole, 'the perfect illusion, terribly beautiful, her colour fairly startling, and she was impossibly young, or seemed so, and a bit distant in the sense that no one ever felt very near her.'

Harold Hobson, the critic of the *Sunday Times*, found his way to Marston Hall to see *The Ortolan* and was similarly struck:

'. . . at one point, when she speaks of a working girl's dreary chances of a cheap pick-up at Saturday night dances, Miss Smith makes a brief foray out of the play's general atmosphere of intellectual efficiency into the realm of theatrical emotion.'

This first notice in the national press was not only typical of Hobson's acumen and ability to spot new talent; it isolates for the first time the Maggie Smith way with unsentimental expressions of sadness. The loneliness of her childhood found an outlet on the stage, and it remained characteristic of her first maturity that her flights into Restoration comedy, as well as her swoops into simple revue material, were invariably shot through with a stinging and truthful pathos.

She signed her first professional contract with the Oxford Repertory Players at the Playhouse on 12 June 1954, as an assistant stage manager at a salary of four pounds ten shillings a week. Her professional commitments, apart from making the tea, included walk-on roles in a series of productions in 1954

and 1955 by Peter Hall and Peter Wood, both of whom were
to become distinguished directors.

Shortly after Frank Shelley had written Margaret's progress
report, the Playhouse was taken over by Thane Parker, chairman of the London Mask Theatre, a company responsible for
the Westminster Theatre and J. B. Priestley's productions.
Parker also administered a little touring outfit called the Elizabethan Theatre Company, which had been formed by a group
of Cambridge graduates including Peter Hall and Peter Wood
(the others, all later well-known directors, were John Barton,
Colin George and Toby Robertson). Parker appointed Hall to
the artistic directorship of the Playhouse, where he stayed for
nine or ten months before accepting a more promising post at
the Arts in London. Peter Wood succeeded him.

In Peter Hall's version of Gogol's *The Government Inspector*,
Margaret played the schools' superintendent's wife in a company which included Billie Whitelaw, Derek Francis, Tony
Church, Peter Jeffrey, Frank Windsor, Michael Bates, Toby
Robertson, Ronald Barker and Clifford Rose. Philip French,
the film critic who was then an undergraduate, vividly remembers her singing 'The Boy I Love is Up in the Gallery' in a
music-hall compilation supervised from the piano by Peter
Hall in a moustache.

'She was absolutely wonderful,' says Hall. 'She sang that
song with such wit and pathos, it was simply spectacular. The
ironic side to her means she can be pathetic without ever being
self-indulgent. I didn't think she would develop the range that
she subsequently has, but I did think she had star quality.'
Hall also directed her as the West Wind 'in a lot of green
make-up' in the 1954 Christmas musical by Vivian Ellis,
Listen to the Wind, which transferred to the Arts with Hall in
the following year (without Margaret Smith, but with Ronald
Barker).

By 1955, Hall had taken over the Arts and hit the West End

with *Summertime*, Ugo Betti's play starring Dirk Bogarde, at the Apollo. Peter Wood took over in Oxford, and Margaret appeared in his productions of Pinero's *The Magistrate* and Sheridan's *The School for Scandal*.

She therefore brushed with the past and the future of the British theatre. Maggie Smith became a star in her own right, but she was also one of the last generation of beneficiaries of the regional repertory system. Peter Hall would go on from Oxford to produce the key new modernists, Samuel Beckett and Harold Pinter, in London, and to found the Royal Shakespeare Company in 1960.

Peter Wood, who later followed Peter Hall to the Arts, directed Pinter's first play, *The Birthday Party*, in 1958. Wood's busy parallel career in television embraced Maggie Smith in her first major small-screen role, also in 1958, and he would work with her many times in the West End, in Los Angeles, on Broadway and at the new National Theatre, of which she was a founder member in 1963.

Even more immediately important than her Playhouse connections was Margaret's involvement in student revues. These were bright days for the University theatre, which had been galvanised in the post-war years by the activities of Kenneth Tynan, John Schlesinger, Sandy Wilson, Tony Richardson, William Gaskill and Lindsay Anderson. The early professional success of such people prompted a rush of energetic talent towards the stage and the rapidly expanding new world of television.

The Oxford Theatre Group was formed in 1953 to take plays and a revue to the fringe of the Edinburgh Festival. It hired professional directors, Casper Wrede and Frank Dunlop, to direct Strindberg's *Miss Julie* and Molière's *Tricks of Scapin*. In the revue, *Cakes and Ale*, Margaret Smith performed three solo items: a song about a cinema usherette, 'Première', for which lyrics had been written by Ned Sherrin and music by

Andrew Johnston ('It's my première tonight, and I'm scared as scared can be . . .'); a marionette musical number by Johnston, 'Invisible Strings', which became her party turn; and a dance narrative by Leonard Webb called 'Engagement Pending' ('Though I get all the sleep that is required, I always seem to wake up feeling tired').

The professional highlight of the 1953 Edinburgh Festival was the Old Vic production of *Hamlet* starring Richard Burton and Claire Bloom. The actor playing Bernardo ('Who's there?') was Jeremy Geidt, and his visit to the damp attic in Riddle's Court off the Lawnmarket, where the OTG performed, was particularly significant. His brother-in-law, Peter Dunlop, was to become Margaret's long-term agent and confidant as a direct result of this encounter.

Geidt, who now works in Boston as 'senior actor' with Robert Brustein's American Repertory Theatre, recalls that the audience at *Cakes and Ale* was pretty sparse. But he was totally smitten by 'this Titian-haired beauty, sitting on a stool in a haze of cigarette smoke'. With a mutual friend, Margaret later visited Geidt in his dressing room at the Assembly Hall and said, 'I hear you think I'm good; what do I do now?' Geidt said he would arrange an introduction to Peter Dunlop of Fraser and Dunlop in London. And he did.

At some point over the next year, Margaret visited Peter Dunlop's office, situated at the wrong end of Wardour Street over a tailor's shop. On his desk, Dunlop kept a heavy Venetian glass stone. In the course of the interview, Margaret fiddled with it, picking it up and putting it down. Dunlop eventually said, 'Oh, for heaven's sake, leave that alone' and you can imagine now the electrified reaction of hurt dignity that was flashed by the girl across the desk, the pained, piercing look of 'Well, if that's how you feel about it . . .'

Despite this incident, the agent and the actress took to each other immediately. Dunlop, who had acted through Charterhouse and Cambridge and on the London stage, was not remotely theatrical. He much preferred his family circle and country life. He was Margaret's type of agent and they remained together for nearly thirty years, although she never signed a contract. 'She couldn't be bothered,' says Dunlop with a chuckle. She went back to Oxford and waited for something to turn up.

Even without professional work, she was in demand. As Ned Sherrin says, if you wanted success with a University show, you tried to get Margaret Smith in the cast. And, on a personal level, there were countless admirers for this waif-like, clownish chanteuse whose timing and stillness on a stage marked her out from the crowd.

One of the most fervent was John Beary, a young actor four years her senior who was smitten during a six-month attachment to the Playhouse as an ASM and bit player: 'We were both innocent, and both romantics. We walked into the night along the Oxford rivers, and cuddled in punts moored under bridges.' Now a director and writer in America, Beary's devotion is undimmed, though he concedes that he lost her when she was 'taken up' by the undergraduates.

One such was Michael Murray, in later life a professional actor, who became Margaret's favoured 'boyfriend' after Beary, and another keen admirer was Andrew Johnston, who wrote much of the University revue material and, on graduating, pursued a notable career in advertising. Both, along with the rest, were kept at arm's length. Margaret was a properly brought-up young girl and was in no great hurry to yield her mysteries. She soon learned to protect herself from regular exclamations of sexual adoration. The physical side of life was fairly unimportant to her, and her upbringing certainly pre-empted any idea of dalliance, let alone promiscuity.

In December 1953, yet another undergraduate was entranced by the vivacious redhead, and his long-term campaign was ultimately to prove successful. One has to say at this point that the romance between Margaret Smith and Beverley Cross is one of the most touching and unusual love stories in the British entertainment business. At first intermittent, then interrupted for about ten years by Maggie's tempestuous affair with, and marriage to, her National Theatre leading man, Robert Stephens, the relationship with Beverley has proved to be the bedrock of Maggie's professional and emotional life.

Beverley came up to the University, to read history at Balliol College, in the Michaelmas term of 1952. He therefore missed Margaret's Viola, but he was aware of her reputation when he met her for the first time during rehearsals for a charity gala organised by Ned Sherrin in aid of the Greek earthquake victims. Margaret did several of her increasingly renowned sketches, including her Joan Greenwood impersonation (as Gwendolen in the just-released Anthony Asquith film of *The Importance of Being Earnest*), and Beverley played his guitar.

Beverley joined the queue of unappeased Oxford suitors, tucked in just behind Michael Murray and Andrew Johnston. The friendship simmered on the back burner for a few years before it became serious at the end of the decade. Margaret was far more interested in reading than she was in canoodling. Having grown out of the runaway adventures of the Blue Door Company, she came across a more acidic, more sophisticated and deeply sympathetic literary rebel: Holden Caulfield in J. D. Salinger's *The Catcher in the Rye*.

If there is one literary example for Maggie's acute allergy to phoniness, it is Salinger's young hero, the world-weary urban cousin to Mark Twain's Huckleberry Finn. She was deeply impressed by Salinger's book about a boy who ran away from school and had harsh words for everyone, including Laurence Olivier and the Lunts.

She had been given some Salinger stories to read by John

Beary, who had laid his hands on copies of the *New Yorker*, where they were published, through the Ford Foundation. The whole Playhouse company was badgered into reading Salinger by his new champions, Beary and Margaret Smith. Beary then wrote to Salinger, telling him about Maggie, his 'comrade-in-arms', and asking for his advice. Salinger replied to them both, telling Maggie that she had better get a move on and marry this boy who doted on her. Beary, who formally proposed marriage to Margaret in 1953, says that Salinger told him to make up his mind one way or the other.

The correspondence must have been one of the very few Salinger entered into in Britain, apart from that with his publishers, before becoming almost entirely reclusive in 1965, 'the Greta Garbo of American letters'. As the poet Ian Hamilton recounts in his fascinating quest for Salinger, the author gave his last interview to a couple of American schoolgirls in 1953, at just about the same time as John Beary was writing to him.

The Catcher in the Rye was not yet the cult manual of adolescent outsiderism it became in the 1960s, and was not all that widely read. The paperback only became available in 1956. Although it prefigured the 'youthquake' whose icons were James Dean and Elvis Presley, the appeal to Margaret, and to the teenage Hamilton in Darlington, County Durham, lay in its gloriously impatient tone of voice and in Holden's coruscating contempt for cant, pretension and, above all, phoniness.

Maggie was deeply affected not only by *The Catcher in the Rye*, but also by the short story *For Esme – with Love and Squalor*, whose war-damaged American hero is offered succour by a precocious young girl he meets while stationed in Britain towards the end of the Second World War.

It is almost unbearable to learn that Meg, incensed by her daughter's literary adventurism and certain that such carryings-on would lead to immoral contamination of some kind, destroyed the letter Maggie received from the American author. This bitter experience probably put Margaret off letter-writing for good (she is a lax correspondent to this day) and did nothing to improve her relationship with her mother. It must have steeled her, too, in her determination finally to escape the asphyxiating intimacy of the semi-detached house in Cowley and its drab air of gentility.

Material from the 1953 Edinburgh revue, and the gala, was incorporated in a BBC television programme, *Oxford Accents*, transmitted on 26 February 1954 as part of a series on Oxford. The linking commentary was delivered by Brian Johnston, the cricket correspondent, and the event may be said to mark the television débuts of both Maggie Smith and Ned Sherrin, who was given a 'producer' credit.

In the summer term, Margaret was photographed in the press with the twenty-one-year-old President of the Oxford Union and future Cabinet Minister, Michael Heseltine. They were discussing details of a cabaret for the presidential ball. In later life, Maggie Smith and Michael Heseltine, nicknamed 'Tarzan' or 'Goldilocks' on account of his flowing mane of blond hair, would share the same hairdresser.

The OTG's revue for Edinburgh in September 1954 was *On the Mile*, presented in the late-night spot in Riddle's Court after a production of *The Dog Beneath the Skin* by W. H. Auden and Christopher Isherwood. Philip Purser of the *Daily Mail* confessed that he fell 'swiftly, completely in love' with the 'infinitely talented' young actress and invited her to accompany him to see Ruth Gordon in *The Matchmaker*, the official Festival's main attraction. Years later, Maggie would remind Purser that he had started her off: 'That's when I realised you can be a comic and yet be an actress. If she [Ruth Gordon] can do it, I thought, so can I.'

An amalgam of the best Oxford revue material was presented

twice in London in October 1954 and September 1955 at the New Watergate Theatre Club in Buckingham Street, off the Strand. Peter Dunlop's partner, Jimmy Fraser, who handled the film side of the business, went along one evening in the second season with Leonard Sillman, a New York producer who was planning a Broadway presentation of 'New Faces'. Margaret's reviews were good: she was described as 'a rich comic talent' and 'a comedienne of some versatility'.

Sillman was impressed and invited Margaret to meet him in his hotel suite. Her initial reaction was sceptical. She had no intention of falling for that old trick, the one where a slick American producer with a suite at the Savoy fancies a girl in the revue and asks her over to challenge her defences. She stood him up. The next day a colleague told her she was mad, did she not realise that this man presented new talent on Broadway? She agreed, reluctantly, to go and see him. She had very nearly blown her big chance.

Ian and Alistair began to appreciate the company of their sister, whose visits to London were increasingly frequent. The boys were working as dogsbody assistants in an architectural firm and decided that they would separate to acquire experience and later form a joint practice (they never did). In 1951, Alistair had worked with a company designing the gardens in Battersea Park for the Festival of Britain before starting his two years of National Service with the Royal Engineers (Ian was rejected on health grounds).

The brothers had moved from Peel Street to another flat in Kensington, and by 1954 had moved again into a large top-floor flat in Belsize Park, Hampstead, with two other architectural colleagues. The two friends soon disappeared and the apartment began filling up with Margaret and other aspiring, out-of-work actresses. Ian remembers this as a 'very jokey' establishment: 'And also very proper, I might say. Margaret had really blossomed, but the Swinging Sixties weren't remotely in sight. Margaret was buzzing around, almost waiting for something to happen.'

Peter Dunlop found her little bits of television work. She was a hostess on ITV's quiz game *Double Your Money*, which required her to look decorative and to introduce the show's star, Hughie Green, thus: 'We'd like you to meet the man with the biggest head in television, the man with the greenest hue . . . Hughie Green!'

With Jeremy Geidt, she 'walked on' in the first BBC television version of John Galsworthy's *The Forsyte Saga*. Geidt recalls that he and Margaret, playing a young couple at a party, asked the director, Tony Richardson, if they should chatter only when the microphone boom materialised above them. Richardson launched into a long Stanislavskyan lecture on how really good actors never stop acting. When the scene restarted, Smith and Geidt danced meaningfully around the studio and, oblivious to the action on the set, carried on acting, and dancing, down the stairs, out of the building and into the car park, while Richardson was reduced to a state of white-knuckled fury on the balcony.

As he recounts the incident, Geidt has a memory flash of bright eyes, smiles, irreverence and high spirits: 'Magical moments, like a diamond shining, giggles while strap-hanging on the underground.' But, he says, this same Margaret Smith was 'incredibly self-anchored; she had what the Georgians called "bottom". She knew who she was, and she had this absolutely fearless quality.' The wide world beckoned.

Back in Oxford, Meg and Nat were compelled to face the inevitable. So was the Oxford Playhouse, whose management was on the economic rocks. The company was disbanded in 1956. Almost immediately, a new set-up, the Meadow Players, was launched under the administration of Elizabeth Sweeting and the artistic direction of Frank Hauser. There was no place for Isabel van Beers and her school, which was wound up in

1957. The University bought the lease in 1961, and the Playhouse acquired its other title, the University Theatre.

Although University drama continued as a going concern among the Oxford undergraduates, there were no more opportunities for formal training until 1982, when the young graduate George Peck started the Oxford School of Drama. The new school, which is housed in a converted farmhouse near Woodstock, is forging links with the professional theatre in Oxford and London and is funded by a rich American patron, Mrs Bern L. Schwartz, through a benefaction to St Catherine's College.

Mrs van Beers withdrew to pursue her teaching work on the schools' circuit. She remains proud of such pupils as Miriam Margolyes, David Dacre and David William. But Margaret Smith still holds special sway in her affections: 'No youngsters today are as interested in working as hard as she was. Margaret was very special.'

Leonard Sillman assembled his cast for *New Faces 1956* with an opening date of 14 June at the Ethel Barrymore on Broadway, and one of the unknowns he engaged was Margaret Smith. Equity informed her that they already had a Margaret Smith on their books. Could she please change her name? She could. She became Maggie Smith and went to New York.

4

New Revue and Old Vic

M AGGIE SMITH, the new comedienne of Broadway, was twenty-one years old, five feet and five inches tall, with blue eyes, red hair and a bright, occasional smile. She lived in Greenwich Village and she was paid $350 a week by Leonard Sillman, of which ten per cent went to her agent, Milton Goldman, who acted in New York for Fraser and Dunlop. She was not happy. She sent Meg a magazine cutting in which she was photographed wearing a silk evening gown and a forlorn expression. Across the bottom she wrote: 'I look very sad! Mummy, I'm not as sad as I look.'

Working for Leonard Sillman, a pushy hoofer from Detroit who had once employed Tyrone Power as his chauffeur, was not a barrel of laughs. Maggie was required to play several old ladies when *New Faces 1956* opened in Boston, but she put her foot down and had them deleted before New York. Sillman was a devious and unpleasant character by all accounts, but he did have a nose for talent. Typically, he thought great acting was to do with being stingy. There *is* something, however, about his theory of the hoarding of gifts, the teasing of an audience, that is attractively convincing.

In his 1959 autobiography, Sillman applauds the discretion of gesture and the utter simplicity of Maria Callas, Chaliapin in *Boris Godunov*, Laurette Taylor, Judith Anderson and Margaret Leighton in *Separate Tables*. He continues: 'That marvellous hoarding of movement until the precise, the perfect moment is a rare thing in the theatre . . . The young English actress, Maggie Smith, who appeared in the last *New Faces*, has it, and it will make her a star.'

The title 'New Faces' had been suggested to Sillman by the financier Otto Kahn, as a contrast to Ziegfeld's expensive Follies. The first show was in 1934. Henry Fonda sang, and Imogene Coca (the matchless zany in Sid Caesar's television *Show of Shows* series) did a striptease. Tallulah Bankhead, according to Sillman, smoked like a furnace throughout the opening night's performance.

In 1936, Gypsy Rose Lee nearly appeared alongside Van Johnson but withdrew at the last minute. Sonny Tufts was in the 1938 version, but 1943 was a non-vintage year. Sillman's reputation took a dive. After the war, Maxwell House Coffee (with whom, ironically, Maggie was to make her only television advertisement, during the run of *Lettice and Lovage*) sponsored 'New Faces' on the radio, and CBS TV gave their new revue show not to Sillman but to Ed Sullivan.

But in 1952 Sillman had bounced back with his fourth *New Faces* in which a comic actress called Alice Ghostley was an overnight sensation and young Eartha Kitt stopped the show with 'Monotonous'. It ran for a year, and then went on tour.

In 1956 Sillman was ready to fire once again with a new assembly of hopefuls. They came from all over: India, Sweden, the Virgin Islands, Italy, France and Puerto Rico. The star, however, proved to be T. C. Jones (long since forgotten and dead), a drag artist from San Francisco who opened the show as the husky Tallulah with a throaty, mannish laugh and a series of insults aimed at the serious theatre of Stanislavsky and Elia Kazan.

The critics were sold on T. C. Jones. Walter Winchell devoted a column to him. In their reviews, neither Brooks

Atkinson in the *New York Times*, nor Walter Kerr (later a devoted fan) in the *Herald Tribune* mentioned Maggie Smith, though the cast album and production photographs suggest there was something worth noting.

A cod Ziegfeld tribute to the all-American girl closed the first half. Following 'Miss Jungle Madness' and 'Miss Fisherman's Tail', Maggie jerkily descended the staircase as 'Miss Bowls of Sunshine', covered in dozens of oranges, and sang, to a slow foxtrot rhythm, in a voice of adenoidal, strangulated lack of conviction: 'I'm a vision of beauty, and the beauty part, is the beautiful feeling, I feel in my heart.' Long afterwards, Maggie met a man who graphically explained to her how he had cut his head open while banging it on the seat in front of him during a laughing fit prompted by this number.

There was a company sketch about the United Nations written by Neil Simon (and his brother, Danny), the writer with whom Maggie was later to work in Hollywood on *Murder by Death* and *California Suite*, and a send-up of Shirley Temple as a screeching 'no-talent' who learned to walk at the age of seven and to talk at the age of thirteen.

Maggie's big second-half number, 'One Perfect Moment', was a still life, a portrait of a Victorian belle frozen at a table groaning with fruit, fowl, wine and sherbet. As she litanised the pleasures of a private dining room at Claridge's, a bottle of tokay and a gypsy violin, she lamented their passing value. At this point, the table started to tilt and the comestibles to slide out of reach. In a cut-glass voice broken up with gurgling, Maggie remarked that everything was as it should be, down to the raspberry 'i-ay-ay-ice', as she suddenly lunged after both the disappearing dessert and the rest of the song.

Maggie's Englishness was exploited. In one sporting sketch where cricket was derided, she responded, aghast, 'Anybody who'd say that would strike the Queen!' Although the Broadway list of that season included such archetypal American hits as Paul Muni in *Inherit the Wind*, Sammy Davis Jr in *Mr Wonderful*, and *The Pajama Game*, New York was in the grip of one its periodic bouts of showbiz Anglophilia. Rex Harrison and Julie Andrews, who had opened in March in *My Fair Lady*, were the toasts of the town, and Maggie was soon taken up.

She became good friends with Julie Andrews and her husband, the designer Tony Walton, and through them met the agent Lou Wilson, who rescued her from the shark-like attentions of Milton Goldman. Alice Ghostley, too, became a life-long friend who would collect her first Oscar for her in 1970. She joined in the celebrations for Liza Doolittle's twenty-first birthday (Julie Andrews was twenty-two, the same age as Maggie) at the 21 Club on 1 October.

In November, the artist Feliks Topolski invited her to a party with Rex Harrison, Harrison's lover Kay Kendall (he was still married to Lilli Palmer, but later married Kendall, who died of leukaemia in 1958), and the distinguished Scottish-born actress Eileen Herlie. Lou Wilson took her on a trip to Puerto Rico.

Maggie liked New York, up to a point. But the showbiz social whirligig was never her scene and she was relieved when *New Faces* closed after a seven-month run. She returned to England, and the boys' Belsize Park apartment, to capitalise on her Broadway status.

The obvious next step was to establish her revue credentials on British soil, and Maggie was signed up by the ambitious and stylish young impresario Michael Codron for the London première of *Share My Lettuce*, 'a diversion with music' by Bamber Gascoigne, which featured an offbeat, quirky score by Keith Statham and Patrick Gowers, and one lyric by Michael Frayn.

More importantly, Codron teamed Maggie Smith with Kenneth Williams, another rising star who had made his

name as the Dauphin in a 1954 revival of Shaw's *Saint Joan*
and in Sandy Wilson's exuberant musical *The Buccaneer*.

Gascoigne had launched *Share My Lettuce* at Cambridge
University, where he was an undergraduate. It caught something of a new surrealism in revue pioneered by the choreogra-
pher John Cranko's *Cranks*. It was bright and bubbly, slightly
bizarre, with no hint of the 'satire boom' inaugurated by
Beyond the Fringe three years later. Gascoigne says he 'sat and
stared in fascinated amazement at all that went on' and recalls
the wonderfully snide verbal wit of Williams in rehearsal and
the fun and vitality of Maggie Smith. He thinks she was a
little plumper round the shoulders in those days.

Codron needed a hit. Having trained, after St Paul's School
and Oxford, with the impresario Jack Hylton, his determination to go it alone had not impressed his father. Nor had a
couple of flops. *Share My Lettuce* proved a life-line leading
to innovative West End presentations of Harold Pinter, John
Mortimer, Sandy Wilson, more revue, and something like
complete solvency in the mid-1960s with *There's A Girl In
My Soup*.

Kenneth Williams shared his lettuce with a white rabbit
which he kept in a box. There were eight colour-coded performers – Williams was 'lettuce green', Maggie 'orange' – who
were heralded by a bebop-ish overture in the early style of
Leonard Bernstein. The sketches included a Pinteresquely
menacing encounter in a railway compartment and an
almost mathematically precise party scene in an army mess
where all the officers were called Michael and all their girlfriends Susan.

In 'Party Games', Maggie played the rapidly articulating
hostess: 'Here's a pencil and pad and you won't find it bad
these are games that we all of us know; pass 'em on as you
write 'em and ad infinitum it's just party games that make a
good party go.' Kenneth Williams said that Maggie sang this

number while fiddling with a rope of beads, twirling them round her neck and then, amazingly, around her waist. 'Just as they seemed to be heading for her ankles, she deftly altered their course and the beads ended up round her neck again. She finished the song looking as immaculate as when she started.'

The show opened on 21 August at the old Lyric in Hammersmith. Williams, said Milton Shulman in the *Evening Standard*, 'capers across the stage like a tipsy pixie getting sloshed on champagne bubbles,' while Richard Findlater in the *Observer* lauded this 'elegant, faintly macabre, and immensely funny' new talent.

Williams had been around a little while. Nearly nine years older than Maggie, he came from an ordinary London Cockney background (his father was a gentlemen's hairdresser in King's Cross) and had found his show-business feet towards the end of the war, and just after it, entertaining the troops while based in Singapore.

His army colleagues there included the Scottish actor Stanley Baxter, the film director John Schlesinger and the playwright Peter Nichols. This period was immortalised in Nichols's 1977 stage play *Privates on Parade*. Williams specialised in impressions of Winston Churchill and the music-hall star Nellie Wallace.

On being demobbed, Williams worked around the country in repertory theatres and made his first real impression in *Hancock's Half Hour*, a BBC radio series starring the melancholy Tony Hancock, in which his fruitily intoned camp persona, unprecedented in public broadcasting, delighted the listening multitude.

Williams was outrageous, but brilliantly fast and funny. His acting had a brutal, Japanese style to it, and his mask-like pixie face was likened by Kenneth Tynan to that of Jean-Louis Barrault in farce. As well as in the Shaw and the Sandy Wilson musical, he had made a West End mark as Elijah in Orson Welles's production of *Moby Dick*, and as Maxime, alongside Alec Guinness, in Peter Glenville's production of Feydeau's *Hotel Paradiso*.

Williams was a complex and private man who abhorred the idea of physical contact but could dominate any social gathering by frankly adopting his outrageous comic identity like a second skin. Extremely well read and highly civilised, he lived alone, always in spartan conditions, even after the series of *Carry On* films, on which he embarked in 1958, made him wealthy. He died in 1988, probably accidentally, after taking an overdose of barbiturates.

He had first seen Maggie in that Oxford revue at the New Watergate. He told Tynan that he had gone along with John Schlesinger and had been immediately struck by her magnetic quality:

'She was like an extraordinary cat, and indeed her eye make-up was positively feline. When we worked together, the way she invented that business with the rope of pearls was definitely a result of her thing about Bea Lillie. I loved her urchin quality, too. She's physically adroit and can fold her arms in such a way that they disappear. The other quality in her work is a sort of basic American feel that must have come from *New Faces*.'

The Times enthused about Williams's unknown co-star, who 'proved that rarity on the English stage, a true *comedienne* whose youth in no way prejudices the sense of timeliness in her art. She is, in fact, a "find" with the urchin gift of combining humour, sophisticated or slum-like, with a touch of tart pathos.'

As a short-order waitress she duelled with Williams at top speed, he lending a fruity provenance to 'broccoli', she a coarse bossiness to 'cheese' and 'wine', the latter syllable extended for pseudo-snobbish diphthongal effect. As a tea-lady on Platform

Eight, she stood alone each night crying, 'Tea, tea, tea' and pathetically confiding, 'They look at what I've got for sale, but not at what I'd willingly give to any man.' In her quavering, Liza Doolittle-ish voice, she waited for the right train to come along. And as a harassed débutante at a party where she could remember nobody's name, she was left utterly alone amid the dying chatter of departing guests.

It is the lot of all gifted performers to be 'discovered' in their early years with the regularity of a cuckoo emerging from its clock. But Maggie's comic personality, the essence that was to make her a star, was already apparent. Codron knew she was special:

'She was always extraordinary, even at the very beginning. She came down to Hammersmith and took one look at a set that was on the stage for another show and said, "I didn't know they still designed sets like that!" I was flabbergasted. But her assurance had nothing to do with pomposity or silliness; she was completely herself, and very funny.'

Share My Lettuce transferred to the Comedy Theatre in the West End in September and moved on to the Garrick in the New Year. Maggie groaned, 'This must be the longest tour in town.' More substantial television work began to be offered. The first major role Maggie played on British television was that of Susie, a dumb blonde waitress, in *Boy Meets Girl*, a Hollywood comedy by Bella and Sam Spewack which Independent Television broadcast in its 'Play of the Week' slot in June 1957.

One consequence of West End exposure was being spotted for the movies. Dennis van Thaal, Michael Balcon's chief talent scout at Associated British Studios, Elstree, signed her on a seven-year contract at the same time as Shirley Ann Field and Ann Firbank; they joined a stable which included Richard Todd, Sylvia Syms and Janette Scott. Very little was subsequently found for Maggie to do. She always rejoiced in the first monthly fan-mail report she received. It consisted of one word: 'Nil.'

However, during the run of *Share My Lettuce*, she did make her first feature film, *Nowhere to Go*, written by Seth Holt (who also directed) and Kenneth Tynan. She had only crossed Tynan's path once hitherto, when, as an Oxford schoolgirl, she claims to have knocked him over with her hockey stick in the High while jumping off a speeding bus. She had no idea who he was, but told her brothers that she had felled a man in a purple suit. They knew that only one man wore a purple suit in post-war Oxford: the already famous and flamboyant undergraduate Tynan, whose middle-name was not Peacock for nothing.

Perhaps as an act of unconscious revenge, Tynan had been unimpressed by *Share My Lettuce*, which he dubbed 'inconsequential', and by her part in it. She was, before she had even started, 'the slightly old-fashioned Maggie Smith'. Maggie later told Tynan that she had learned the art of 'the inconsequential' by watching Beatrice Lillie, 'who did the craziest things, or things that didn't matter.'

Tynan was now working as both a drama critic on the *Observer* and a script editor at Ealing Studios. Maggie was cast as Bridget Howard, a rich, lonely, slightly snooty but inquisitive girl who has run away from five schools and who now befriends an unsuitable confidence trickster, played by the well-built Canadian actor George Nader.

One of only two black and white movies Maggie Smith made (the other was *The Pumpkin Eater*), *Nowhere to Go* was Seth Holt's first film in a career which never fulfilled its promise. Tynan once recommended Holt to Ned Sherrin as one of the three best conversationalists in London. But Holt never became a media celebrity. Instead, he made horror films and died suddenly in 1971, six weeks into shooting *Blood from the Mummy's Tomb*.

The opening prison break-out in *Nowhere to Go* is a rightly renowned sequence of great excitement, and a fine cast includes the silent-screen star Bessie Love as a wealthy widow, Bernard Lee as a dangerously smiling 'Mr Big', Harry H. Corbett as an obstreperous crook and André Melly as an Irish night-club girl.

It is a flinty, technically assured film, full of shadows and twists, with a good jazz soundtrack by Dizzy Reece. Bridget stays loyal to 'Greg', takes him home for Christmas in the family cottage in Brecon and ends up being arrested herself. Under that cover, Greg tries to steal a getaway bike, is surprised by a farmer and fatally wounded.

As he lies dying in the road, Bridget returns from the police station to find his last message – 'Tell your friends to look somewhere else' – and walks away over the fields into the middle distance, sad and alone once more, a prisoner of her own background and the British class system.

Maggie was a different kind of young film heroine, edgy, sensitive and intelligent. One popular newspaper declared that she made 'bosomy blondes old-fashioned', while the more sedate C. A. Lejeune in the *Observer* looked forward to seeing her again: 'She looks as crisp as a celery stick and speaks like a girl who has a good mind of her own.'

Since working with her at the Oxford Playhouse, Peter Wood had developed a parallel career in television. The West End producing company, H. M. Tennent, run by Hugh 'Binkie' Beaumont, had an arrangement with ITV to present new work, and one of Wood's 1958 projects – the year in which he also directed Pinter's *The Birthday Party* – was *Sunday out of Season*, 'a gentle, sensible little play', according to one critic, by a West Country potter called Peter Draper.

For 'Binkie-vision', as the set-up was known, Wood wanted to cast the girl he remembered from Oxford as a defensive student from London University who goes to a small Welsh seaside resort to recover from an unhappy love affair. She embarks on a tentative new friendship with a local boy whose father is suffering from silicosis and who is also in flight from emotional turmoil. This role was taken by Alec McCowen, who had worked with Wood at the Arts and who had already made a West End reputation in several plays, including that same production of *The Matchmaker* (opposite Ruth Gordon) Maggie had seen in Edinburgh.

McCowen was enormously taken with her: 'I remember thinking, when is she going to do something? I looked at her face and nothing seemed to be happening. But when I looked on the monitor, I realised everything was happening. Her acting was all in her head and very underplayed. It was a tender little play and she gave a very sensitive performance.'

Peter Wood says that he had to hold the viewfinder up to his eyes so that the actors could not see him snivelling. 'The periphery of the emotional situation was very precise; they acted beautifully, in concentric rings. Alec's role was tenth cousin to Jimmy Porter [in *Look Back In Anger*], only Welsh, and Maggie had come to commune with herself.'

It was because of *Sunday out of Season* that both McCowen and Maggie were invited by Michael Benthall to join the Old Vic in 1959. One detail of this transaction still rankles with McCowen. During early rehearsals for that first season, the actors were marking out the moves when Benthall shouted at Maggie and McCowen from the back of the stalls: 'You'll have to speak up, we can't have any of this television acting here.'

This insult to two of our most conspicuously audible actors was doubly hurtful because they were only 'blocking': 'But he was a man, Michael Benthall,' says McCowen, 'who used to give with one hand and take away with the other. He didn't much like people liking him, I don't think.'

Maggie completed a hectic television schedule which

included Christopher Fry's *A Phoenix Too Frequent* and
Somerset Maugham's *For Services Rendered*. Most of Maggie's
early work on television has been lost or wiped. The cavalier
attitude of its own custodians towards the nation's small-screen
culture, in the age before video recordings, is a scandal of the
post-war era; in Maggie's case, the loss is particularly regret-
table if one judges it by the quality of her performance in the
Maugham, which has luckily been preserved.

She plays Lois, the youngest of three daughters in a country
household torn apart in the dreary aftermath of the First World
War. Maugham's bitter 1932 play was confirmed as a Chek-
hovian classic by this production, and its urgency and pathos
are well served by the immediacy of a 'live performance' on
television.

Lois's father is a smugly complacent lawyer who sits down
to tea and declares that 'this old England of ours isn't done
yet' as his eldest daughter, brilliantly played by Ursula Howells,
goes mad singing the National Anthem off key. Her loved
one, a disoriented naval war hero (Robert Urquhart), has shot
himself because her offer of financial help is construed as a
gesture of mere pity.

Lois's other sister has a boozy, farming husband (Jack
Hedley) who propositions her, but she decides to pre-empt a
life of predictable tedium by running off with an old roué
(William Fox) whose second wife overhears the elopement
plans on the telephone and delivers a nearly disruptive bombshell into the family drawing room. In the corner sits the
brother, another veteran, the blinded Sidney (Anthony Newl-
ands), who denounces patriotic morality and the deceitful politicians who send young men to graves with their hollow cant
and hypocritical bunk.

Maggie as Lois is threatened less by bombs than by bomba-
zine. She wants out, action, the bright lights, something to
look forward to. She paints a serious, thoughtful portrait of a

girl waking up to her own ability to exert power over men. She exudes confidence and poise, and does not use her 'revue' intonations, but the clear, cool voice of the real actress. It is a lovely performance, truthful and sharp, in a very good company.

At the end of 1958, Maggie appeared briefly in the only out-and-out West End flop of her career, *The Stepmother* by Warren Chetham-Strode. The débâcle was most keenly felt by Kate Reid, the distinguished Canadian actress who was making her London début. She played the new wife of a man haunted by the memory of his crippled first wife, and Maggie flitted on as a variety agent's secretary called Vere Dane, stealing the notices in a scene where she instructs an office boy in the art of coping with a would-be trainer of performing elephants.

On tour, Maggie's humour and pathos were noted in the *Yorkshire Post*. Desmond Pratt said that her brash Cockney forthrightness was mixed with 'a deep sympathetic understanding of the secretly forlorn'. *The Times* approved 'a delightfully wristy performance'. Kate Reid recalls that Maggie's hair was dyed 'very very blonde, almost pink' and that she cried a lot in rehearsals.

Maggie took this role partly on the rebound from a strange rebuff by Charles Laughton, in which her old Oxford admirer, John Beary, also played a part. Beary had been working in Ireland, but was now employed by the impresario Oscar Lewenstein as an assistant to Laughton, who was appearing in, and directing, *The Party* by Jane Arden. Laughton had not been on the London stage since playing Captain Hook in *Peter Pan* in 1936.

Laughton's role was as an unstable, institutionalised alcoholic whose daughter, Ettie, is holding a party which she capriciously cancels the minute she learns that her mother has invited her father home for the weekend. Laughton went to see Maggie in *Share My Lettuce* at Beary's suggestion, invited her to audition and subsequently to dinner.

Beary saw the whole affair as his great chance of reclaiming Maggie. Laughton said that she 'showed some signs of genius' and reminded him of Laurette Taylor. But on the next morning, the final girl came in to audition. It was Ann Lynn, and she was cast as Ettie on the spot.

Beary says that Maggie was so shocked by this seeming rejection that she decided at that moment to do no more revues and to enter the lists as a serious actress. She became a contender. And Beary was romantically thwarted for the second time.

In June 1959, the *Sunday Times* identified a representative cross-section of the British cultural élite, and the film critic Dilys Powell nominated in their number Maggie, whom J. W. Lambert apostrophised as 'a popper-in of great talent'. In August, Maggie returned to Edinburgh with the Old Vic company as Lady Plyant in Michael Benthall's production of Congreve's *The Double Dealer*.

Benthall had run the Old Vic since 1953, and Maggie was one of several newcomers who bridged the gap between these last days of the old rep and the incoming era of subsidised theatre. In 1963, Laurence Olivier would take over the Old Vic as the first artistic director of Britain's new National Theatre, and Maggie would be one of his twelve contracted actors, most of them unknown or recruited from the Royal Court. At the end of the 1950s, she represented the transitional phase, as well as that future in embryo, along with Judi Dench, Barbara Jefford, Alec McCowen, Stephen Moore and John Woodvine.

It did not seem like it at the time. John Moffatt remembers that she fitted in to a very happy company which is 'unfairly despised' because of what happened afterwards. The leading actors were Fay Compton, Joss Ackland, Walter Hudd, Robert

Harris, John Justin and Donald Houston. In 1960, Judi Dench and John Stride would make their names in Franco Zeffirelli's production of *Romeo and Juliet*. Michael Elliott ran the final Old Vic season after Benthall left in 1962, and then everything changed.

Judi Dench, Moyra Fraser, Maggie, John Moffatt, Alec McCowen and Joss Ackland became a particularly close group of friends within the company. They had Sunday lunches in each other's houses and suppers after the show. For McCowen, it was 'by far the happiest company I have ever worked in. That company symbolises for me the theatre and my time in it. Some of the productions were terrible, but not all.

'The happiest show I did there was *The Merry Wives of Windsor*, which was appalling, but a riot to be in. It was always very hard to get up the stairs in the interval because Moyra Fraser and Maggie had invariably collapsed with laughter and were rolling around hugging each other in these huge skirts.'

Although Maggie was ever a worrier and self-doubter, McCowen says she 'was not so much a moaner in those Old Vic days.' He noticed the difference, the more downbeat approach, years later when they filmed *Travels With My Aunt* with George Cukor. 'Every morning on *Travels*, the greeting would be "Don't feel like it today" or some such phrase; but then this spirit for comedy bubbles out in a totally mysterious way.'

Judi Dench shared a dressing room with those very merry wives. 'Maggie always had the most beautiful clothes. She taught me always to buy not one pair of shoes but two or three identical pairs of what suited you. I had never met anyone like that before, and I've always done this ever since.

'She came to see me at the Vic the year after she left and she was wearing the most beautiful white coat. I jumped on her back and she spilt a glass of tomato juice all down the front. But I don't think she had two of *those*! To me, she's always been immensely funny, and always so chic with that wonderful, shiny hair.'

Dench and Maggie got to know each other in Edinburgh because Miles Malleson, a senior character actor who was as renowned for his bottom-pinching exploits as he was for his halitosis, was pursuing both of them. Judi Dench says, 'We were rather frightened of him, but I expect he only wanted to take us out to tea.'

The Double Dealer had not been produced since 1916, and Alan Pryce-Jones in the *Observer*, lauding Congreve as 'a supreme poet of the corrupt ephemeral', declared, presciently, that such a rare approach to playwriting needed a National Theatre to do it justice: 'Since the contemporary theatre has no experience of Restoration comedy, the company must be congratulated on doing as well as they do. They must not, however, sneeze when they take snuff.'

The London reviews were generous, but it was Bernard Levin in the *Daily Express* who really threw his hat in the air, and not for the last time: '. . . shining over all there is the captivating, brilliant, champagne-bubble performance of Miss Maggie Smith as Lady Plyant. Miss Smith is a walking, talking flame. She has a squeal of pretended virtue with undertones so lascivious that it turns my bones to water. And I swear she never puts foot to ground throughout, but floats a yard above the stage.'

Lady Plyant is a tyrant at home, a coquette abroad. Maggie, consigning her elderly husband to a permanent state of subjection and sexual starvation, must have driven poor old Miles Malleson as potty on stage as she did off.

The spirit of independence in marriage and the enunciation of wittily brutal conditions laid down within and without the married state are hallmarks of the comic heroines who became Maggie's speciality: Rosalind, Beatrice, Silvia, Mrs Sullen, Margery Pinchwife, Maggie Wylie and Amanda Prynne. From

Shakespeare to Restoration comedy, J. M. Barrie to Noël
Coward, Maggie knew instinctively how to make herself
stylishly available on her own terms.

Levin declared that *As You Like It*, in which Maggie played
Celia to Barbara Jefford's Rosalind and Alec McCowen's
Touchstone, marked the end of a seven-year lean spell at the
Vic, and that the theatre was now 'a place to visit for pleasure
rather than duty'.

But new notes of critical dissension marked the beginning
of a debate over mannerism which was to loom large across
the years in any critical discussion of Maggie's acting. In the
Sunday Times, J. W. Lambert entered the first caveat: 'Maggie
Smith mangles her phrases [as Celia] with a quite striking
absence of ear'; and Edward Goring in the *Daily Mail*, noting
that previous queens in *Richard II* at the Old Vic included
Peggy Ashcroft, Margaret Leighton, Renée Asherson and
Claire Bloom, stated that Miss Smith 'is more suited to comedy
. . . The flat, tremulous voice manages a tear-choking note
but carries stronger echoes of Maggie, almost of our Eth of
The Glums. Regal robes and one of those medieval gilt hairnet
affairs sit uneasily on the dizzy bombshell of *Share My
Lettuce*.'

Her extraordinary inflections have always both highlighted
unexpected phrases and declared her own idiosyncrasy. Alec
McCowen can still hear today the sonic imprint Maggie left
on Celia in phrases such as 'lame me with reasons' ('lame'
given syllabic extension and a mocking, viperish tincture); 'like
a dropped acorn', said of Orlando found lolling under a tree;
'I like this place and willingly could waste my time in it' on
arrival in Arden; and 'Alas, poor shepherd', a poignantly heart-
felt ejaculation.

McCowen, no technical slouch himself, says that this
colouring of the words, the unexpected highlighting of phrases
that normally pass unnoticed, put her, for him, in the same

class as Edith Evans. 'We knew she was a very special actress, even in that company; we were all pretty good. But to do this with Celia! Barbara Jefford was a bloody good Rosalind, but she must have been quite surprised.'

Maggie was disappointed not to be playing Rosalind herself. She was also passed over for Gwendolen in *The Importance of Being Earnest* (again, Barbara Jefford, still young but vastly more experienced, got the role). Michael Benthall made amends by giving her the leading role in J. M. Barrie's *What Every Woman Knows* and thus set the seal on her stardom.

The opening night was 12 April 1960. The *Daily Sketch* reported twelve curtain calls under the heading of 'Maggie – a Star at 24'. The *Daily Mail* review was headlined 'Maggie's night at the Old Vic', and the critic reported 'very loud cheers' and 'the arrival of Maggie Smith as a fully fledged comedienne'.

Barrie's play, dating from 1908, when it was seen as a loose retelling of the early career of the Labour Prime Minister Ramsay MacDonald, had not been seen in London since 1943. For the first time, Maggie was able to conjure the Celtic side of her background in the character of Maggie Wylie, an allegedly spinsterish ugly duckling whose father and brothers marry her off to a working-class upstart who has breached the family home in order to steal knowledge from their library.

The 'wee wifey' becomes the inspirational support for the Scottish autodidact's political success, but she is taken advantage of, and proceeds to redefine her position by renegotiating it with evidence of marital infidelity. Some critics, including Alan Pryce-Jones, thought Maggie was too straightforwardly entrancing: 'Far from being unmarriageable, she would have had all Kirriemuir at her feet at a turn of the wrist.'

The production was given for only twenty-five performances, but the acclaim was tumultuous. John Moffatt, playing a diplomat, remembers that, on the First Night, he came on 'and she had her back to me; it was the first time I had met her in the play and she was bent over a desk. She turned, and it was one of those extraordinary moments when I didn't see Maggie Smith there. I saw this other Maggie, Maggie Wylie, and it quite startled me. I hadn't seen this in rehearsals. I suddenly thought: this is a great actress.'

The impact of Maggie's Maggie Wylie was considerable. The West End, and in particular the all-powerful Binkie Beaumont, sniffed out a new star. John Moffatt, looking back, is adamant about her right to supremacy. 'Maggie always behaved instinctively like a great star. There was never any question of dirty words or taking her clothes off. This was, and is, inconceivable to her because of an idea of what the public will accept. And it was nothing to do with being "grand" or "theatrical". With Maggie, the work always came first.

'When I was a young man, there were many great untouchable stars in the West End: Cicely Courtneidge, Marie Tempest, Noël Coward, John Gielgud and Beatrice Lillie. Maggie is the last one of that breed. And her privacy, her dislike of giving interviews and appearing on television chat shows, is all part of that. She respects the public too much to disappoint them with bad manners or odd behaviour.'

The London publisher Hamish Hamilton wrote to Maggie on the very next morning: 'Your performance is enchanting, and I wish Barrie could have seen you. I'm sure he would have agreed that you are every bit as good as Hilda Trevelyan [the original Maggie Wylie], and much better than anyone else since. I haven't enjoyed an evening in the theatre so much for ages. My congratulations and thanks.'

One month after *What Every Woman Knows* opened, 'Binkie-vision' presented the première on ITV of Noël Coward's *Hay Fever*. Although Maggie's loyal champion Philip Purser thought that the 1925 comedy was 'rather a fraud' and that the production, directed by Casper Wrede (who had

Day trip to Sandringham, September 1938, with her mother
and brothers Ian (left) and Alistair

Margaret aged ten parading her
membership of the Vera Legge
School of Dancing in her
Oxford garden

Margaret as Viola for the OUDS, 1952

Meg and Nat in Washington DC for Ian's first wedding, 1965

Right Maggie in her breakthrough role: Maggie Wylie in J. M. Barrie's *What Every Woman Knows*, Old Vic, 1960 (*Houston Rogers*)

Below Maggie on tour in 1960 in Beverley Cross's *Strip the Willow* with (left to right) Michael Blakemore, Morgan Shepherd (behind), Cyril Luckham and Michael Bates (*David Sim*)

Playing Hilde Wangel, Michael Redgrave's salvation in Ibsen's *The Master Builder*, Old Vic, 1964 (*Angus McBean/Theatre Museum*)

As Desdemona with Laurence Olivier as Othello at the Old
Vic, 1964 (*Angus McBean/Times Newspapers Ltd*)

Above The new Lunts. Robert Stephens and Maggie received great acclaim in Zeffirelli's *Much Ado About Nothing*, Old Vic, 1965 (*Zoë Dominic*)

Left Born in a trunk? As Avonia Bunn in Pinero's *Trelawny of the Wells*, Old Vic, 1966 (*Zoë Dominic*)

The perfect secretary? With Peter Ustinov in *Hot Millions*, 1968
(MGM)

With Robert Stephens in *The Prime of Miss Jean Brodie*
(BFI/20th Century Fox)

As Margery Pinchwife in *The Country Wife* at Chichester,
1969 (*John Timbers*)

directed Maggie in *The Ortolan* at Oxford), suffered from its curiously haphazard camera work, the event was important in many respects, not least the distinction of its cast list.

Maggie played the bashful, giggling flapper, Jackie Coryton, alongside Edith Evans as Judith Bliss, George Devine as David Bliss, Paul Eddington as Sandy Tyrell and Pamela Brown (the actress, not the author) as Myra Arundel. This last role Maggie was to make her own ('This haddock is disgusting') in the famous National Theatre revival four years later, when Edith Evans would repeat her somewhat over-age version of Judith.

Coward had been off the agenda for a few years and had suffered setbacks in the theatre. *The Times* wondered at Edith Evans never having played Judith before and surely anticipated 'Dad's revival' (as Coward himself called it), which began with a 1963 production of *Private Lives* at the Hampstead Theatre Club, in declaring *Hay Fever* to be Coward's best play 'and one of the most perfectly engineered comedies of the century'.

The Bliss family entertain four guests for the weekend and subject them to mild humiliation and eccentric diversion between Friday evening and Sunday morning. Jackie is an effectively dumb role which Lynn Redgrave later occupied with considerable flair at the National. Maggie had her eye on Myra (*The Stage* complimented Pamela Brown on her 'darkly etched vampire') and, in the long term, Judith, the devastatingly harebrained and incorrigibly vain actress who is teetering on the brink of middle-aged retirement. Meanwhile, *The Times* found this version 'a delicately timed, stunningly stylish production', and noted Maggie Smith's 'beautiful study of flaxen inanity'.

Maggie appeared 'by permission of Associated British Picture Corporation Ltd, and the Old Vic'. She was now definitely in demand. Michael Codron wanted her to appear in another

revue with Kenneth Williams, but she was determined to continue her education as an actress.

While Maggie made waves at the Old Vic, Codron presented two more shows with Williams, *Pieces of Eight* (1959)
and *One Over the Eight* (1961). The Williams/Smith partnership was not over, though. They remained in touch and would
team up again before long in the West End.

Maggie was flat-sharing with a girlfriend, Juliet Duncombe,
in Eldon Road, Knightsbridge, and spending a lot of time with
Ian Bannen, a Scottish actor six years her senior who had been
in the Stratford-upon-Avon company with Beverley Cross and
who, in 1958, had scored two great personal successes in the
plays of Eugene O'Neill, *The Iceman Cometh* and *Long Day's
Journey Into Night*.

Bannen was, and is, a soft-spoken, introspective character
whose melancholic disposition was ideally suited to the dark
complexities of O'Neill. And, like the loyally besotted John
Beary, he was a Catholic. Maggie was very taken by him, and
also by a close friend of Bannen's, a stage-struck cleric called
Adrian Arrowsmith, who began giving Maggie instruction in
the Catholic faith. There was even talk at one stage of a great
wedding in Westminster Cathedral.

In Oxford, Nat and Meg must have been horrified at the
thought of their daughter converting from their Presbyterian
and Anglican persuasions. In the event, the friendship with
Bannen petered out and Maggie never became a Catholic,
although it was a close-run thing. Bannen only married much
later in life, after a turbulent career in movies and television.

Beverley Cross reappeared on the horizon. His first play,
One More River, had opened successfully at the Liverpool
Playhouse with a young actor called Michael Caine in the
cast, and it was scheduled for an October 1959 presentation
by Laurence Olivier's production company at the Duke of
York's in London. He knew very well that this might bring

him closer to Maggie once more, and although he was married to another Oxford contemporary, Elizabeth Clunies-Ross, he declared himself 'absent without leave', and reported devotedly to the stage door of the Old Vic in order to renew his lifetime's mission of courtship.

5

West End Calling

T HE reappearance of Beverley Cross was to have a decisive effect on Maggie's career. His rock-like imperturbability complemented her anxiety and defensiveness. Beverley's companionship is the essential safety net for the high-wire tension of Maggie's performing style.

Beverley's mother, Eileen Dale, was a dancer and actress who claimed to have been pestered at the stage door of the Hippodrome by a 'frightfully dull' man called Evelyn Waugh (their brief correspondence is lost). She also appeared in the London premières of *Our Town* and *A Streetcar Named Desire*. In 1936, when Beverley was five, Eileen married George Cross, a theatrical manager of such stars as Godfrey Tearle and Jack Buchanan, and later a long-serving house manager of the Ambassadors Theatre.

Beverley attended the naval college at Pangbourne during the war, joined the army and then postponed his arrival in Oxford by taking a berth in the Norwegian merchant navy. After Oxford, he joined the Shakespeare Memorial Theatre Company at Stratford-upon-Avon, but was discouraged from developing his acting career by a remark of John Gielgud, in whose production of *Much Ado About Nothing* he played Balthazar: 'You'll never make an actor; you wear your doublet and hose like a blazer and flannels.'

He stopped acting almost immediately and wrote two novels,

some television plays and *One More River*. His varied writing credits to date include the money-spinning version of Marc Camoletti's French farce, *Boeing-Boeing* (1962); libretti for the musicals *Half a Sixpence* (1963) and *Hans Andersen* (1974), both starring Tommy Steele; libretti for the Richard Rodney Bennett operas *The Mines of Sulphur* (at Sadler's Wells in 1965) and *Victory* (at Covent Garden in 1970); the new version of *The Scarlet Pimpernel* for Donald Sinden, directed by Nicholas Hytner at Chichester and Her Majesty's in 1985; and innumerable screenplays of which the best known are *Jason and the Argonauts* (1962) and *Clash of the Titans* (1981). It is a fair list, though many good judges feel that Beverley's early promise has never really been fulfilled. In the late 1950s, he was one of the first recipients of the new Arts Council playwriting awards, for each of his first two plays, *One More River* at Liverpool and *Strip the Willow* at the Nottingham Playhouse.

One More River, in Olivier's presentation, directed by Guy Hamilton (who would later direct several of the James Bond movies, as well as Maggie in *Evil Under the Sun* in 1982), with designs by Alan Tagg, arrived in London without Michael Caine. But a strong cast included Paul Rogers as an old bosun trying to mollify a mutiny on board a freighter anchored in a West African river, and Robert Shaw – who made his name in the role – as Sewell, a bullying, autocratic officer who is alleged to have scalded a deck-boy by throwing a cup of coffee in his face (echoes of Gloria Grahame and Glenn Ford in *The Big Heat*).

The boy, who in one impressively ambiguous scene has entertained the gin-sodden sailors by preening around in exotic silks, falls to his death after the scalding incident. The sailors put Sewell on trial. By the time the troubled ship is given the signal to proceed into Port Harcourt, Sewell himself is dead and his innocence surprisingly established.

The play, tense of mood and racily written in three

well-constructed acts, is a naval equivalent of Willis Hall's exactly contemporary hierarchical army thriller *The Long and the Short and the Tall*. But the fashion in new playwriting was moving away from such work, however muscular, towards the rougher, working-class prescriptions for British society delivered by John Osborne, Arnold Wesker and the angry brigade at the Royal Court.

The link between the old West End order to which Beverley aspired and the new Court generation was Laurence Olivier. While his presentation of Beverley's play enjoyed a modest run at the Duke of York's and then the Westminster, Olivier himself was starring in Ionesco's *Rhinoceros* at the Royal Court, where he had scored one of the biggest successes of his career as Archie Rice in John Osborne's *The Entertainer*.

Olivier, still married to Vivien Leigh, was appearing opposite Joan Plowright, with whom he was in love. When *Rhinoceros*, directed by Orson Welles, transferred to the Strand Theatre, Olivier's affair was reported in the newspapers and Plowright was compelled to leave the production because of the uproar – and, it was alleged, gastroenteritis. Plowright stayed on at the Court and made the biggest splash of her career as Beatie Bryant in Arnold Wesker's *Roots*. Guess who stepped in to the Ionesco?

Maggie Smith took over as Daisy to Olivier's Berenger on 8 June 1960 for a six-week run. The show was the hottest ticket in town; it was said to be harder to get into than *My Fair Lady*. Other London hits of the moment included Donald Pleasence in Harold Pinter's *The Caretaker* at the Duchess, Paul Scofield in Robert Bolt's *A Man For All Seasons* (as it happens, the first play I saw on the London stage) at the Globe, Alec Guinness in Terence Rattigan's *Ross* at the Haymarket and the Lunts in Peter Brook's production of Dürrenmatt's *The Visit* at the Royalty. Maggie had joined the élite.

The *News Chronicle* described her as 'cool, crisp and wonderfully matter-of-fact as Daisy, the last woman in the world to join the rhinoceros ranks'. Maggie had little rehearsal time with Welles, but remembers being fascinated by the size of his feet. Olivier was suffering from gout at the time and Maggie set the pattern for their warily competitive relationship by sitting on the gouty leg during rehearsal.

Levin in the *Express* admired the way Maggie tamed her 'natural razor-sharpness . . . into the simple, consoling girl she should be' and *The Stage* averred that she was 'gradually developing into an actress of distinction'. But *The Times* thought that she failed in the final long duet with Berenger: 'Her coming to look after him in a world beset by rhinoceroses is all too casually presented to us as a matter of comparative unimportance, so that her eventual desertion does not shock us as it should. Miss Smith's charm and lightness are not quite all that are needed here.'

This idea that Maggie might be out of her depth in serious drama was one she never shook off, though there is ample evidence from Maggie Wylie onwards – through Desdemona and Hedda Gabler – to contradict it. The force of her comic and indeed sexual presence certainly impressed Olga Franklin in the *Daily Mail*, who reviewed a television adaptation of Somerset Maugham's short story *Penelope*. Maggie played a doctor's wife who wins back an errant spouse by affecting indifference. Franklin said that the production's one weakness was that 'the beautiful Maggie, dressed to the nines with more sex appeal in her little finger than Monroe and Bardot in the nude, made it seem hopelessly unconvincing that her doctor husband should prefer another woman.'

The ripening of Maggie coincided with her appearance in Beverley's crucial second play. After the première of *Strip the Willow* in Nottingham, a new pre-London tour was presented in Cambridge, Newcastle and Brighton in September. Maggie was cast as Kathy Dawson, a politician's mistress sheltering from an imminent nuclear attack in a decaying West Country folly, along with an archaeologist (played by Barrie Ingham) and a private detective (Michael Bates, who had also been in *Rhinoceros*).

For one reason or another, Maggie spent much of the play wearing very few clothes. Those that she did wear were designed by Brigitte Bardot's Parisian couturier, Jacques Esterel. Cross himself described the play as 'a mixture of black magic, strip poker and science fiction'.

It also inverted the Judgement of Paris myth by requiring Kathy to choose the man with whom she would begin pro-creation after the bombs had fallen in the first interval. A Midsummer's Eve party, where the world starts over but the play falls apart, was bolstered in the programme by a quote from the Anonymous Lowlander in 1892: '. . . they danced a jig called Strip the Willow. It was all very wild and gay, but I could see that the lean quartet . . . were as serious and grim as the four horsemen of the Apocalypse.'

Maggie's decorative qualities were politely referred to on the road, but *The Times*, venturing forth to the Hippodrome at Golders Green, last stop before the West End, ran a review under the unpromising headline 'Britain Wiped Out in Comedy's First Act', while the *Daily Telegraph* killed kindly, but killed nonetheless, with 'Horror Comedy a Bit Flat'.

Beverley wrote his personal tribute to Maggie in the form of a stage direction at Kathy's entrance: 'She is about twenty-five and very beautiful. As elegant and sophisticated as a top international model. A great sense of fun. A marvellous girl.'

Binkie Beaumont of H. M. Tennent, who had gone to Golders Green at Beverley's invitation, told him that the West End did not like ironic comedy but that 'the girl is very, very good.' So good, in fact, that he started planning her West End career while putting a stop, for the moment, to Beverley's: *Strip the Willow* never made it on to Shaftesbury Avenue.

Also in the cast was a young Australian actor, Michael Blakemore, who, thirty years later, would direct Maggie in *Lettice and Lovage*. He played an American soldier on security patrol after the fall-out.

'It was an odd play, derived from drawing-room comedy and Peter Ustinov's *The Love of Four Colonels*. But I had this long and very delicious scene with Maggie, which she played in a bathing suit. We tended to giggle a lot, but playing with her was thrilling, because of her sense of stage reality. Like all remarkable actors, she can live in the moment. She organises a part so that every single moment is accounted for, but she still has the flexibility within that framework to do something marginally different each night.

'She is also incredibly generous. The prerequisite of the very best acting is the ability to listen; and there's no actor I know who's a better listener than Maggie. She was on her way to becoming a star in those days, but she wasn't there yet. She was just an extremely brilliant actress that everyone had their eye on and had great hopes for.'

Maggie and Beverley were now living together in the Eldon Road flat in South Kensington. Beverley was otherwise based at the White House at Beaumont in Hertfordshire, which he shared with his chow dog, Tuffet. His first marriage had broken down irretrievably, but there was a delay in arranging the divorce. Most friends of Maggie and Beverley regarded them as unofficially engaged.

Beverley went off on location in Jordan to do some second-unit script editing on the David Lean film of *Lawrence of Arabia* ('action stuff with camels'), while Maggie squeezed in another television role before joining a production of Jean Anouilh's *The Rehearsal*, which Binkie Beaumont was supporting at the Bristol Old Vic and bringing into the Globe.

The television play, only the second that survives on tape from her early career, was *The Savages* by Peter Draper, the author of *Sunday out of Season*. This was another 'Binkie-vision' project in which Maggie plays Rose, a Cockney prostitute who steals the heart of a young boy starved of affection at home. It is a sentimental and naive piece, but not without its moments.

These include John Laurie as an old bed-bound nutty uncle denouncing the civilised life ('They're all savages in smart suits, cannibals, eating people alive') while playing his record of 'The Laughing Policeman', and Victor Maddern as a brothel regular abusing Maggie's budgerigar (like Jean in *Miss Julie*) and telling the boy that it's best not to love anyone at all.

The best scene, though, is that between Maggie and the boy, who tells her that she is the most beautiful person he has ever seen. Maggie has a tumbled, fresh-faced look about her and the sympathetic listening she lavishes on the boy makes a nice change from all the 'entertaining' she has to provide at other times. The cast also includes Ursula Howells as the boy's mother, Rose Hill as the senior prostitute and Fay Compton as a wealthy grandmother.

Maggie was a more respectable child-minder in *The Rehearsal*. She played the young girl employed to care for the orphans in the west wing of a château where a party, rehearsing the performance of a Marivaux play, unconsciously echoes its own romantic intrigues. The girl, Lucile, is heartlessly seduced by the debauched hero, called Hero, played by Alan Badel.

The assistant director was a young working-class son of a Home Counties gardener. His parents lived on the estate and tended the gardens of Stewart Granger and his actress wife Elspeth March (who, thirteen years later, played a cheerful old lesbian in Maggie's soggy venereal disease comedy vehicle *Snap*). He was called Robin Phillips and Maggie later spent a crucial working period of her life with him in Canada, where he was director of the Stratford Festival Theatre in Ontario. But in 1961 he was a nobody. And a dogsbody.

The director, John Hale, left him to run through a rehearsal of the seduction scene, which was not going well, on what happened to be Phillips's nineteenth birthday: 'Badel was very much the star, sitting centre stage, and Maggie was hugging the walls.' When they cried out for help, he tentatively suggested that the scene might be more effective if Maggie sat centre stage and Badel encircled her.

'I don't think it was a particularly clever suggestion, but they tried it, and of course the scene immediately worked. It was quite nice. I could see Maggie's eyes twinkling at the suggestion. She didn't say anything . . . but they whisked me off for a birthday drink because they were so pleased.' Phillips was to become one of Maggie's favourite and most influential directors, but not for another fourteen years!

After the First Night at the Globe on 6 April 1961, Robert Muller in the *Daily Mail* declared the scene to be 'one of the most affecting things to be seen in London at the moment'. Levin in the *Express* commended Maggie's 'pretty dash and honesty'; Hobson in the *Sunday Times* found her 'touching, sincere and sometimes devastating'. Tynan in the *Observer* applauded everything about the play and production except her contribution: '[She] never quite captures the luminous gravity that Anouilh demands; instead of silver she gives us tin,' hinting at Portia's casket scene in *The Merchant of Venice* which Maggie played on television ten years later.

The Rehearsal moved next door to the Queen's Theatre in May, but Maggie was back at the Globe, and reunited with Kenneth Williams and the director Peter Wood, one year later in Peter Shaffer's double bill *The Private Ear* and *The Public Eye*. Her success here ensured that she was discovered yet again. Binkie Beaumont was clasping her to his scheming and all-powerful bosom, and literati even more distinguished than the critics were sitting up.

Evelyn Waugh visited the Globe with Lady Diana Cooper

and wrote to Ann Fleming on 2 July 1962: 'We (Diana and I) went to the theatre and saw a brilliant (to me) actress named Maggie Smith. We couldn't get seats and then said "How about a box?" "Oh yes, of course there's always a box. Do you really want one?" So we sat cheek by jowl with Maggie Smith and admired her feverishly . . . Miss Smith is a fair treat and the two little plays she is in give her a chance to show it. She will become famous. Perhaps she is already and it is like me saying: "Keep an eye on a clever young American called T.S. Eliot."'

In the first 'little play', *The Private Ear*, Maggie was Doreen, an office typist on a first date with a nervous music-lover in his Belsize Park flat; in the second, *The Public Eye*, she was Belinda, the young wife of a jealous accountant who sets an eccentric private detective, Julian Christoferou, on her trail. Julian munches macaroons in a mackintosh and becomes the surrogate lover who never existed in the first place.

The role was taken by Kenneth Williams, but Beaumont considered him too outré for the sensitive musical wooer, and that part was played by a prominent juvenile of the day, Terry Scully, who gave up acting shortly afterwards. According to Peter Wood, the double bill's director, it had initially been offered to Michael Caine, though Caine himself has no memory of this. Widely regarded as the first outstanding young romantic actor who did not sound like a RADA-trained minor public schoolboy, Caine was on the brink of a movie career which would one day pair him with Maggie in *California Suite*.

Shaffer, of course, wrote the two triangular pieces with a view to the same three actors appearing in each. Instead, Williams made a mark as the strange detective and Maggie increased her reputation for versatility. In the first piece, Maggie was naive, ordinary, stumble-tongued; in the second, according to *The Times*, she adapted 'her special amalgam of

height, beauty and simplicity to a girl, supposedly childish,
who enjoys Bellini and the architecture of Robert Adam'.
Many critics expressed disappointment in the quality of the
plays, but Shaffer only offered them as *jeux d'esprit*.

Both Shaffer and Wood took every opportunity to observe
the extraordinary rapport between the two young stars. Shaffer
remembers a Sunday lunch at the Bear Inn, Woodstock, en
route to the pre-West End touring date in Oxford. He asked
Maggie if she liked salmon and she replied that she did if it
was good; if it wasn't, it tasted like old blankets. The phrase
lodged.

The small restaurant was full of sober, respectable families.
The situation acted as a spur, says Shaffer, to Williams, 'who
invented an invisible man standing at the table exposing himself, with Kenny in that very loud fruity voice protesting "I've
had just about enough of this, I'm not interested in your dick,
do you understand that?" and so on. Maggie was in part
delighted, but really rather disapproving. She hardly ever performs like that in private, let alone in public.'

As for their work together, Wood says it was simply dazzling.
'They were like greyhounds, the speed at which they could
bat and ball it.' Wood dismisses as 'facile rubbish' the common
accusation that Maggie picked up her exaggerated campy nasal
twanging from Williams: 'She has an idiosyncratic inflection
process that is all her own. Kenneth, too, had this way of
splitting the inflection, the "ee-aw" thing which is immensely
valuable and which Katharine Hepburn and Jean Arthur also
had. This skill allows you to lift the end of a line so that it is
properly heard and available for another actor to respond to.
It's quite a rare gift nowadays. Maggie and Kenneth adored
each other primarily because of their common speed and brilliance: it was like Boris Becker and Pat Cash meeting each
other on the tennis court for the first time having never played
anyone else as good as themselves.'

Maggie's great moment in the first play arrived when the
hapless would-be seducer fed his Behemoth of a sound system
the love duet from *Madame Butterfly*. Wood devised a six-
minute mime, each move of which was timed 'not to the
bar, but to the note' and, at the point of seductive would-be
resolution, Maggie slapped Scully's face.

Shaffer recalls Maggie not doing a sketch, but suggesting a
woman in a terrible situation in a fake ocelot coat, entangling
herself in that coat, taking a cigarette, burning the coat out of
nervousness. His climactic stage direction in the published text
describes exactly what she did: 'Doreen slaps the boy's face –
then, horrified, takes it between her hands, trying to recall the
blow.'

These were happy days, symbolised by the fact that Beverley,
Maggie and Beverley's stepfather, George Cross, were working
in adjacent theatres on Shaftesbury Avenue: the Apollo, the
Globe and the Queen's. Beverley had a great commercial success with his English adaptation of *Boeing-Boeing*, starring
David Tomlinson; Maggie was working with the actor she liked
above all others, Kenneth Williams, while Richard Pearson,
who played the jealous accountant, became a good friend to
both; and George Cross was managing the Queen's and playing
host to Anthony Newley's hit musical *Stop the World – I Want
to Get Off*.

Williams said that the warm summer 'seemed never ending'
and he would spend weekends blackberrying in the Hertfordshire fields and chasing the dog around the gardens at Beaumont and nearby Broxbourne with Maggie and Beverley. One
blazing Sunday morning, Maggie drove Williams to Becken-
ham in Kent for a day with Richard Pearson and his family.
She wore a pink dress with a matching hatband round a straw
boater: 'It was an open car and, at every traffic light, motorists
and lorry drivers looked twice at this elegant lady motorist. I
felt very proud sitting beside her.'

Feature articles about Maggie began to appear more regularly, and she covered her embarrassment with giggles. She told the *Daily Express* that she had no idea where she was going: 'I just drift into things and I've been lucky. I live for today. I'm restless. I put off everything,' adding with a nice touch of mysteriousness, 'I'm always living behind myself.'

Evasive tactics were momentarily dropped when she told *Woman's Own* magazine that she would not return to revue: 'To go back to anything is bad. In revue you have to make your impact in three minutes flat. It's agony . . .' Nor was she brimming with fashion tips for the readers: 'I can't wear any kind of jewellery, and hats look ghastly on me.'

Her performance in the Shaffer plays secured her the first of her many major awards: Best Actress in the *Evening Standard* Drama Awards for 1962. The judging panel consisted of Peter Hall; the film producer, John Boulting; the assistant controller of BBC TV, Donald Baverstock; and the critics Milton Shulman, Philip Hope-Wallace and T. C. Worsley. Maggie had beaten off challenges from Brenda Bruce, Geraldine McEwan, Dorothy Tutin, Siobhan McKenna and Sheila Hancock. That year's Best Actor was Paul Scofield in Peter Brook's great production of *King Lear*.

Maggie accepted the prize on 28 January 1963 with the words, 'I did seem to get through at O-Level. I do promise you I'll try very hard next term.' She was escorted to the dinner at the Savoy by Beverley, and wore a long black skirt and a bronze-coloured top which, said the *Express*, reflected 'the deep glow of her lovely auburn hair'.

She had left the Shaffer plays and taken a three-week holiday with Beverley in the winter sun on Tobago. 'Next term' would bring a fateful invitation to join the National Theatre. But she was concentrating for the moment on her third big West End role for Binkie and H. M. Tennent, Mary McKellaway, in Jean Kerr's *Mary Mary*, which opened at the Queen's at the end of February (*Stop the World* had completed a run of just over a year).

Jean Kerr was the wife of the prominent American drama critic Walter Kerr. She never saw Maggie in her play because she refused to board an aeroplane. The Canadian actor Don Harron was the trusted repository of her views on how the play should be produced; twenty years later, Don Harron's daughter, Mary, an arts journalist and television producer, interviewed Maggie for the *Observer*. Mary in the play is a journalist, too, precariously married to the publisher Bob McKellaway (Harron). Within a fortnight of their divorce, a question of income tax reunites them. A flirtation with a film star enlivens Mary and rekindles her marriage.

The rows were redolent of Coward's *Private Lives*. But Mary's barrage of wisecracks – 'By the time she is thirty, a starlet has been carefully taught to smile like a dead halibut'; 'This man writes like a sick elf' – was insufficient to save a piece most critics deemed second-rate. Levin, who had moved to the *Daily Mail*, said it was constructed on 'the washing-line principle', with funny lines hung out to dry between the posts holding up the plot.

But the comments on Maggie's performance were uniformly complimentary. The most interesting and sustained appreciation came from Bamber Gascoigne, who had recovered from the agreeable shock of seeing Maggie in his own revue and taken up a column in the *Spectator*:

'Miss Smith's performance is extraordinarily mannered – but then this is largely its strength, since the mannerisms are so completely and unmistakably her own. Most great comediennes have this quality of unique oddity; anyone else borrowing their gestures or tricks would look plain ridiculous, but in them the effect is superb.

'If Beatrice Lillie is suavely made, and Joyce Grenfell is gawky, the word for Maggie Smith is probably akimbo. When

motionless she looks as trim as a kitten, but the slightest shock
– a seductive innuendo from a dark, handsome film star, or
the blast of light when the curtains are drawn in the morning
– is likely to send her billowing across the stage, her legs and
arms flapping about in a welter of confusion like a puppet
whose puppeteer is about to sneeze.'

The breakthrough was now fully accomplished. In movies,
too, Maggie was on the brink of international stardom. Her
seven-year film contract suddenly yielded a sprightly role in
an eminently watchable crime comedy, *Go to Blazes*, for
which the Irish wit and raconteur Patrick Campbell co-wrote
the screenplay.

Maggie played Chantal, a French shop girl in a Berkeley
Square fashion house run by a queenly couturier majestically
played by Coral Browne. They become involved in the esca-
pades of three amiable crooks – Daniel Massey, Norman Ros-
sington and Dave King (making his film début) – a pyromaniac
'Mr Big' played by Robert Morley, and a struck-off fire chief,
played by Dennis Price, who educates the gang in fast getaway
techniques by appropriating an old fire engine and securing
immunity against red lights, traffic police and other civil
obstructions.

The film suffers an almost fatal attack of lethargy during
an over-extended farcical interlude with Derek Nimmo as a
domestic flood victim but the rest is bright and charming, with
lovely vignettes from dear old Miles Malleson as an excitable
antique fire-engine curator and the legendary Wilfrid Lawson
as a junk-yard manager.

Maggie appears at her most lushly glamorous in this film
and she knocks Daniel Massey for six at their first encounter.
Her figure is sensuously outlined in a stylish olive-green dress
when Massey, on the run, backs into a roomful of models and
disrupts a fashion show. He passes himself off as an aristocrat
from the Foreign Office.

Their romance founders when their cover is blown. For not only is the Massey character a fraud, so is Chantal: when Coral Browne tells Maggie the firm is going bust, her French accent evaporates in a Cockney howl of 'Blimey, can't we 'ave a lovely little bonfire, and collect?'

Coral Browne's shop eventually goes up in flames as Massey and Co. raid the next-door bank. But the getaway is interrupted by a real forest fire and, in their efforts to act responsibly for once, the crooks forfeit their booty. Sackfuls of banknotes are blown into the sky. Prison looms once again.

Nowhere to Go was made in a spirit of antagonism towards the Ealing comedies but, in the positive destination of *Blazes*, Maggie relished just as readily the genuine, slightly quaint and old-fashioned article.

The contrast is a clear demonstration that she would never distinguish conclusively between the serious and the trivial in her work; she respected both and was unhampered by too many artistic pretensions. She knew as clearly as anyone, and better than most, the difference, say, between Congreve and Peter Shaffer. But both could supply appropriate raw material for the exercise of her artistry.

Finally, it was in *The VIPs* that Maggie created an international stir. MGM's two-hour blockbuster, scripted by Terence Rattigan and directed by Anthony Asquith, was in part devised as the second film after *Cleopatra* to enhance the romantic fairytale legend of Elizabeth Taylor and Richard Burton, the biggest gift to showbiz gossip writers since the heyday of Douglas Fairbanks and Mary Pickford.

A sort of *Grand Hotel* of the airport lounge, the film crams an array of star actors into a fog-bound Heathrow, where they await a delayed flight to Miami. Elizabeth Taylor is on the point of leaving her shipping-millionaire husband (Burton) for a fling with Louis Jourdan. Orson Welles is a film producer anxious to leave the country for tax reasons, and Margaret

Rutherford twitters inimitably as the Duchess of Brighton planning to raise new money for her crumbling ancestral home. Michael Hordern is the airport manager and David Frost an importunate journalist.

Maggie appeared as Miss Mead, a loyally inventive and romantically disposed secretary to a brash Australian tycoon played by Rod Taylor (the same sort of relationship was repeated opposite Rex Harrison in *The Honeypot*). She fidgets effectively in a sensible coat and beret while Rod Taylor receives bad news; he has one last chance to beat off a corporate challenge in America, but no cash. Meanwhile, Burton goes grovelling to Elizabeth Taylor with apologies and new intentions, but an almighty row ensues.

At this point, Maggie has her big scene, requesting help for her boss from the wealthy Burton. She plays it on the edge of tears, while Burton, boiling inside with his own frustrated devotion, recognises her advocacy as an expression of unrequited love for Rod Taylor and signs a blank cheque. It is a beautiful encounter, expertly and tenderly played on both sides. Burton certainly recognised Maggie's quality. He later said that she didn't just steal the scene; she committed 'grand larceny'. He never worked with her again.

She had kissed the Canadian George Nader in *Nowhere to Go*; her second screen kiss with a hunky colonial leading man (Rod Taylor was Australian) was gratifyingly received and she delicately touched her lips with the tips of her long fingers. Off screen, Rod Taylor had fallen very heavily for Maggie and was even said by Robert Stephens to have proposed marriage to her in the first week of shooting. She did not entirely reject his advances, although he was a married man, and the romance blossomed in their second film together, *Young Cassidy*.

While Maggie continued to draw the town in *Mary Mary*, Kenneth Williams came out of the Shaffer plays and persuaded

Beverley to accompany him on a holiday cruise to the Greek
Islands. Williams was quite happy sipping his eau de vie on
deck, but Beverley ploughed ashore to visit the hallowed sites
on Delos, Lemnos and Skiathos, though he did manage to
drag Williams up to the Parthenon when they dropped anchor
at Athens.

As these two stalwarts of the commercial theatre were trudg-
ing through the ruins, Laurence Olivier was gathering around
him a hand-picked caucus of personnel for the new National
Theatre he had launched at Chichester in 1962. As fellow
directors, he enlisted William Gaskill and John Dexter, both
from the Royal Court, where he knew, through Joan Plowright
and from first-hand experience, that the most exciting new
theatrical energy was being unleashed by George Devine.

Each director had a say in the recruitment of actors. Dexter
and Gaskill insisted on three Royal Court actors, in addition
to Plowright: Robert Stephens, the late Colin Blakely, and
Frank Finlay. In carving up the repertoire, Gaskill agreed to
do a Restoration comedy, Farquhar's *The Recruiting Officer*.
He told Olivier that the only actress he knew who could play
Silvia was Maggie Smith, whom he rated 'the new Edith
Evans' on the basis of her Old Vic performance in *The Double
Dealer*.

Joan Plowright, now married to Olivier, obviously had his
ear on account of its proximity to hers on the pillow. She had
also been aware of Maggie for some time. She remembers
rehearsing *The Entertainer* and reading Jean Rhys and, not
surprisingly, feeling a bit low. Two friends took her to see
Share My Lettuce and she thought Maggie was 'divine':

'Way before the National Theatre started, Larry was drawing
up a list of people to be considered, and I persuaded him to
go to the Old Vic to see Maggie as Lady Plyant in *The Double
Dealer*. I had already seen it; she was quite brilliant. Larry
came back and said that an actress who can play comedy as

well as that can also play tragedy, if she really wants to.'

As a result, Olivier, who of course now knew Maggie at first hand from *Rhinoceros*, invited her to lunch at the Ivy, the theatrical restaurant opposite the Ambassadors Theatre. She was a percentage star in the West End, earning seven and a half per cent of the gross box-office take, with a more than promising film career taking shape. The offer had to be good.

Olivier was unable to put a great salary on the table, but in addition to Silvia, he unexpectedly threw in Hilde Wangel in Ibsen's *The Master Builder*, and Desdemona in *Othello*. Maggie was so surprised she nearly choked on her food. Binkie Beaumont, she knew, had more plans for her. And, in spite of the Old Vic season, she felt she was inexperienced in the highbrow classical repertory. She gave Olivier a definite 'No' and rushed home in a blind panic to Eldon Road.

Beverley was horrified at her decision. He talked her down, and round. First thing next morning, Maggie sent Olivier a telegram reversing her decision and accepting his invitation to join the National Theatre.

She was one of twelve actors placed on a three-year contract. Robert Stephens was another and, as Beverley jovially admitted in later life, in persuading her to join the National at the Old Vic, he pushed her into the whirlwind of a relationship with Stephens, followed by marriage and two children with him. For a time in the 1960s, it seemed as though the English-speaking theatre had found, in Maggie Smith and Robert Stephens, its new ideal star couple, fit successors to the Lunts and the Oliviers. And, up to a point, it had.

In November 1963, *Time* magazine picked out Maggie Smith and summarised her career as she prepared to test her mettle with Olivier. Earlier in the year she had given a most revealing interview, one of the very few, to Nancy Banks-Smith in the *Observer*. Nothing she has said before or since summarised so well the life she had found as an actress in flight from both the pressures of the real world and the deficiencies, as she saw them, in her own personality:

'I'm never shy on the stage. Always shy off it. You see, the theatre is a different world. A much better world. It's the real world that's the illusion. It's a world whose timetable is more precise than anything else on earth. Outside, trains can run late. But trains in the theatre are always on time . . .

'It's strict. It's secure. The theatre is full of people looking for prefabricated security. They find it there. Nowhere else. Outside, marriages crash . . . life goes wrong . . . the thermometer freezes. Inside, the walls are padded against the world.'

6

Surprises at the National

Throughout her career, Maggie has had a habit of stepping from one job to another with scarcely a break and often a too busy period of overlap. She joined Olivier's National as a West End star, and indeed extended her night shift on Shaftesbury Avenue in *Mary Mary* throughout the opening rehearsal period. She left *Mary Mary* on the last night of November 1963, and ten days later opened as Silvia in *The Recruiting Officer* at the Old Vic.

The curtain had gone up on the new National on 22 October, with a fair-to-middling production of *Hamlet* guest-starring Peter O'Toole. *Saint Joan* and *Uncle Vanya*, both great successes, joined the repertoire from the Chichester Festival Theatre, where Olivier had been preparing and half-launching the operation for two summers.

The Recruiting Officer had not been seen in London since 1943 and it was the first real test of how the mixture devised by Olivier and his subalterns would work. Olivier himself appeared as Captain Brazen, alongside Max Adrian as Justice Balance, ex-Royal Courtiers Stephens and Blakely as Captain Plume and Sergeant Kite, with new names Derek Jacobi and Lynn Redgrave in support. An unknown Michael Gambon played a tiny role.

William Gaskill, who had been flatteringly wooed away from the Royal Court by Olivier, recalls the flurry of excite-

ment which attended these early days. 'I don't remember
Maggie coming in like a visiting star, not for a moment. I did
a lot of improvisations, so everyone was in the same boat. The
starting up of the company was exhilarating and that generated
a kind of equality, with of course Larry having the status that
he always had. Everyone was in a sense less experienced and
less important than he was.'

The production is renowned in retrospect as signalling the
restoration of Restoration comedy. It was light and clear, with a
beautiful outdoor Shrewsbury townscape based by the designer
René Allio on the redbrick Queen Anne buildings of the main
street in Amersham. It had architectural airiness without pas-
tel-coloured cuteness. Bamber Gascoigne, who had succeeded
Kenneth Tynan on the *Observer*, said that 'every scene on this
stage acquired an air of sharpened reality, like life on a winter's
day with frost and sun.' The old 'gadzooks' fan-flapping Restoration frills and frippery were out. The playing was tough,
quick, ebullient. Felix Barker in the *Evening News* confidently
proclaimed that 'a new tradition was born in the English
theatre . . . [with] no straining after effects, no twiddly bits' in
Gaskill's quietly orchestrated production.

Olivier's entrance, after a big build-up in the early scenes,
was at first subliminal, as he flashed hilariously across the back
of the stage without a word. Maggie spent most of the evening
in travesty, with a cork-black moustache and knee-high black
boots which, as B. A. Young said in *Punch*, gave her 'a curious
gait with a suggestion of the goose-step about it; just to see her
walk across the stage is a comic treat in itself.'

Gaskill thought she was not immediately happy in the role,
but improved as the production matured in the repertory. Her
amorous pursuit of Captain Plume resulted in a fraternal
clinch with Robert Stephens, who exclaimed, oddly bemused,
''Sdeath! There's something in this fellow that charms me!'

There was indeed. He and Maggie embarked on a

clandestine affair in early 1964 that was initially an inevitable consequence of working proximity. In March, at Lynn Redgrave's twenty-first birthday party, only two people – Lynn and her father's dresser, Christopher Downes, who became a close and constant friend to both Maggie and Robert – knew of the liaison.

Robert was married, for the second time, to the actress Tarn Bassett. They had a daughter, Lucy, born in 1963, who is now an international lawyer with ambitions to be a judge in Paris. Robert's first wife, Nora Ann, with whom he had a son before the Royal Court days, was not an actress, and in later life married the lawyer of the Reverend Ian Paisley, the leader of the Democratic Unionist Party in Northern Ireland.

Robert had met Maggie at a party several years earlier and considered her 'a rather sad-looking creature'. During rehearsals of the Farquhar she made him laugh a lot: 'She was very raunchy. She didn't drink like a fish, but she swore like a trooper. I thought it was just going to be one of those theatrical romances which can happen, but she was much more serious about it than I was.'

Robert Stephens was three years older than Maggie. The son of a West Country master builder, he left home in Bristol to train in Bradford with Esmé Church and arrived in London via a stint with the Caryl Jenner touring company and repertory in Morecambe. Tony Richardson, George Devine's assistant at the Royal Court, brought him down to join the English Stage Company as a founder member in 1956. It was there, in 1958, that he played the title role of *Epitaph for George Dillon* by John Osborne and Anthony Creighton. The production transferred almost immediately, but only briefly, to Broadway. The future looked good.

And so, for a considerable time, and mostly with Maggie Smith, it was. But Robert was, and is, a complex, troubled and, ultimately, deeply flawed character whose immensely likeable volatility became too much part of his stage persona. William Gaskill, who had also been introduced to the Court by his fellow Yorkshireman Tony Richardson, was the director of *George Dillon*. He once pinpointed Robert's special quality as an actor: the ability to understand the nature of failure.

In the last act of *George Dillon*, after the hero has enjoyed some success as a hack writer, he is given a present by his family. Gaskill recalls that, as he unwrapped it to discover a typewriter, Robert registered layers of reaction that convinced you this man would never write anything worthwhile in his life. There was a similar moment of volcanic poignancy at the end of *The Recruiting Officer*, when Plume renounces his job: '. . . the recruiting trade with all its train of lasting plague, fatigue and endless pain, I gladly quit . . .' Stephens invested the lines with what Gaskill calls 'a shadow quality', bringing to the conclusion something over and above what the play actually says.

Robert had returned to the Court after New York and joined Olivier's new venture at Chichester in 1963. He had already played the Dauphin in *Saint Joan* and Horatio in the O'Toole *Hamlet* before Maggie came spinning into his life as Silvia.

The relationship, artistic and personal, gathered speed throughout 1964, an amazingly busy year in which Maggie played Desdemona and Hilde Wangel opposite first Michael Redgrave and then Olivier, and Robert scored his greatest National Theatre triumph as Atahuallpa, the Peruvian sun god in Peter Shaffer's historical epic *The Royal Hunt of the Sun*.

Within the same twelve months, Maggie's second major film, *The Pumpkin Eater*, was released, and she answered a call from Rod Taylor to play opposite him in the Dublin shooting of a film about the early life of Sean O'Casey, *Young Cassidy*.

This hectic year ended with the all-star National production of Noël Coward's *Hay Fever* and preparations for Franco Zeffirelli's riotously Italianate *Much Ado About Nothing*, in which Maggie and Robert seemed to seal their joint pact with the public as Beatrice and Benedick.

The cast of *Othello* assembled to read the play on 3 February 1964. As recounted in a famous rehearsal log book kept by Kenneth Tynan, Olivier, who had been talked reluctantly by his dramaturg into playing the last great tragic role available to him, 'delivered the works – a fantastic full-volume display that scorched one's ears, serving final notice on everyone present that the hero, storm-centre and focal point of the tragedy was the man named in the title. Seated, bespectacled and lounge-suited, he fell on the text like a tiger.'

Olivier had enrolled at a gymnasium and worked hard at unravelling a new baritonal lower octave to mix in with his steel and whiplash tenor. His make-up was incredibly elaborate. He aimed at a blue-black Nubian colour and, at every single performance, covered himself from top to toe in three layers, allowing each one to dry. This process took three hours. His dresser then polished him with a piece of chiffon so that he shone. His hair was cut very short so that his wig could be glued to the back of his neck, deleting the possibility of a recalcitrant hedge effect when his neck muscles bulged. Finally, he was sprayed in a very fine mineral oil.

He was literally, and metaphorically, untouchable. Maggie felt that in the scene when she welcomed him back at Cyprus, there should be physical contact. Olivier refused, and she exclaimed in one rehearsal, 'I've come all the way from Venice to see you, you've won the war, I'm pleased to see you, what do you want me to do, back away in fuckin' 'orror?' Olivier took Robert, who was not in the production, on one side and said, 'Please tell her to stay away from me on the stage. I don't mind if *she* looks like a cunt, but I'm buggered if *I'm* going to look like one.'

The production opened on Shakespeare's birthday, 23 April. There was a brittle wariness and rivalry between Olivier and Maggie. She was possibly the only member of the company of whom he was secretly afraid, simply because he knew how good she was. She could give as good as he gave, and was probably twice as fast. One night Olivier took her to task for the diphthongs she would form on her vowel sounds. As the daughter of an important senator, he felt she would speak impeccably and not sound quite so common.

She took the point and poked her head round his dressing room as he sat there in all his black and naked glory: 'How Now Brown Cow!' she mockingly, immaculately and laboriously intoned. Olivier either didn't get the joke or refused to be riled: 'That's much better, Maggie darling,' he said. Christopher Downes remembers, too, that Maggie sent the boss a postcard of Cassius Clay, then at the height of his boxing fame, on which his boastful tag-line – 'I'm the greatest, I'm the greatest' – was prominently displayed: 'He didn't get it at all. He had very little sense of humour about himself.'

The late John Dexter was the director of *Othello*, and he encouraged Maggie to be stronger, stiller and more serene than are most Desdemonas. According to Riggs O'Hara, the American actor who lived and worked with Dexter for thirty years, the director saw the steel and iron in Maggie and disliked the more girlish, vulnerable side of her acting.

In his diary notes, Dexter wrote after the early casting sessions: 'Nobody wants her [Maggie]. I do. A strong-willed mature woman who's been around and knows what she wants. She wants that big black man. Isn't everyone tired of pretty blonde ingenue Desdemonas?'

Maggie surprised everyone in the role. As O'Hara says, 'She sailed down from the back of the stage through that copper arch in a blue paisley dress with that wonderful brown chiffon over-sash Jocelyn Herbert had designed for her, the air billowing out under it; it was quite spectacular. I'd never seen her be that magisterial.' John Gielgud thought she was 'extraordinary casting' but that she pulled it off splendidly. Tynan thought that she revealed something new – 'an ability to play serious characters whose approach to sex was affirmative and aimed at total erotic fulfilment'.

In spite of Olivier's 'hands-off' instruction, the couple kissed when Othello arrived in Cyprus, with a hint of dreamy sexuality on both sides. In pleading for Cassio, Maggie played sweetly but strongly right down the middle of the argument.

And when Othello struck her round the face with the proclamation he had received from Lodovico her reaction was not, as Tynan noted, the usual collapse into sobs, but 'one of deep shame and embarrassment, for Othello's sake as well as her own. She is outraged, but tries out of loyalty not to show it. After the blow, she holds herself rigidly upright and expressionless, fighting back tears. "I have not deserved this" is not an appeal for sympathy, but a protest quietly and firmly lodged by an extremely spunky girl.'

This scene spawned another anecdote often recounted by Maggie, corroborated by Robert and by Derek Jacobi, who played Cassio. Some months into the run, Olivier was trying to persuade Maggie that she should appear in Thornton Wilder's *The Skin of Our Teeth*, but Maggie was resisting the idea, and one or two other suggestions. Olivier was so incensed that he slapped her with particular force across the face with his hand rather than with the proclamation. She was knocked cold and Edward Petherbridge, playing an attendant supernumerary at the start of his distinguished National career, emitted an audible gasp of 'Oh, Mag!' Frank Finlay had to improvise a new piece of business for Iago: carrying an unconscious Desdemona from the Senate House.

Diana Boddington, Olivier's loyal and devoted stage manager, vehemently denies this story. She says it was Orson

Welles who nearly killed his Desdemona, Gudrun Ure, and
she stage-managed that production, too. 'My only problem
with Larry's *Othello* was the long dress Maggie wore. Larry
played in bare feet and as Maggie came on upstage she at first
used to bring on with her all the cigarette ends that she'd
gathered in her progress along the corridor from the dressing
room. Larry used to go berserk. The only solution, finally,
was to ban smoking in the corridors on *Othello* days.'

Most of the reviewers moved into top sonorous gear to try
and do justice to Olivier's performance. The production itself
was competent enough, but Frank Finlay's Iago was clinically
devious and efficient rather than crawling with theatrical mal-
ice. Olivier had no intention of being upstaged by his lieutenant.

But some dissenters, notably Alan Brien and Jonathan
Miller, took exception to Olivier's adoption of what they
described as nigger-minstrel characteristics. The languorous,
rolling gait, the swaying from the hips, the full-throated impre-
cations and the open-palmed, eye-rolling, tongue-lolling
insouciance all conjured a white man's vision of an exotic,
alien paramour, very probably with enormous sexual apparatus, who had transgressed the decorum of polite society.
Which is exactly Shakespeare's point about Othello. It was
Olivier's unapologetic sensuality which raised hackles.

Looking back, the performance was delicately poised at the
very last moment at which the liberal theatre-going audience
would accept the impersonation of a demonic black character
by a white actor. Subsequent made-up Othellos have dodged
the problem by playing martial dignitaries (Brewster Mason
and Donald Sinden) or Moorish outcasts (Paul Scofield and
Ben Kingsley). And when Michael Gambon hinted that he
might approximate to Olivier's tidal waves in an intimate and
heavily cut Scarborough revival directed by Alan Ayckbourn,
the show never saw the light in London.

Olivier's daring interpretation, certainly unrivalled by any white or black actor since, was probably the last great romantic tragic performance of our theatre, which is why Alan Dent in the *Financial Times* was correct to invoke shades of Kean, Salvini and Macready, even if he hadn't seen them. Irving Wardle (who had succeeded A. V. Cookman on *The Times*) mentioned Frederick Valk and Anew McMaster, modifying the historical throwback by noting the reversal of the modern trend of presenting *Othello* as Iago's play with the central figure a massively vulnerable dupe.

The epileptic fit was amazing, terrifying, and the final death-bed aria over Desdemona's corpse – 'Wash me in steep down gulfs of liquid fire,' arms supplicating with the elements – before slashing his throat with the concealed stiletto, one of the most purely animal feats of acting I have seen. Franco Zeffirelli told Tynan: 'It's an anthology of everything that has been discovered about acting in the last three centuries. It's grand and majestic, but it's also modern and realistic. I would call it a lesson for us all.'

Maggie herself was quietly touching, though *The Times* felt she was on distant terms with the part: 'Obviously a mettlesome girl who would not for an instance have endured domestic tyranny, she introduces facetious modern inflections (for instance her giggling reference to "these men" in the bedchamber scene) which clash destructively with the character.'

In July, the production moved down to Chichester for just sixteen highly acclaimed performances. Robert Stephens was already embarked on *The Royal Hunt of the Sun* on the open festival stage. John Dexter, directing, had been attracted to the play by the challenge of a single stage direction: 'They cross the Andes.' Robert's primitive icon was in part homage to Olivier's Othello, but mostly an extraordinarily vivid and powerful performance in its own right.

No one knew what an Inca god might have sounded like, so Robert created an entirely new world of vocal sound based on bird cries, throat clickings and glottal stops. He also became a burnished figure of sensual athleticism. Shaffer remembers Maggie sitting in on rehearsal and giving them both a lift back to the house in Bosham which Maggie shared for the season with Derek Jacobi and Edward Hardwicke.

She was flitting around between London and Dublin (where she was filming *Young Cassidy*) and Jacobi recalls how, at one point, she returned from Dublin and announced she was going to bed for two days. On the third day, he took a cup of tea upstairs and opened the door to find Robert there too.

The Master Builder, directed by Peter Wood, had opened at the Old Vic in June, and was promptly hailed by Bernard Levin as the National's 'first catastrophe'. Michael Redgrave as Solness appeared not to know his words, and people in the theatre, as well as in the audience, assumed he was drunk. In fact, he was suffering from the onset of Parkinson's disease and would switch alarmingly from one scene to the middle of another in the next act. As Hilde, the reviving demon from the architect's past, Maggie was in the firing line, desperately trying to keep the show on the road.

Olivier was furious with Redgrave and made that fury quite clear. After the First Night performance on 9 June, he burst into Redgrave's dressing room, dragging Peter Wood after him, and delivered an almost incoherent tirade, telling Redgrave in no uncertain terms that there was nothing wrong with 'this boy's' (Wood's) production and that he would play Solness himself. He did so on tour in Oxford in November, prior to returning to London and dividing his Solness between two Hildes: Maggie and Joan Plowright.

When the press was invited to see Olivier's Solness, one reviewer was bold enough to say that Maggie acted Olivier off the stage. On the second night, Robert was sitting in her dressing room when Olivier called by and said, *en passant*, 'Oh, by the way, I understand that one of the critics says that you almost act me off the stage. If I may say so, darling angel, heart of my life, in the second act you almost bored me off the stage, you were so slow.'

Slowness was about the last accusation you could ever level at Maggie. Robert watched the performance that night and witnessed her rip through the play like a jet-propelled aeroplane.

'She picked up her cues so quickly, you couldn't slip a razor blade between the lines. Larry fluffed and dried all over the shop. He paid for his mistake by being made to look like a complete monkey. It was after that experience that he said to me in the street he would never act with her again. Nor did he. They were both brilliant, but in completely different styles. He worked inwards to a role from the outside; she works always on her breathtaking comic instinct, about which she can tell you absolutely nothing.'

Even at loggerheads, Maggie and Olivier struck great sparks off each other. Peter Wood says that one morning of rehearsal for *The Master Builder*, the scene of their first encounter, was 'the greatest moment in the theatre I have ever known'. Gaskill saw one performance 'at which they were electric. I shall never forget it; it was as good as anything I've ever seen, a kind of excitement had taken over.' Irving Wardle summarised the transformation:

'This Solness is a thirsting vulgarian who has hoisted himself to middle-class status, but whose manners still compare coarsely with those of the doctor and his bloodlessly genteel wife. His fear of heights, later to take on a cloudy significance, is thus firmly rooted in the fear of losing his precarious foothold in society . . . Maggie Smith's Hilde has developed almost beyond recognition . . . her scenes with Solness now carry an erotic charge which visibly augments the characters and forms a natural bridge to the mighty symbolic outbursts of the last act.'

Internal relations were not made any easier by the fact that Joan Plowright scored less of a success in the role of Hilde than did Maggie. She had also been ill, suffering a miscarriage which prevented her from opening opposite Olivier as planned. But when she did face the critics, Clive Barnes in the *Daily Express* said that the play sagged with Plowright and that Olivier could not strike the sparks that flared up with Maggie's Hilde, a creature of 'fire and ice'.

Maggie herself was too busy to take much notice of Olivier's anguish. She probably enjoyed the fact that he needed her lustre in the company but resented its shine. Younger company members appreciated her industry and example. Lynn Redgrave found both she and Robert endlessly helpful and encouraging. 'I loved watching Maggie, and learned an awful lot. It must have been hell for her rehearsing at first with my father, but she was extraordinarily sympathetic to him. He, I know, thought she was brilliant.'

Her stock continued to rise in the film world. It is an odd coincidence that just as the erotic fulfilment Tynan noted in Desdemona and Hilde must have been fuelled by the affair with Robert, so she played crucially catalytic girlfriends in her next two movies at a time when three men – Beverley, Robert and Rod Taylor – were competing for her decisive favours.

In Jack Clayton's exceptionally frank *The Pumpkin Eater*, with a screenplay by Harold Pinter adapted from Penelope Mortimer's novel, Maggie plays the relatively small role of Philpot, a children's nanny in the household of Peter Finch and Anne Bancroft. The latter is excessively philoprogenitive, that is to say, cannot contemplate sex without parturition. She has eight children by three marriages. Maggie is a fecklessly destructive foil to Bancroft's invincibly productive wife and she is easy pickings for Peter Finch, though the affair is cloaked in secrecy and never explicit.

We first see Maggie in the kitchen, sitting skittishly on the sink with legs and arms akimbo, informing Bancroft that she (Philpot) is frigid. Finch is a scriptwriter; Maggie, lolling mischievously in her bedroom, opines to Bancroft that 'it must be wonderful to have a man working in the house.'

An indelible comic mark is made on a deeply depressing, sometimes slow, but fascinating black and white film, with Bancroft sinking further into decline and despair, breaking down in Harrods and failing to rescue the marriage after visits to an abortionist, a doctor, a psychoanalyst and even her first husband (played by Richard Johnson).

Dilys Powell in the *Sunday Times*, detecting the influence of Antonioni, applauded a 'beautifully devised' film which, for once, looked *with* women instead of at them. Years later, Clayton pulled off a similar feat with Maggie in the central role of another piece about tragic disintegration, *The Lonely Passion of Judith Hearne*.

Maggie's Dublin sojourn yielded a piece of work which would provide good material for a specialist film buff's interrogation on television's *Mastermind*. Which film did John Ford abandon after shooting just twenty minutes? In which film does Rod Taylor, as an Irish playwright built like an Irish navvy, say 'All the world's a stage, Mick, but some of us are desperately under-rehearsed'? In which film does Flora Robson play Rod Taylor's mother? And in which film does Michael Redgrave as W. B. Yeats walk on a stage and shout at a rioting audience, 'You have disgraced yourselves again'?

The answer to all four questions is *Young Cassidy*, which must be classified as one of several compellingly bad but undoubtedly interesting films Maggie has made. It tells the story of playwright Sean O'Casey, 'John Cassidy', his life and his loves, and his association with the Irish Citizens Army and the Abbey Theatre during and after the Easter Rising. It ends with him boarding a ship for England. Tynan, who was writing film reviews in the *Observer* while working at the National, sneered, 'This is O'Casey spruced up for export and audience identification.'

The project was beset with bad luck. Sean O'Casey, who vetted the use made of his volumes of autobiography, died during the shooting. John Whiting, who had been commissioned to write the screenplay, died a few months before shooting started. And John Ford, whose career was winding down, took to his bed with illness after getting only a few reels of film in the can.

Lindsay Anderson had first been broached about the subject and had thought of Richard Harris as the roistering O'Casey the producers had in mind. But, by the time Ford became involved, the MGM executives forced him to have Rod Taylor. Ford supervised a few scenes between Taylor and Julie Christie, who played the first of Cassidy's three girlfriends (the others were Pauline Delany and Maggie), and also the funeral of Cassidy's mother. Although *Young Cassidy* is still labelled 'a John Ford film', the bulk of the work was taken over by Jack Cardiff.

The movie opens with a slightly work-soiled but mostly glistening Rod Taylor digging in a sewer. At home, Flora Robson makes stew and Jack McGowran dresses up as Richard III. The tram strike looms, Rod writes a pamphlet. Suntanned, fleshy, square-jawed and large, Rod declares that 'there is too much in this country going to waste' and starts filching books from a bookshop where Maggie Smith slaps his wrists and charges him sixpence.

Maggie's character, Nora Creena, appears, respectfully portrayed, in one of O'Casey's plays, *Red Roses for Me,* and also in one short chapter of his autobiography. She was far too religious for O'Casey to bear and he wrote, 'Free thought to her would be but blasphemy and ruin eternal.'

Instead, Maggie plays a sturdy slip of a girl, her long ginger hair tied in a black bow at the back, in whose eyes O'Casey sought 'a soft, shy shelter', as a sensible, sensuous support system to his ambition. Their courtship is the central theme of the film, pushing aside all other political and cultural developments. On a spree in the countryside, Rod pulls Maggie down on top of him and the camera cuts to a bubbling, picturesque river. There follows a rather sweet and sickly sequence of post-coital languor, with a certain amount of kissing, cuddling and singing. Maggie, it must be said, looks positively radiant and old hot Rod pretty pleased with himself.

When Cassidy and Nora visit Lady Gregory at Coole Park, we are treated to the sight of an imperious Edith Evans waited on by a skivvy played by O'Casey's real-life daughter, the actress and director Shivaun O'Casey. Rod carves his initials on the tree alongside those of Yeats, Shaw and Augustus John, and is told by Michael Redgrave's monocled poet that he, John Cassidy, is the Irish Dostoevsky and that he must be prepared to be inspired by the Arctic waste, not the warmth of his girl's body.

The uproar at the first night of *The Plough and the Stars* is summarised by the brother who accuses Cassidy of showing his countrymen to be knaves and fools, and of 'putting our room on the stage and me in it'. Redgrave's Yeats, however, tells Cassidy that the world and its playhouses belong to him. Encouraged, Rod asks Maggie to marry him in the dark of an empty Abbey auditorium. 'No, Johnny,' she says, abandoning him to the world; she needs a simple life, not his terrible dreams and anger, and she backs away up the aisle and out of the theatre. Rod boards a ship and the credits roll.

In her personal life, Maggie made a similar decision. The hurly-burly of life with a Hollywood star was not something she ever seriously contemplated. Beverley's quiet loyalty was taken for granted, but he was beginning to lose touch. His first wife was still being difficult about a divorce and while Maggie had become embroiled at the National, he had spent time in Australia directing the première there of *Boeing-Boeing*.

Maggie, thanks to Beverley's encouragement, had discovered a new life at the Old Vic, and her creative partnership with Olivier and, especially, Robert Stephens, held promise of unlimited excitement and glory. Most importantly, the work was challenging and adventurous, though the inscrutable, incorruptible William Gaskill thought that the bloom had already gone off the National's ensemble pretensions:

'In the second season at the Vic we had Noël Coward trying to get Dame Edith to remember her lines in *Hay Fever*, Franco Zeffirelli camping it up in *Much Ado* and a set for *The Crucible* that looked like a gnome's tea-party. I could see the socialist ensemble was not going to happen.'

Another way of looking at it was that the National Theatre was entering a richly popular phase and that the ideals of a committed company formed along the lines of the Berliner Ensemble were an impracticable option, anyway. They probably always were with Olivier at the helm and the flamboyant, eclectic Tynan, the archetypal champagne socialist, at his side.

The actors themselves knew they were part of something exciting, whatever its intellectual pedigree, and they worked harder than ever. At the centre of the company, Maggie and Robert became box-office magic, attractions second only to Olivier himself, and a couple living out their supposedly private bliss in the glare of public adulation.

Entr'acte: Maggie among her Peers

'A STAR is someone with that little bit extra,' said Noël Coward, but the definition crumbles when you try to define 'bit extra'. An audience knows a star when it sees one. On screen, the cliché is that the camera loves a star. In the theatre, certain basic qualities of stardom are quantifiable: total audibility, eye contact throughout the house, animal magnetism, the precise ability to convey the process of thought, and watchability, even with the back turned on the audience.

In Maggie's case, the very pronunciation of her name stirs expectation and raises the spirits. As Bernard Levin says, 'There's a glow around her, on stage and off, and everybody knows about that glow. It's real.' And yet, of all palpable stars, she is the last to place a boorish insistence on her status.

Some big stars, such as Vanessa Redgrave and Charlton Heston, are perfectly charming and approachable people, but even in those two cases, the portcullis will descend at moments of crisis: they become elevated and remote. Maggie is unusual in that she behaves at all times as if she has no power or status whatsoever.

On the night of her son Toby's professional stage début in *Tartuffe* in 1991 at the Playhouse in Charing Cross, she stood unostentatiously in the foyer sipping a glass of champagne with Beverley, impervious to the First Night throng and totally unrecognised. At the same time, Maggie-watchers knew that the 'Do Not Disturb' signs were up. She was nervous for Toby. Had an old friend or colleague dared to penetrate the transparent membrane of her solitude, there's no knowing what might have happened.

In the nineteenth century, and even into the middle of this one, all great actors were a race apart. Sarah Bernhardt and, less outrageously but no less publicly, Eleonora Duse, were fêted and revered like royalty throughout Europe. In England, Ellen Terry was as generally loved as any public figure of the day. The phenomenon of the disappearing great actor – Paul Scofield, Alec Guinness, Maggie and, to a certain extent, Olivier himself – is an odd result of the modern insistence on privacy when faced with the threat of instant global exposure in the age of gossip magazines and electronic media.

Some star performers whose reputations are not dependent on organised hype – unlike, say, Joan Collins, or Cher, or Madonna, or Michael Jackson – now wish to reclaim their privacy. Paradoxically for a show-off, Maggie Smith chisels away at her work with the monastic dedication of the instinctive recluse.

In a golden age of British acting, she is distinctly quiet and 'invisible', even compared to such leading peers as Glenda Jackson and Vanessa Redgrave, who are, respectively, two and three years younger, and Judi Dench, who is just three weeks older. We do not know what she thinks of the world, except that she distrusts most people in it. She rarely appears on television as 'herself', gives very infrequent, guarded interviews to the press, lends her name to no causes, her signature to no petitions, her prestige to no boards of directors. Life is difficult enough without the hassle of good works and deeds. And the pettiness of the theatre, the rapacity of the film companies and the vanity of acting, you feel, are phenomena Maggie just lives with as the price she pays for the demon within.

The director Peter Wood says that 'psychological shingles is what she's got, an inflammation of the personality ends.' The designer Anthony Powell is reminded of 'flayed anatomy, with those missing layers of skin, stripped away to show the formature of muscles and bones. She is more scared of being touched and hurt than anyone I know.'

The stage offers security in spite of all its dangers. In the theatre, Maggie forfeits her individuality in a curious distillation of her personality, and at last knows who she is, what she should wear and to whom she must speak. Off stage, she is beset with confusion and indifference on all these points.

Or at least, that is the appearance. 'Dealing with her gift' is the spine of her life, according to Brian Bedford, one of her favourite leading men, and nothing much else interferes with that task. She worries endlessly at a text, like a dog at a bone, not to find a new laugh, nor to perfect a new trick, but to make a line, a passage and then the whole play, come alive again. Night after night, from first to last.

She works hard in rehearsals, but never with a closed mind. William Gaskill says that Olivier would arrive at rehearsal with his performance intact, deliver it like a gift and adjust it thereafter if necessary. Maggie never has anything finished before she starts, which is why rehearsing with her is so exciting.

And unlike many actors half her age, she practises her scales and arpeggios. She is fanatical about not putting on weight. 'Red lorry, yellow lorry' is a drama student's articulation exercise (the phrase repeated, fast, *ad infinitum*) she has never stopped using, like a trusty old toothbrush. She trains, in fact, like a dancer.

And, like a great dancer, she can be radiant at will. Peter Shaffer remembers seeing Margot Fonteyn dance Aurora in *The Sleeping Beauty* when she might have been thought too old for the part. 'One saw within three or four minutes that here was a young girl conjured by the psychic resources of the artist, and Maggie can do that. She has this wonderful radiance which enables her not only to look as glamorous as anyone you've ever seen, but also to illuminate the moral corners of a play.'

She herself has never believed in her own beauty. The courage she needs to go on the stage at all is the prerogative of only the most exceptional performers. The photographer Zoë Dominic believes that Maggie is akin to Maria Callas, who feared that the audience would destroy her each time she went out to sing. The vulnerability of the great artist invests the audience with this dangerous power. No such risk is taken by the average actor.

Any attempt to 'place' Maggie in the annals of British acting is bound to consider her alongside Judi Dench and Vanessa Redgrave. These two are left to contest the crown of Peggy Ashcroft, while Glenda Jackson seems certain to pursue a life in politics. Dench and Redgrave are, in a way, the Gladys Cooper and Sybil Thorndike of our day, while Maggie is certainly the Edith Evans.

She has had notable success in many of Edith Evans's roles – Millamant, Mrs Sullen, Rosalind, Cleopatra, Judith Bliss – and is the nearest we come to the idea of the chastely intelligent Anne Bracegirdle, for whom Congreve wrote his most famous female roles.

There are more similarities with Evans. Dame Edith's background, like Maggie's, had not a whiff of theatrical tradition. She was the only child of a minor civil servant in the post office. Her mother, like Maggie's mother, in Bryan Forbes's phrase, 'set great store by the proprieties.' Her talent was instinctive, imaginative and untrained (she first went to work in Pimlico as an apprentice milliner) and she had a way of finding words such as 'basin' inherently funny. Later in life she became a Christian Scientist, and like Maggie never had to brazen it out in the provinces: 'God was very good to me,' she once said. 'He never let me go on tour.'

She knew Bernard Shaw – she was his Lady Utterwood in *Heartbreak House*, his Serpent in *Back to Methuselah*, his Orinthia in *The Apple Cart* and, after a protracted scuffle, his Epifania Fitzfassen in *The Millionairess* – but was not all that devoted: 'He kissed me once. But I derived no *benefit* from it.'

Nothing was allowed to interfere with her theatre work, which amounted to sixty glorious, uninterrupted years after she had been discovered as Cressida in Streatham Town Hall by William Poel. She had no children and was loyally supported by a self-sacrificing husband whom she knew from her teens, and whom she married in 1925 and hardly ever saw, as he worked abroad for British Controlled Oilfields.

Like Maggie, Edith Evans was intensely private off stage. She had no real interest in the material world and no ambition in conventional show-business terms. And she first went to the Old Vic as a West End star. Unlike Maggie, she did hardly any revue, made few films until much later in life ('I don't think I have a film face; it moves about too much,' she once told reporters) and wrote quite a lot of letters. Her *amour fou* was an unlikely affair with Michael Redgrave, who played a boyish Orlando to her forty-nine-year-old Rosalind.

Maggie could wrest Millamant and Mrs Sullen from Edith Evans because the performances were a fading memory among critics and audiences. But Evans's Lady Bracknell, with its almost self-parodying haughtiness and deadly swoop on 'a hand-bag', bedevils any actress, thanks to its notoriety from the 1951 Anthony Asquith movie. Maggie herself used to do impressions of these intonations in her revue days.

When Judi Dench played Lady Bracknell (at the National Theatre in 1982), she brilliantly side-stepped all comparisons by portraying the tension and melancholy of a much younger dowager, non-stentorian and with the bloom still on, whose husband, dining alone with his meals on trays, was a considerable brake on her social and indeed sexual potential.

Her success in the role did not obliterate Edith Evans, and Maggie had to start all over again when she finally delivered her reading. But it was quite a good swipe. And Dench has also had her RSC triumphs as Hermione/Perdita in *The Winter's Tale*, and as Viola, Portia, the Duchess of Malfi, Beatrice, Lady Macbeth and Imogen in *Cymbeline*. She followed her Lady Bracknell at the NT with an equally unexpected, and equally memorable, Cleopatra. Any competition Maggie mustered at that time was confined to Canada, so that the impression, in Britain at least, was that Judi Dench had become our leading tragedienne.

The release of feeling, a sort of glorious shiver with an instantly recognisable crack in her voice, characterises all these Dench performances. The renewed monstrosity of Bracknell will be something left to Maggie to accomplish when she gets round to her second Aunt Augusta (Lady Bracknell's name was adopted by Graham Greene for his travelling aunt). Dench generously concedes that it is Maggie's extraordinary way of looking at the world that marks her out, her delightful sense of the absurd: 'She does things in such a daring way that she leaves me standing. She also leaves me laughing.'

Everyone loves Judi Dench, just as everyone loved Ellen Terry. But her drive is of a different calibre to Maggie's, less gnawing, less obsessive. John Moffatt says that Maggie, like Paul Scofield, is possessed by a demanding and driving genius, but that she also skirmishes in the realms of camp by inhabiting a world that is peculiarly her own, rather as Beatrice Lillie did. Maggie loves a line of Bea Lillie's, said of a hopeless case leaving the stage: 'She'll never find the kitchen, she's that moody.'

And, as Maggie's performances are often a series of elaborately contrived masks that proceed to disintegrate, she further arouses interest in what she might *really* be like under the skin. As Peter Hall says, 'When the public sees Maggie Smith in a play, the public becomes voraciously interested in what kind of person Maggie Smith is.'

There are various points of similarity between Maggie and Judi Dench, but that is not one of them. Judi Dench is known to be a cosy, comfy creature with good manners, good breeding and a pronounced liability to burst into giggles and gales of laughter. Everything is more dangerous, acidulous and beadily *observed* with Maggie.

This is not a value judgement on their respective talents. But Maggie, especially in comedy, presents the role, while Dench puts herself in its centre and works outwards, negotiating the limits of her own characterisation at the same time as she meets the rest of the actors and the surrounding production. This method leads, not all that surprisingly, to the occasional aberration in the costume and wig departments, where Dench is often reprehensibly careless. Maggie never makes such mistakes.

With Vanessa Redgrave, the contrast is even greater, and has been well made by Simon Callow. 'To work with Maggie and then with Vanessa,' says Callow, 'is to go from alpha to omega. They are the Gielgud and the Olivier in the sense that they represent absolute opposites. Vanessa inhabits poetic states and becomes infused with them; but what they are, and where they come from, is entirely mysterious. Maggie, on the other hand, is interested in a particular truth at every moment, and she goes at it like a forensic scientist. She never stops. Vanessa is so much more intuitive, and random; she throws a casual light over something, and because nobody's ever had such a strong beam before, you see all kinds of things reflected.'

Callow believes that Maggie, like Olivier, finds a kind of sanity only in technical craft: 'They are both tremendously needful personalities who don't go into "acting" at all, and must externalise what they do. But if it were *only* that, you wouldn't be interested in them. Maggie plucks at the script and says, "What am I supposed to do, I mean, I mean, you say, I mean, it's supposed to be funny." Then you say, "It's supposed to be funny," and she will press a button and go into comic mode, and what you have written or translated becomes like Congreve.

'For Vanessa, you have to create a whole imaginative framework, which takes about five hours to get across. You can't just say, "This woman hates men." Once Vanessa finally takes such an idea into her imaginative world, she takes it on completely. But one idea, put simply to Maggie, can instantly go through her whole performance. She is ecstatic at such moments and becomes the most beautiful, physical and most alive woman you have ever seen in your life.'

The hands, the gestures, what Robin Phillips once called 'those witty, witty elbows', the quizzical tilt of head, all are part of a technical mechanism whose inner working remains a mystery. Alec McCowen says that with most actors he can see how the wheels go round. With Maggie, he can't. Others have puzzled for years over her way of making a line, or a word, sit up and bop an audience on the nose. She once complimented the Irish actor Joseph Maher for 'never answering last night's question', by which she meant that he played off exactly what came to him from the other actors. Maher confessed that he thought that was what actors were supposed to do. 'You find me five people who can,' Maggie snapped back.

Maher also notes the insertion of an intake of breath, even a tiny 'd'you know', as a missing beat in a line that might not otherwise stand up and be funny. This is a good example of a purely instinctive technical gift, and only used very sparingly.

Nicholas Pennell, who acted in Canada with Maggie, also

thought long and hard about this trick, and reckons it is a way of ensuring that the line sounds as if it is being spoken for the very first time. Little repetitions come into it, too, sometimes almost imperceptibly. Pennell has heard a particular phrase repeated, very quickly, not to reiterate meaning, but to cancel it, so that attention is engaged by starting on an entirely different tack.

Pauline Kael said of Diane Keaton in Woody Allen's *Annie Hall* that she raised anxiety to an art form. The phrase has often been reapplied to Maggie Smith as a way of dealing with that peculiar tetchiness and angularity, as well as the speed of thought and motion, which is her ineradicable trademark. Because of her concentration and intellect, the fluffiness of her acting never curdles, though detractors sometimes complain of emotion that is entirely self-generated or mannerisms that are over-familiar.

Maggie's reaction is to shrug sympathetically and mutter that she can't help being lumbered with her own deficiencies, as she adopts yet another gloomy view of the perennially hostile world. She uses her moods of depression to reactivate her determination to work out the best way of doing the next line, the next scene, the next play, the next film. Another profound aspect of her mystery is the fact that so much is buried and bottled up inside. As Angela Fox, mother of Edward, James and Robert, says, 'You couldn't act like Maggie unless you'd known deep personal emotion. Vanessa's the same.'

Peter Wood, who once labelled her 'Miss Downbeat', and has known her all her professional life, claims Maggie realises that, like Scofield and Ralph Richardson, she has 'the precious essence' and is careful not to spill a drop of it. This accounts in part for her defensiveness and reluctance to talk about acting.

There is a famous story of Ellen Terry rehearsing a play for the first time with Dion Boucicault. The Irish playwright and director had introduced into his staging something nobody else had ever heard of: blocking. He blocked out the actors' moves. This was especially new to Ellen Terry, who was used to being told by Henry Irving, 'Just stand by me, dear.'

Boucicault described at great length what he wanted: she was to move up here, go down there, cross the stage at this point and deliver the last lines as if she had lost the most valuable treasure in the world.

'And then,' said Ellen Terry, 'I suppose I do that indefinable something of my own for which you pay me so much money.'

'Dead right,' says Peter Wood. 'That is what Maggie does. By the exercise of an awesome technique. And you don't meet it very often. In fact, hardly at all.'

7

The New Lunts

HAVING made her mark at the National in two demanding tragic roles, Desdemona and Hilde Wangel, which altered the public's perception of her, Maggie renewed her comedy career with especial relish. In the middle years of the 1960s she and Robert enjoyed the razzmatazz of being 'the new Lunts'.

They were married in 1967, shortly after the birth of their first son, moved house, acquired a country property, had another son, and were cast in leading roles in major films: Maggie as Miss Jean Brodie, Robert as Billy Wilder's Sherlock Holmes. Maggie's film would make her an international star. Robert's failed to do the same for him and married life became much trickier. The time arrived when they could no longer share equal billing.

These tensions were disguised for some years within the apparent democracy of a theatre company. Maggie and Robert were cast in *Hay Fever* which, in spite of the problems with Edith Evans as Judith Bliss, became one of the National's greatest hits.

On the first day of rehearsals, Noël Coward addressed the cast: 'I'm thrilled and flattered and frankly a little flabbergasted that the National Theatre should have had the curious perceptiveness to choose a very early play of mine, and to give it a cast that could play the Albanian telephone directory.'

Although about ten years too young for the part, Maggie always saw herself as Judith Bliss, and her sights on it must have been sharpened now. She 'covered' the role and very nearly took it over. As things turned out, she made a fantastic comic creation of the vamp Myra Arundel, and will forever be associated with the show-stopping delivery in Act Three of the previously unremarked line 'This haddock is disgusting.' (The haddock was not really that bad; stage management provided mashed bananas.)

Derek Jacobi, who played Judith's son Simon Bliss, recalls how battle lines were drawn between Dame Edith and Maggie at the first dress parade. 'Maggie came on in this ravishing black cocktail number for Act Two which had an eye-catching long fish-tail fan at the back. The Dame put her elbow on the sofa where Maggie had to sit, and as Maggie got up, there was this great tearing sound and the fan came off. "Oh, that looks so much better, Maggie," said the Dame.

'At the next rehearsal, Maggie returned not only with the fish-tail back on, but also with an immensely long cigarette holder around which, before she sat down on the sofa, she twirled the fish-tail. She then sat down, unpeeled the holder from the fan and put it in her mouth. Of course this remained in the show and more or less stopped it every night.'

Dame Edith was far too old for Judith, but Coward, who directed, was monumentally patient, a fact enshrined in Tynan's account of one of the Master's most renowned mots. Dame Edith insisted on saying in rehearsal, apropos of the weekend cottage's Thames-side situation in Cookham, 'On a very clear day you can see Marlow.' Finally Coward could stand it no longer and yelled from the back of the stalls, 'Edith, the line is "On a clear day you can see Marlow." On a *very* clear day you can see Marlowe *and* Beaumont *and* Fletcher.'

The actress herself became suddenly aware of her predicament as she travelled up to Manchester for the out-of-town

opening with her friend, Gwen Ffrangcon-Davies. She was
going through her lines and came to the scene where she is
defending her flirtatiousness to her own children: 'Anyone
would think I was eighty the way you go on.' She stopped,
stared at Ffrangcon-Davies and said, 'But I *am* nearly eighty.
I'm seventy-six. I can't play this part.'

On arrival in Manchester, Dame Edith took to her hotel
bedroom and refused to emerge until earnest representations
had been made by Coward, Olivier and John Dexter. She told
Coward, who found her moaning on her bed, that she had 'a
dry mouth and a dropped stomach'. She agreed finally to play
the dress rehearsal, to which an audience had been invited,
only after Coward had decided 'to give the Dame hell' and
had berated her for being a disgrace to herself, the theatre *and*
Christian Science. The audience was sent home.

When the play was run for a second time, the Dame was
allowed back to the hotel, and Maggie stood in as Judith.
Diana Boddington was stage-managing and remembers a riot:
'Well, Maggie just sent up Edith's performance something
rotten. The mimicry was unbelievably funny. We were all –
Noël, Larry, everyone – laughing so much we were lying
around on the floor.'

No doubt hearing that Maggie, or 'the little Smith girl' as
she called her, was more than capable of stealing her thunder
as Judith, Dame Edith agreed to play the week in Manchester
on the odd condition that Gwen Ffrangcon-Davies was allowed
to sit in her dressing room, presumably as a last line of defence
against any dreaded Maggie intrusions.

But Maggie never allowed respect to swamp her adversarial
instincts. She knew, and loved, the Dame's reported comment
on *Share My Lettuce*: 'It is unprofessional, and cissy.' Lynn
Redgrave recalls that, later in the run, Dame Edith imperiously accosted Maggie backstage: 'I understand that you are
covering the role of Judith Bliss. I should like to tell you here

and now that I shall not be off.' Maggie, quick as a flash, replied, 'Well, I sincerely hope not, because the cossies won't fit!'

'The Dame, God rest her soul,' says Jacobi, 'was not the most generous of actresses. She was certainly hideous to us youngsters, giving us notes and summonses and tellings-off and I think to a certain extent Maggie was standing up to her for everyone else in the cast.'

Nothing, not even these peccadillos, could tarnish Dame Edith's reputation or the profound respect in which she was held. But by this time in her career she was a rather sad and loveless old lady, and many Maggie-watchers feel that her example in private life was something Maggie was afraid of. One way of ensuring against complete emotional isolation would be to have children.

Dame Edith had a few loyal friends, but no family. And not much peace at the Old Vic this time round. Jacobi remembers that Maggie and the Dame occupied adjoining dressing rooms and, between shows on matinée days, Maggie would play a favourite record, 'Baby Love' by the Supremes, at full blast 'so that the Dame could not sleep and would be too tired to cause trouble in the evening performance.'

On the First Night, 29 October 1964, Coward sat in the stalls next to Judy Garland, just behind Lena Horne and quite near Rudolf Nureyev. It was that sort of evening. In a programme note, Tynan reminded a generation for whom Pinter was the new master of elliptical style that 'Coward took the fat off English comic dialogue; he was the Turkish bath in which it slimmed.'

Style apart, Herbert Kretzmer declared in the *Express* that *Hay Fever* was 'one of the few plays I have seen that is about nothing at all.' Each member of the Bliss family invites a guest for the weekend. Charades are played after dinner. The guests leave in the morning before breakfast. A generally observed point was that the guests now seemed more eccentric than the hosts, whereas the reverse was true when Marie Tempest led the 1925 première.

Certainly none was more eccentric than Maggie's Myra Arundel in green cloche hat and matching shoes, looking, said Felix Barker in the *Evening News*, 'like an Anita Loos heroine drawn by Aubrey Hammond'. Myra is described in the play as a girl who goes about using sex as a sort of shrimping-net. With her fluttering eyelashes and anaconda smile, Maggie was a picture of enamelled, nauseated horror as she stroked Derek Jacobi's hair and found her fingers covered in grease, or scooped her train into position with the cigarette holder and faced yet another incompetent assault upon her lethal defences.

If *Hay Fever* unleashed a comic genie from the National's bottle, the Zeffirelli production of *Much Ado About Nothing*, so despised by Gaskill and some of the more high-minded critics, let slip the dogs of merry war. The costumes were coloured and padded out to resemble Sicilian confectionary dolls. Maggie looked at her most edibly beguiling in a red dress and blonde wig. Robert was a swarthy swaggerer with heavily pomaded hair and massive dark glasses. The contest between Beatrice and Benedick was that of two razor-sharp habitual antagonists who were in love with each other to start with.

It opened on 16 February 1965 and stayed in the repertoire for several years. The audience loved it. Philip Hope-Wallace in the *Guardian* gave the most vivid overall picture of its free-wheeling *opera buffa* provenance: 'The lancers in Messina? But that is nothing. Some of the girls have strayed out of Goya or Fuseli, the lordlings are from Visconti's *The Leopard*, Dogberry leads them in a chorus of *La traviata*, Leonato has escaped from *Don Pasquale* and later turns up (in mock mourning for his daughter) got up like Papa Ibsen. There is a town band; a female bicycle; umbrellas; human statuary; bowler hats and a measure of mugging and gesticulating which make the films of Gloria Swanson or the farces of Labiche look like *tableaux vivants* of unwinking decorum.'

Against this, the killjoys, led by Bernard Levin (who reported 'one of the more excruciatingly tedious evenings at present obtainable this side of Hell'), booed from the cheaper seats as well as from the review pages. But however reprehensibly glib was Zeffirelli's irreverent approach to the comedy, we can see it now as the first of a whole string of major Shakespearean knees-ups in the latter half of the century. Within two decades, the RSC would present other comedies by swimming pools, on motorbikes and as thinly disguised sub-Broadway musicals.

One serious point at issue had been Tynan's recruitment of the poet Robert Graves to 'clarify' some of the more recherché jokes and references. Over three hundred minor alterations were proposed and many adopted. But Maggie refused point blank to accept any alteration on 'I had rather lie in the woollen', and proceeded to show Tynan and Graves how to convey the meaning *and* gain the laugh. One key to Maggie's greatness in Shakespeare is her genius for unlocking abstruse meanings with unerring perception and comic timing.

Albert Finney made his NT début as Don Pedro and played him, said Levin, 'as though he had a red-hot poker stuck in his trousers, staggering about backwards and talking like an itinerant ice-cream pedlar with a cleft palate.'

Another NT débutant was Ian McKellen, whom Maggie herself had recommended as Claudio on the basis of his touching performance in James Saunders's *A Scent of Flowers*. Finney subsequently blossomed in *Miss Julie* and *Black Comedy*, both with Maggie, while McKellen did not find the groove and postponed his passage to the top flight for a few years.

Maggie was unhappy before the opening. She told Christopher Downes that she was going to put on a wig and dark glasses and go to the Isle of Man. But anyone who saw this deliciously irresponsible and joyous production has memories of two particular Maggie moments. When Don Pedro concluded that, out of question, she was born in a merry hour, Maggie stopped the scene for just one half line of piercing pathos with 'No, sure, my lord, my mother cried . . .' and immediately revived the antic mood on 'But there was a star danced, and under that was I born.' The pain of childbirth was the price of her jocund animation, and Maggie turned the scene right round on the proverbial sixpence.

Later, in the church, she is asked by Benedick what he might do to soften Hero's agony at her supposed betrayal. Zeffirelli had wanted her to play for another big laugh. Instead, she yelled, 'Kill Claudio' with a totally unexpected savagery. This outburst of towering, disinterested rage stunned the audience to silence and so petrified the scene that you felt the entire production might have to be abandoned, like an unruly football match suddenly blanketed in freezing fog. Robert held a very long pause and whispered, almost under his breath, 'Not for the world.'

Two weeks after the opening of *Much Ado*, Maggie took part in a Sunday night Bach-Handel concert at the Royal Festival Hall to raise money for the Save the Children Fund. She admitted to Sydney Edwards in the *Evening Standard* that she could play Bach's easy pieces for the piano, but confined herself to the recitation of a script based on a play by Colly Cibber and a contemporary account of a temperamental clash between two of Handel's sopranos. She was asked about her NT touring schedule: 'I'm going on tour – to Glasgow, Nottingham and Manchester. It always happens to me. I make a film and get sent to Cricklewood and everybody else goes to Tahiti.'

In addition to gadding around the industrial north, the National maintained its connection with Chichester on the softer South Downs, where they presented a fourth summer season in 1965. Maggie opened in July in a double bill of Strindberg's *Miss Julie* and a new farce by Peter Shaffer, *Black Comedy*.

Miss Julie was cast first and Tynan approached Shaffer with a commission to write something to go with it. Shaffer revealed that, ever since he had seen the Peking Opera, he had wanted to write a farce involving the 'black theatre' of one of their most famous sketches, where battle is joined on a fully lit stage by combatants plunged into total darkness.

Although late with a film script, Shaffer was told to get on with it by Olivier who, Shaffer recalls, as a result of Tynan's enthusiasm, simply looked straight through him and said, 'It's all going to be thrilling.' Shaffer immediately developed a complete writer's block because he'd agreed to do it before working out a plot. Olivier's only suggestion was that Maggie's part shouldn't be too long as she was working very hard and seemed to be frail.

The plays went into rehearsal in Chichester and although the Strindberg, translated by Michael Meyer and directed by Michael Elliott, was relatively straightforward, John Dexter was directing the Shaffer from a script that seemed to change every day. Maggie's role as Clea, the jilted mistress, was an unresolved hotchpotch. One day, according to Riggs O'Hara, she stood up and said she had the perfect answer: 'As I slit my wrists in the first play, why don't I cut my throat in the second?'

The exciting thrust stage caused problems, too. The claustrophobic Strindberg was of necessity opened out, with a large ramp bringing the actors into the arena. And the exigencies of farce meant that, in the Shaffer, the actors had to transmit their reactions and sight gags through 180 degrees. It was remarked that the killing of a budgerigar was received with far more dismay and disapproval in Chichester than was the valet's seduction of his mistress; Maggie had not quite focused her voice on the tragic intensity of the last few minutes.

Both productions were seen to better advantage when they arrived at the Old Vic in the following March. You could sense more of Miss Julie's gathering horror and there was clearer delineation of both her social superiority and her sexual desire.

Ronald Bryden in the *New Statesman* took a well-timed and perceptive long view of Maggie's career. Over her performance as Miss Julie, he said, hung the burning question of whether she could go on to become the National's tragedienne: whether she might some day tackle Hedda, Phèdre and Cleopatra, or continue on her present course towards Rosalind, Millamant and Wilde's Gwendolen.

As it turned out she would have to go to Canada to play Cleopatra, Millamant and Rosalind. Hedda was a few years off. Phèdre still beckoned, but Gwendolen has now surely been subsumed by Lady Bracknell. In 1965, the issue of her tragic aspirations remained, for Bryden, in the balance. She was much less a seductress, he felt, than a hypnotised victim, although she managed a momentary comeback in the second half with her long history of a twisted upbringing.

Although one or two critics acclaimed this Miss Julie as a great performance, Bryden was nearer the mark in alleging that the bloodthirsty diatribe against men, as well as the desperate lesbian appeal to Christine, was beyond her range. It was a pointer to what she might achieve, rather than a fully accomplished tragic portrayal. The play's impact was softened, muted.

Although some critics were mean and sniffy about *Black Comedy*, the piece was a riotously funny addition to the repertoire and one of the most expertly played farces London had ever seen. Suddenly Feydeau did not seem beyond the National's grasp. Indeed, Jacques Charon was on his way from the Comédie Française to direct A *Flea in Her Ear* in the winter.

The play opens with an effete sculptor, Brindsley Miller (Derek Jacobi), showing his debby, squeaky-voiced fiancée, Carol (Louise Purnell), into a flat he has furnished with antiques 'borrowed' from a neighbour, Harold Gorringe, in order to impress her father, who is about to arrive. They set the scene in complete darkness. They are then plunged into full stage light by a power failure. The subsequent action is, for both Brindsley and the apartment, a progress through disintegration.

Gorringe (Albert Finney) returns unexpectedly, so Brindsley has to keep his furniture under wraps and in the dark. Dexter moulded his cast into a furniture-removal organism in a wonderful seven-minute climax of plastic mime, bottoms and jaws sticking out in all directions as chairs, tables, a lamp and a sofa were clandestinely smuggled across the passage and back to Gorringe's flat.

In a preface to his collected plays, Shaffer records that the First Night turned into a veritable detonation of human glee: 'A stern-looking middle-aged man sitting directly in front of me suddenly fell out of his seat into the aisle during this section of the play and began calling out to the actors in a voice weak from laughing, "Oh stop it! Please stop it!" I cannot remember a more pleasing thing ever happening to me inside a theatre.'

A motley crew of unwanted visitors included Maggie as the irate ex-mistress queering Brindsley's romantic pitch. So this, she haughtily declared, was what he meant by a blind date. Shaffer arranged a delayed entrance for Maggie in order to allow her to wind down from *Miss Julie*, and she came on and topped everyone with a classic display of mischievous outrage culminating in her impersonation of Brindsley's ancient Cockney cleaning woman, Mrs Punnet.

Maggie spilt the beans from a great height dressed only in

a borrowed pyjama top: 'Water? Good 'eavens, I must have upset something. It's as black as Newgate's knocker up 'ere. Are you playing one of your saucy games, Mr Miller?' The point about the performance, though, apart from its surface brilliance, was the element of desperation in Clea's attempt to hang on to Brindsley. She had walked out on him after four years and had thought of nothing else for six weeks. Her affection was riddled with guilt, and her revenge tempered with pathos and the threat of loneliness.

It would be crass to suggest that Maggie's coruscating Clea fed off the confusion in her personal life, but by the time Robert and Maggie were back in London in 1966, Beverley was rumly contemplating the four or five years he had spent as Maggie's unofficial fiancé. He had divorced his first wife and left his two daughters to be with her, and now Robert was about to be divorced by Tarn Bassett. Things were coming to a head.

The National visited Oxford in April with the double bill and also Pinero's affecting backstage comedy *Trelawny of the Wells*, in which Maggie had taken over as Avonia Bunn, a part which, like Clea, allowed her to parade a splendid pair of legs. John Higgins told *Financial Times* readers that she played Avonia as 'a fourth-rate trouper with a heart as high as the Post Office Tower and a turmoil of emotions that run from jubilation to despair in a matter of seconds.'

She won round after round of applause, not least on the line where a prolonged whine of aghast sympathy greeted the news that her poor Gadd had been fobbed off with the Demon of Discontent: 'Ooh, that's a rotten part. I assure you, Rose, as artist to artist, that part is absolutely rotten.' As rotten, in fact, as Myra's haddock had been disgusting. Robert Stephens gave a marvellous, heart-rending performance as the budding new playwright of the future, Tom Wrench, a companion portrait to his George Dillon and a roseate premonition of

Chekhov's cynical poet Trigorin, one of Robert's outstanding performances ten years later.

By June, Robert had taken over Harold Gorringe from Finney in *Black Comedy*, and the farce was paired with a new John Osborne script, *A Bond Honoured*, directed by Dexter, in which Maggie and Robert played an incestuous sister and brother. The text was derived from Lope de Vega's *La Fianza Satisfecha*. The central character, the murderous Leonido, becomes a new version of the lone-wolf Osborne anti-hero, launched on a tidal wave of rage and invective.

The setting was Sicily. Robert as the Oedipal Leonido raped his mother, blinded his father, seduced his sister, Marcela (Maggie), beat up a priest, renounced Christianity, insulted a Moslem king and was finally crucified as an 'outrageous saint'. Philip Hope-Wallace drily observed that it was 'all rather like *Turandot* without the music, or *Hassan* without the benefit of Basil Dean'.

The violence was all verbal. When Maggie died, she made a turn and pulled red ribbons out of her belt to indicate the blood. It was a strict and very classical, rather Oriental, production, designed by Michael Annals (who had worked with Dexter on *The Royal Hunt of the Sun*), and Maggie was again disciplined by Dexter to control her natural gestural brio. She wore a not very becoming black wig and black contact lenses.

Dexter was renowned for the abrasiveness of his tongue and the total demands he made on actors. A side effect of his obsessive style was that he could be deeply unpleasant to them. Maggie never worked with Dexter again. Riggs O'Hara recalls meeting Maggie years later at one of Olivier's Christmas parties. She was moaning about some director or other. He asked her why, in that case, did she never ask for John? 'And she said she could no longer stand being shouted at.' O'Hara coldly enquired whether she wanted a director, or a friend.

The friendship with Robert was overpowering her loyalty to

Beverley. For a time, the domestic equilibrium was maintained. Kenneth Williams recounts how he visited Maggie and Beverley in Hertfordshire in May 1965.

In June, with Maggie tied up at the National, Beverley and Williams departed on another holiday together. This time it was a month-long jaunt to Crete and Turkey, and Beverley worked out the itinerary: London to Athens, boat to Istanbul, then Heraklion, then boat to Naples, and home. Once again Beverley went off in search of the sites of classical legend, including the palace of Agamemnon, Knossos, Phaestos and Sitea.

At home, the crunch finally came in the summer of 1966, when Maggie disappeared to Rome for a few weeks to make a film with Rex Harrison called *The Honeypot*, an amazingly cumbersome rewrite by Frederick Knott, and the director Joe Mankiewicz, of Ben Jonson's *Volpone*.

Robert followed her there, and Maggie finally wrote to Beverley with the bad news. He had been aware of the developing romance with Robert since his return from Australia, where he had spent three months directing *Boeing-Boeing*.

'I was more than hurt, I was murderous. So in order not to murder anyone, I got married again quickly and went to Greece and France to keep out of their way.' His second wife was Gayden Collins, a model, and Beverley kept travelling, and working on his screenplays and libretti, for the next six or seven years. He had waited for Maggie before and he would wait for her again.

In *The Honeypot*, whimsically subtitled 'Anyone for Venice?', Maggie reverted to supportive secretarial type with an eye on the main chance, as in *The VIPs*. Her character, Sarah Watkins, is a registered nurse and travelling companion to Susan Hayward. She progresses to a big scene with Rex Harrison – playing Cecil Fox, the richest man in the world –

by massaging Susan Hayward's back and being kissed in a gondola by yet another self-satisfied square-jawed hunk.

At least Cliff Robertson as McFly, the Mosca sidekick to Harrison's fading Volpone, was a slight acting advance on George Nader and Rod Taylor. Cliff and Maggie end up sharing the rich man's spoils and each other. The film fades romantically on the couple walking across an empty, rain-drenched St Mark's Square.

The slowness and clumsiness of the film are hard to credit, especially to Joe Mankiewicz. Hayward, a whisky heiress from the Deep South, is one of three beautiful women summoned by Rex to his deathbed – the others are Capucine and Edie Adams – prior to his division of spoils which nobody needs but everybody wants.

When Susan Hayward is found dead in bed, the plot becomes clogged with a murder mystery. Maggie visits the palazzo to warn Rex of an attempt on his life and stays to hear the story of it. A slightly stilted moral dialogue ensues in which Maggie defends the 'tender' side in people, rather than their 'legal tender'.

She enters and departs this curious scene in a dumb-waiter contraption. Rex also reveals his secret ambition to be not a dumb waiter but a ballet dancer. When he dies, and the will is read, he is discovered to be bankrupt, with four mortgages on the old palazzo. Cliff and Maggie – who has quietly turned the tables on everyone – become the ultimate beneficiaries by amalgamating the estates of Rex and Susan Hayward.

The film is frustrating in that Harrison and Maggie never fulfil a promising partnership. As Tynan said, 'Both of them possess incomparable equipment for playing the scorching social comedy that no one now seems capable of writing.' It must be a matter of great regret, too, that the partnership was never tested again, on screen or stage.

Maggie continued her habit of coming out of a mediocre

film quite well: in her sensible suit and cropped hair and, as the
Sunday Times said, 'with her searching gaze, her untheatrical
manner and her sense of humane comedy', she once again
looked like a major screen talent biding her time.

By the end of the year, with Beverley gone, Robert had
moved in to Eldon Road. Maggie continued playing Myra
Arundel, Beatrice, Desdemona and the double bill in the Old
Vic repertoire. She started to do less when she realised that,
at the age of thirty-two, she was pregnant. Joan Plowright
took over, not all that happily, in *Much Ado*, which Robert
redirected on behalf of Zeffirelli (Robert was shortly afterwards
appointed an associate director of the NT), and Desdemona
was passed, very safely, to Billie Whitelaw.

Maggie was named in Robert's divorce from Tarn Bassett
and the baby arrived in the Middlesex Hospital on 19 June
1967. *The Honeypot* had overshot its schedule by many weeks,
and Maggie had not seen a gynaecologist in Italy. The baby
was the wrong way round and had to be delivered by Caesarian
operation. Maggie said later that this made her feel as though
she had just popped out to Harrods for it.

The boy was named Christopher, after his godfather
Christopher Downes. Everyone had expected a girl, including
Zeffirelli, who had pre-christened the baby 'Daisy'. Maggie
received a telegram from Zeffirelli in Italy which read: 'Congratulations on Christopher. I shall spend all my life trying to
turn him into Daisy.'

Ten days later, Maggie and Robert were married in Greenwich registry office. This was arranged by the National's press
officer, Virginia Fairweather, who wanted to keep the wedding
private and well clear of the inevitable media glare at Caxton
Hall. Fairweather explained to the Greenwich officials that
Maggie's brother, Alistair, lived in nearby Blackheath (true)
and that Maggie had been staying there for several weeks (less
true).

Virginia and Christopher Downes were the witnesses, and the quartet was in and out the Greenwich back door and sipping celebratory champagne in Eldon Road by midday. The sipping stopped while Robert went off to perform a *Royal Hunt* matinée. In the evening, the party decamped to a favourite Italian restaurant in Beauchamp Place known privately as the 'Trattoria Hysteria', and a few other friends arrived. Albert Finney's present was the recently released Beatles' *Sergeant Pepper* album.

The first the public knew of all this – indeed, the first official announcement of any sort on the subject – was an article written by Barry Norman, then showbiz correspondent of the *Daily Mail*, on 20 August 1967. The ginger baby was two months old, and Robert said that his arrival had slowed Maggie down: 'She isn't so *frantic* to be working.'

The whole business had confused Maggie's parents, though of course they took great delight in their new grandson. On the day of the wedding, 55 Church Hill Road was besieged by reporters, who parked out in the public house across the road. Nat was convinced that Maggie only married Robert because she was pregnant by him.

Nat retired in the same year and offered his life's work of jottings, pamphlets, papers and sundry little publications to the Bodleian Library. He was so upset when they rejected his offer outright that he took all the papers down to the bottom of the garden and burned them in a rage of bitterness and disappointment. He resolved on the spot to renounce his medical and scientific interests and to devote the rest of his life not only to keeping the archive of his daughter's career, but also to catching up with her world of literature and the theatre. He went down to Blackwell's bookshop in Broad Street and stocked up on Penguin classics and Elizabethan poetry.

Maggie's maternal purdah didn't last long. Almost immediately, she and Robert made television versions of two cut-glass old English comedies: Somerset Maugham's *Home and Beauty* and Frederick Lonsdale's *On Approval*. The latter also starred Judi Dench, who remembers that they all 'corpsed' terribly and were threatened with the sack. Dench then came down the stairs wearing a tartan cloche hat, which was 'too much' for the fourth member of the cast, Moray Watson, who promptly 'collapsed all over again'.

By the end of the year, Maggie was back on a film set, starring opposite yet another distinguished old bear of English comedy, only slightly less grizzled than Rex Harrison, Peter Ustinov. Ironically, Maggie was offered the part of Patty Perwilliger in *Hot Millions* because the shooting had been delayed and Lynn Redgrave, the original casting, had become too heavily pregnant to continue.

On the parturition front, Maggie came full circle by introducing little Christopher, aged eight months, to show business in this film. As Christopher Downes says, it's a touching detail and could yet be as significant as Judy Garland having little baby Liza Minnelli alongside her in *In the Good Old Summertime*.

Christopher's screen début comes in the scene where the apparently incompetent Maggie has taken a job as a bus conductress. She helps a mother and child off the bus and lingers on the pavement to admire the swaddled infant. The bus moves off and Maggie turns in panic to chase it down the street. Having lost that job, she tries her hand at being a cinema usherette – echoes of that early Ned Sherrin sketch where Maggie sang 'It's my première tonight' – and causes chaos by directing customers to the wrong seats. She finally blows it by asking the manager for his ticket.

Maggie starts the film as a failed traffic warden who has a room in the same lodging house as Ustinov, alias Marcus Pendleton, a.k.a. Caesar Smith, an embezzler turned criminal computer programmer. Overstressing her character's inclinations towards flirtatious scattiness, Maggie inveigles herself into Ustinov's firm as his new secretary.

She is brittle, funny and defensive, somewhat frozen, with long false eyelashes which reinforce a strange resemblance to the puppet Lady Penelope in *Thunderbirds*. But she melts in the touching scene where she and Ustinov eat an improvised sausage supper and discover a shared love of music. They are, of course, a pair of lonely misfits. Ustinov's cosy, reassuring manner elicits a sudden, moving declaration: 'I'm so lonely I could scream it from the roof-tops.'

In their next scene together, Maggie proposes marriage. Soon, she is sitting at home, pregnant, while Ustinov disappears, mysteriously, to one of his various European 'offices'. Through the London contact of a deliciously nasty and lubricious executive played by Bob Newhart ("Ere, what we doing in the park?' asks a mini-skirted Maggie when Newhart offers her a lift home), she ingeniously uncovers the criminal operation. She then quietly outmanoeuvres them all.

She has been embezzling funds from Ustinov – whose businessman alter ego, Caesar Smith, is really Robert Morley – and reinvesting them with spectacular financial results. She is offered a place on the board, but declines it with the imperishable line, 'A woman's place is in the 'ome, innit, making money!' The film ends with Maggie playing the flute in a Haydn concerto conducted by Ustinov in a sequence recorded in Watford Town Hall.

In a sense, *Hot Millions*, which was scripted by Ustinov and Ira Wallach, and directed by the Canadian Eric Till, is a feminist comedy. It is not a great film, but it is entertaining and it did give Maggie plenty of scope to combine comedy with pathos. There is also an implied paradigm of her own career at this stage in its assertion that you can both have a successful home life and shoot to the top of the professional tree.

Maggie must have taken some assurance from this, though she soon found out how difficult it was to balance the private life with the public demands of her talent. For her, the career always came first, not out of cunning or strategic necessity, but out of her incurably obsessive drive to be working. And she had a sure instinct about what work to do.

To start with, she and Robert were equal married partners. The liberating physical relationship with Robert and the birth of the first of her two sons had enriched Maggie's womanhood, with incalculable benefits to her acting. But neither she nor Robert yet knew how very difficult it would be to sustain such an exhilarating partnership.

8

The Prime of
Miss Maggie Smith

THE PRIME OF MISS JEAN BRODIE, released in 1969, eight years after the publication of Muriel Spark's novel, remains today the film most readily associated with Maggie Smith. It certainly symbolises the period of her working life in which she first achieved her greatest fame.

It is a good film, not a brilliant one, and Maggie becomes camp, a term most memorably discussed by Susan Sontag in her *Notes on Camp*. The aesthetic sensibility of camp is usually associated with homosexuality. The camp connoisseur takes refined and intense pleasure in the style-conscious works of Oscar Wilde and Aubrey Beardsley, of Ronald Firbank and Ivy Compton-Burnett. Camp is not necessarily a minority taste, nor is it necessarily anathema to good art. *Swan Lake*, certain films of Visconti, and Dame Edna Everage are camp, and Maggie Smith certainly commands a comparable, if not greater, level of broad popularity as a camp pin-up.

And yet, as Peter Hall says, Maggie only really resides on the cusp of camp. She does not go the whole hog, like the late Coral Browne. There's too much going on inside. But Maggie had certainly commanded a camp following in *Share My Lettuce* and *Mary Mary*. As Jean Brodie, the Edinburgh schoolmistress of the 1930s whose pupils were the 'crème de la crème', she had a much wider audience and a proportionately larger camp following.

For the first time, her stardom was totally secure. She had, as Peter Wood describes it, 'a telepathic ray' with an audience in the theatre; on screen, the same thing happened. Maggie won her first Oscar and entered the international arena on her own terms. As Cecil Wilson said in the *Daily Mail*, 'After repeatedly stealing other peoples' pictures, she now becomes a star in her own right.' *Jean Brodie* was the first X-rated movie to be chosen for the annual Royal Film Performance.

Robert was also in *Jean Brodie*, and indeed gave a fine performance as Teddy Lloyd, the raffish art master who paints a nubile schoolgirl (Pamela Franklin) in the nude, has an affair with her, yet desires the spinsterish Miss Brodie all along. But from the moment we see Maggie stiffly cycling through Edinburgh in her sensible coat and hat, signalling a right turn into the Marcia Blaine School for Girls with the grim determination of a comically blinkered road menace, the movie belongs to one person.

Muriel Spark's novel had been adapted for the London stage in 1966 by Jay Presson Allen, and the title role taken by Vanessa Redgrave, followed by Anna Massey. Presson Allen did the screenplay for the producer Robert Fryer, who was adamant that Maggie should play the role. Executives at Twentieth Century Fox were much keener on the idea of Deborah Kerr.

It is tempting to see Maggie's creation as a subtle revenge on her Scottish puritanical mother and indeed on the Oxford High School, which had, as Maggie admitted in an interview, more than a touch of Marcia Blaine. In her gingery blonde, glistening Marcel-waved wig and no-nonsense, shoulder-shuffling walk, Maggie was a comic totem of unbending rectitude.

Her dictatorial aphorisms in the classroom – 'Prop up your books in case of intruders', 'Give me a girl at an impressionable age, and she is mine for life' – were cloaking something more sinister, a seditious intent to inculcate enthusiasm among her charges for the men she most admired, Mussolini and General Franco.

This darker side of Jean Brodie's fanaticism escapes Maggie. You do not really feel that the performance acknowledges the mixture of bland academic exhortation and dangerous brain-washing in Spark's heroine. (Her declared motto of 'Lift, enliven, stimulate!' was reworked for Lettice Douffet by Peter Shaffer as 'Enlarge, enliven, enlighten!'). Her 'gels' must be prepared, she says, 'to serve, suffer and sacrifice'. And she precipitates the death of one of them (played by a young Jane Carr) who rushes off to Spain and inadvertently joins the Fascists, while her brother is fighting for the Republicans.

Maggie plays a Brodie who lives immune to the world and even her own beliefs. But she presents an almost chillingly perfect portrait of bottled-up sexuality and dazzling irony. Walk with your head up, she instructs the gels, 'like Sybil Thorndike, a woman of notable mien'. The joke here, of course, and one of which you sense Maggie is unaware, is that Sybil Thorndike was also a woman of notable left-wing spirit. Maggie's laugh is gained on the glacial camp delivery of the line, without a trace of sarcasm.

Miss Brodie is betrayed finally by the girl who is her sexual substitute in the life of Robert's infatuated married art master. Maggie's anguished cry of 'Assassin!' is not as blood-curdling as it might be. The real nastiness of her character has been swamped in the enamelled perfection of her comedy performance.

The film opened almost simultaneously in New York, where the critical response was tumultuous. In the *New York Times*, Vincent Canby said there had not been such a display of controlled, funny, elegant theatricality since Laurence Olivier soft-shoed his way through *The Entertainer* nine years pre-

viously, and was one of many to comment on Maggie's complicated and judiciously executed amalgam of counterpointed
moods, switches in voice levels and obliquely stated emotions.

The cultish impact, and this is the first evidence of an
intensely camp admiration that has attached to Maggie ever
since, was registered by the influential columnist Rex Reed,
who said that Maggie had made the profoundest effect on him
of any actress since Kim Stanley in *The Goddess* in 1957. He
drooled on prophetically in *Holiday* magazine about 'one of
the most magnificent screen performances in the history of the
medium by Maggie Smith who takes the film into the realms
of immortality. Words could never do justice to her work, to
the skill and wit and sureness. If critics could give Oscars, she
would already have one from me.'

Whatever the quibbles, Maggie's Miss Brodie, far more
severely and accurately Scottish than Vanessa Redgrave's
admirable stage performance, would enter a pantheon of
flawed, inflamed schoolteachers on celluloid: Robert Donat in
Goodbye Mr Chips, Bette Davis in *The Corn is Green*, Michael
Redgrave in *The Browning Version*, Sidney Poitier in *To Sir
With Love*, Sandy Dennis in *Up the Down Staircase*, and
Robin Williams in *Dead Poets Society*.

While filming continued on *Jean Brodie*, the ever-solicitous
Christopher Downes was helping Maggie and Robert to house-
hunt. Maggie's agent Peter Dunlop also gave advice and
extended his range of interests in Maggie's life from contracts
and tax demands to domestic requirements, especially nannies.

Something larger than Eldon Road was now needed, and a
1902 villa on four floors near the Fulham Road seemed just
the job. The house was in Queen's Elm Square, a little estate
of fourteen houses with cellars, three spacious floors and a
black and white gabled façade at the top. It remains in Maggie's
possession to this day.

While the move was in hand, Maggie, Robert and baby

Christopher stayed in Penelope Gilliatt's house in Chelsea. Gilliatt's marriage to John Osborne had just broken up, and their daughter, Nolan, was brought back to England by the nanny, Christine Miller, to visit her father.

'Big Chris', as she was affectionately known by the boys when older, immediately hit it off with Maggie and helped out with the baby because Christopher's own nanny had suddenly left. She stayed with Penelope Gilliatt and Nolan for over ten years and later worked for Maggie and Beverley in Canada.

Christine Miller remembers a house full of laughter. One day, she had her four wisdom teeth removed. She couldn't open her mouth properly, so Robert volunteered to make 'something wonderful' for supper. The result was an 'absolutely brilliant' steak tartare, which the afflicted nanny was able to suck through what remained of her teeth, gratefully unmindful of the lumps of pepper. These lumps promptly lodged in her gums, causing excruciating pain, while Maggie and Robert fell about, hysterical with cruel laughter.

It began to make economic sense to think of a second home, a place in the country, and Maggie turned to her architect brothers for advice. Or rather, she turned to one of them. Ian had gone to America in 1959 and stayed there, building up a successful practice in civic architecture and specialising in big stores and university developments. Slomanson Smith & Barresi Architects still thrives and operates internationally out of offices in Bleeker Street, New York. Ian married in 1965, was divorced four years later, and remarried, acquiring a stepdaughter in the process.

Alistair had married in 1963 and settled with Shān and their son, Angus, in Blackheath, where they became friends and neighbours of the actress Margaret Tyzack and her husband, years before the two Maggies won their Tonys in *Lettice and Lovage*. Prior to that, they had lived round the corner from

Eldon Road. Shān had done a lot of Beverley's typing for him.

Alistair's firm, Norman and Dawbarn, which specialised in designing hospitals and aerodromes overseas, was based in Guildford, Surrey. In 1968 he and Shān decided to move nearer the office. The plan was to find a big house suitable for dividing in half and sharing with Maggie and Robert. Guildford was only about thirty miles from London and easily reached at weekends.

The first place Alistair saw was Tigbourne Court, an 1899 house of considerable interest and quality designed by Edwin Lutyens, probably the most gifted and influential of British architects since Sir John Vanbrugh and Nicholas Hawksmoor. Lutyens was very active in this part of Surrey at the turn of the century, and Tigbourne Court at Witley, one and a half miles from Chiddingfold and a few more from Guildford, was one of his most original and unusual inventions.

The main gate looms suddenly on a busy road: a symmetrical entrance screen disguises an unusually asymmetrical house. The loggia of the main entrance has a three-gabled wall above, and each of the other entrances has an independent forecourt formed by the shape of the building and the use of different paving. The walls are of Bargate stone, drilled with lead, and there are red bricks in the chimney stacks and window surrounds. There is a pergola leading to a magnificent garden of four acres, landscaped by Gertrude Jekyll, and a well.

This was a very far cry from the cramped living conditions of Maggie's childhood. But there was no intention of turning the address into a fashionable weekend bolthole for favoured showbiz chums as, for instance, Olivier and Vivien Leigh had done with Notley Abbey. Maggie has never been a great party-goer, let alone anything at all of a party-thrower.

At first, the two families occupied one half of the house while the other half was redecorated, and then Maggie and

Robert moved into the main suite of rooms. Alistair and Shān stayed in the servants' quarters, which nonetheless had six bedrooms. Shān supervised the gardening and developed all the local contacts needed to run such an establishment. When Maggie and Robert appeared at weekends, usually late on Saturday nights, the two families could be as intimate or as separate as they wished. The arrangement worked very well.

Maggie fitted in a quick guest appearance in Richard Attenborough's posh, gargantuan but irresistible film-directing début, a version of Joan Littlewood's *Oh What A Lovely War!* She appeared, in Judith Crist's phrase, 'raucous and insidious as a Lilith of the music hall', a bespangled coquette singing the recruiting song 'I'll Make a Man of Any One of You'. In a way, she expressed the soul of the film, which is about enlistment through seduction, and death as a payment for experience. The sudden close-up on the grotesquely made-up Maggie at the end of her song is one of the movie's most indelibly vulgarian images.

With transatlantic stardom and two new homes came another major award and a second dose of maternity. In March 1969 Maggie received the Variety Club award for film actress of the year in *Hot Millions* (other recipients included Jill Bennett and John Gielgud for stage performances in plays by John Osborne and Alan Bennett, and a twenty-eight-year-old Tom Jones as show-business personality of the year).

One month later, on 21 April, Toby was born. Like Christopher, he was delivered by Caesarian in the Middlesex Hospital. He had been expected two days later, but Maggie was impatient to get it over with and remembers more or less pushing Tommy Steele's wife out of a hospital bed so that she could jump into it. Within six weeks, Maggie was rehearsing for a Chichester Festival Theatre revival of Wycherley's *The Country Wife*.

*

Maggie had been stung into action by a major rebuff at the National Theatre, where Olivier had asked her to choose between Viola in *Twelfth Night* and Rosalind in *As You Like It*. When Maggie sought to take the matter further, Olivier, who was increasingly jealous of Maggie's and Robert's appeal to the public, tartly informed her that he was going to produce an all-male version of *As You* (he did, with Ronald Pickup as Rosalind) and a revival of *The Way of the World* with Geraldine McEwan in the 'Maggie role' of Millamant. This news was hurtfully imparted by letter after a particularly convivial weekend Maggie and Robert had spent with the Oliviers in Brighton. The hurt was not lessened by the fact that Olivier had posted the letter before his guests arrived.

Meanwhile, Maggie told Catherine Stott in the *Guardian* that she found babies fascinating once 'they stop being the wobbly turnips they are for so long . . . One has lived selfishly for so long that it is suddenly rather an appalling thought that you really need to think about so many people, small people who really *need* to be thought about.' Robert needed to be 'thought about' too, perhaps. During the Chichester period he collapsed for the first time with one of his subsequently regular bouts of acute depression aggravated by heavy drinking and overwork.

Margery Pinchwife was Maggie's first new stage role for three years. The Chichester season was no longer an extension of the National. John Clements had succeeded Olivier as artistic director, and his *Country Wife* production team reflected his sober West End pedigree: it was directed and designed by two venerable scions of the Binkie Beaumont era on Shaftesbury Avenue, Robert Chetwyn and Hutchinson Scott.

The plot revolves around the untrue declaration of an incorrigible rake, Horner, that he is impotent and therefore to be trusted with other men's wives. Margery, like Lady Plyant in *The Double Dealer*, is married to a jealous old fool, and in her major scene she writes a letter of rebuttal to Horner, dictated by Pinchwife, through which she refracts her own lascivious invitations.

Maggie risked the bucolic accent of the country cousin but made it a specifically consistent one. In a prim cap and low-cut dress, sensuously wielding the fateful quill pen, she emanated a twinkling air of wistful sexuality. Ronald Bryden observed how, in trailing a nasal, farmyard drawl about the stage, she made Margery's stifled talent for living seem like some monstrous escaping vegetable, burying the rest of the play knee-deep in eager, luxuriant greenery. She put the seal on her performance, as any great Margery must, in the letter scene where, panting and hanging her tongue almost to her chin, she climbed half on to the writing-table with anxiety, and caught the quill successively in her hair, her eye and her inkwell.

Christopher Downes likened Maggie in this scene to Ethel Merman doing a big Cole Porter number. Its effect on the audience was galvanic. The night Downes went, the inkwell fell off the table and Maggie caught it just before it hit the floor. He thought this one of the most incredible pieces of 'business' he had ever seen, but Maggie assured him afterwards that it had never happened before. At the end of the scene, 'poor old Gordon Gostelow' as Pinchwife came on with the line, 'What have you done?' and of course, says Downes, 'got a huge laugh; he was ever so pleased with himself.'

Although Maggie has made several recordings of Shakespeare, and there is both a record and a film of the NT *Othello*, *The Country Wife* is the only play she has ever recorded in an original production for BBC Radio. She did so in 1985, with Jonathan Pryce as a darkly lubricious Horner (Keith Baxter was less dangerous at Chichester), Barbara Jefford as the fulsomely insatiable Lady Fidget and John Moffatt as the surely definitive Sparkish.

Maggie's radio performance, though slightly riper, is very much a re-creation of the Chichester version: as crisp and rosy as a fresh young apple, with a precise Oxfordshire accent and a musicality unsullied with mannerism. When you hear Maggie, spuriously concerned about her husband, her 'dear Bud', ask, 'Why dost thou look so fropish? Who has nangered thee?', savouring those two unexpected syllables of 'frop' and 'nang', you cannot imagine anyone else ever sounding so charmingly mock-innocent or so deliciously flavoursome.

These months mark the high point of Maggie's stage career in Britain. The fact that Robert played Archer and Tesman to her Mrs Sullen and Hedda, two of her greatest stage performances, indicated that, although the marriage still prospered, Robert's visible, public role in it was becoming an exclusively supporting one. And by winning an Oscar, Maggie changed her footing within the profession and upped her market value way beyond Robert's.

The Beaux' Stratagem opened in Los Angeles, where the NT was on tour, in January 1970. Billy Wilder took Jack Benny to the First Night. According to Christopher Downes, the great comedian recognised the gift for which he himself was renowned above all other entertainers. 'Gee, what about that girl's timing!' he said of Maggie to Wilder.

The three-week season in the huge and intimidating Ahmanson Centre was the first of several appearances Maggie and Robert made there over the next few years. She had a ready-made Hollywood following, on account of the success of *Jean Brodie*. And in the New Year's Honours list back home, she had been appointed Commander of the British Empire, CBE, along with Joan Plowright and Kenneth More.

The Los Angeles season also featured Olivier's production of Chekhov's *Three Sisters*, in which Robert played the louche battery commander Vershinin, and Maggie Masha, the middle sister whose dull marriage to a schoolmaster is briefly, and tragically, enlivened by her infatuation with the visiting army officer. Masha was really Plowright's role, but she had been unable to make the trip.

The Ahmanson was picketed during the opening night intermission by student radicals accusing the National Theatre of being 'an airless mausoleum'. The reviewers thought otherwise.

Maggie's reception was ecstatic. The Los Angeles drama critics gave her their Best Actress award. Olivier never allowed Maggie to share Masha in London with Plowright. He could not afford another blow to his wife's pride comparable to those she had already suffered over Hilde Wangel and Beatrice. In any case, Plowright was an exceptionally fine Masha. The production was recorded, like the *Othello*, on film.

Christopher and Toby were left at home with their grandparents while Maggie and Robert took a house in Malibu for the duration and soaked up the adulation. In the *New York Times* of 22 February 1970, under the headline 'The New Young Lunts?', Walter Kerr (husband of the author of *Mary Mary*) applauded two performers who subtly signalled that they were fighting hard for an eternal promise that was probably going to turn out to be false. When they were at last torn apart, Kerr noted Maggie's arrival at sounds below the level of speech that would interest, and perhaps surprise, Jerzy Grotowski.

This reference to the fashionable Polish avant-garde guru hinted at something disturbing and elemental in the performance, and the significance of acting with her volatile and seductive husband adds another layer to the mixture. Robert's flirtatiousness was almost his professional trademark. On being chided by Olivier for this, he retorted, 'But I learned how to do it all from you!'

Maggie told the author and critic Ronald Hayman, 'I think of Robert as an actor when we're working, and not as my husband. But I can see that it's easier for an audience to watch two people who are married playing two characters who are married. It's all done *for* you.'

For his part, Robert told Hayman that their work on stage was never staled by custom or familiarity: 'I'm always constantly surprised by Margaret. There are certain actors and actresses with whom you can never vary anything . . . But I wouldn't say that I knew beforehand the way in which Margaret was going to speak some line. I'm constantly dazzled by a different reading or a different approach to a line.'

If they were the new Lunts, there seemed little chance of a repeat of the famous occasion when Alfred Lunt and his wife Lynn Fontanne 'dried' on stage together. The deathly silence was broken by the audible delivery of the next line by a prompter. Still neither actor spoke, and the prompt came again. Silence. Another prompt. Alfred turned crossly to the stage-management corner and hissed, 'We know what the *line* is, but which one of us says it?'

Maggie also relished the story about Lunt's failure to get an easy laugh on a line in which he requested a cup of tea. After weeks of puzzling over this, Fontanne finally asked her husband why he didn't simply ask her for a cup of tea instead of asking the audience for the laugh.

The Lunts, like Robert and Maggie, had made their own way as actors before appearing together for the first time in the 1924 production of Molnar's *The Guardsman*, source of both the above anecdotes. The difference was that they were married while working separately for a long time prior to that historic success. Marriage for Robert and Maggie was inextricably linked to their work together, specifically at the National.

Maggie eventually performed Molnar's comedy not with Robert, but with Brian Bedford in Canada. There were, however, many plans to exploit the marriage on stage and screen,

most of them emanating from Robert. It is ironic that this
should have been so at the very time when Maggie, in Farquhar and Ibsen, portrayed the richly comic and profoundly
tragic consequences of a wretched marriage.

She and Gaskill picked up exactly where they had left off in
The Recruiting Officer, and by the time *The Beaux' Stratagem*
returned from Los Angeles and opened at the Old Vic on
8 April, Maggie's Mrs Sullen was a full-blown masterpiece of
comic acting.

At six o'clock that morning, Maggie heard that she had won
the Best Actress Oscar in Hollywood. Her friend from the *New
Faces* days, Alice Ghostley, collected the award on her behalf
in the Music Centre adjacent to the Ahmanson. She had
unexpectedly beaten off challenges from Jean Simmons in *The
Happy Ending*, Liza Minnelli in *The Sterile Cuckoo* and Jane
Fonda in *They Shoot Horses, Don't They?*

Her triumph was shared, at a distance, with John Wayne,
who belatedly won his first Oscar for *True Grit*, and John
Schlesinger who was declared Best Director for *Midnight
Cowboy*, which was also voted Best Picture. This was third
time lucky for Maggie: she had been nominated twice in the
supporting actress category for *The VIPs* and *Othello*. Gaskill
recalls thinking how oddly low-key, and typically English, was
that First Night reception at the Vic for someone who had just
won an Oscar.

Farquhar's last play is about divorce, with many precise
references to Milton's great pamphlet on the subject. Two
buccaneering gallants, Archer and Aimwell, arrive in the
sleepy town of Lichfield and upset various applecarts. Archer
homes in on Mrs Sullen, a London beauty driven frantic by
boredom and shrewish by a sodden, elderly husband.

Gaskill cleared the stage, and his designer partner on *The
Recruiting Officer*, René Allio, delicately, but not preciously,
conjured an English cathedral city in russet canvases and

Queen Anne interiors, with an ochreously shaded High Street and a glimpse of the church beyond.

The atmosphere was light and vaporous, conducive to the tasteful expression of high spirits. Benedict Nightingale in the *New Statesman* noted Maggie's artful aggression and its effect on Robert: 'A purr becomes a quiet growl becomes an ecstatic snap of the jaws: the cat turns chameleon turns crocodile, and it's scarcely surprising that Stephens responds as he does. Who ever saw such biological bravura in a woman? Swagger and sally as he may, a kind of artless, rather awkward wonder never quite deserts him: he seems a man transfixed.'

Of all Maggie's stage performances, it is Mrs Sullen that inspired the most impressively evocative writing from the critics, just as Edith Evans had started critical adjectives dancing in 1927 when she scored the biggest success of her career thus far in the role. J. C. Trewin said that Evans had set the play 'to her own music', while Ivor Brown thought it likely that 'years hence we shall bore posterity by quoting this magnificent performance to incredulous and careless youth.'

Maggie was just as inspirational. Her tilted nose and chin conveyed a heavenly contempt for men that was irresistible; her surreptitious smile betrayed a willingness to forgive a lesser species; her presence doomed men to eternal victimisation in the sex war; her performance was shot through with nuances, like veins of colour in a painting; and her swooping descent from decorum to appetite was epitomised at the moment when Robert's Archer refused her money with a bow and she stood, purse held in her still-outstretched hand, while her eyes ran like zip fasteners up and down his extended leg.

She was a tight-laced beanpole, graceful, swaying and tender, who thawed among her own languid phrases and angular gestures. Her playing drew from Ronald Bryden a splendidly phrased comparison with some exquisite Douanier Rousseau giraffe, peering nervously down her nose with huge, liquid eyes at the smaller creatures around, nibbling off her lines fastidiously in a surprisingly tiny nasal drawl.

The overall and overwhelming beauty of Maggie's Mrs Sullen derived from the fact that her humorous façade masked the imminent possibility of tragedy and despair. And it proved, perhaps more so than any other of Maggie's London performances, that the best of comedy always fends off disaster and that whereas farcical comedy ends in laughter, the true spirit of emotional comedy could just as easily end in tears.

William Gaskill thought she had matured immeasurably as an actress since they had worked on *The Recruiting Officer*, and remembers most the way she handled the speech which closed the first half. Gaskill adored Farquhar, but knew this poetic passage was feeble. He wanted to cut part of it, but Maggie asked for it back and, he says, 'shaped it wonderfully. She played it in a pure classical style, quite breathtakingly':

> Wedlock we own ordain'd by Heaven's decree,
> But such as Heaven ordain'd it first to be;
> Concurring tempers in the man and wife
> As mutual helps to draw the load of life . . .
> Must Man, the chiefest work of art divine,
> Be doomed in endless discord to repine?
> No, we should injure Heaven by that surmise;
> Omnipotence is just, were Man but wise.

Maggie and Robert themselves were getting along quite well, but they were certainly not of 'concurring tempers'. In late June they opened at the Cambridge Theatre in *Hedda Gabler*, and John Moffatt, who was playing Judge Brack, overheard quite big rows through the dressing-room walls. Robert would occasionally forget to waken Maggie at the appointed time as she slept between matinée and evening performances, and she would fly into a rage. The National had extended its activity into the Cambridge, and the Ibsen was joined in repertoire there by *The Beaux' Stratagem* in August.

Ingmar Bergman's celebrated Stockholm production of *Hedda Gabler* had visited the Aldwych Theatre as part of the World Theatre Season of 1968. Bergman had never directed a play outside Sweden, but was coerced into doing so in London by Olivier, to whom he habitually referred, with heavy sarcasm, as 'the Lord'. Michael Meyer, whose translation was used, has recounted the dim view Bergman took of the play and expressed his own view that the production was a very striking evening, but only for someone who neither knew nor liked Ibsen.

The text was heavily cut. Great liberties were taken, some of them repeated in later productions, most notably the collaboration between the director Deborah Warner and the Irish actress Fiona Shaw at the Abbey in Dublin in 1991. There was no portrait of General Gabler and there were no vine leaves in Loevborg's hair. Instead of the controlled revelation of Hedda's pregnancy, Maggie appeared in a wordless prologue, pushing frantically at an unwanted bulge in her stomach, apparently on the point of vomiting.

But there was something unexpectedly electrifying about this production, and certainly about Maggie's performance. Robert Stephens says, quite unequivocally, that it is the best production of anything he has ever been in. John Moffatt says that, years later, he talked about it with Maggie and they agreed they had not encountered an experience like it since, nor a director: 'What that man could do in a few seconds, the way he could transform a performance with one little remark. I could go on all day about it.'

Bergman was going to set up the re-creation of his Stockholm version for about ten days and leave London to fulfil other commitments while Olivier took over. The billing would read something like 'Ingmar Bergman's production supervised by Laurence Olivier'.

But he suddenly found he could rejig his plans and return for a week or so before the opening. He repeated an experiment he had tried, with success, before. He left the actors with masses of notes, asked Olivier to relinquish his 'assistant director' role (Olivier was only too happy to oblige) and instructed them to rehearse for a maximum of four hours a day, on their own. No one was to disturb their work.

In his autobiography, Bergman says that the only reason he did *Hedda* in the first place was that the brilliant actress Gertrud Fridh had no leading part that autumn. He set about his task with some reluctance, but found that 'the face of its weary supreme architect was unmasked' and that 'Ibsen lived desperately entangled in his furnishings, his explanations, his artistic but pedantically constructed scenes, his curtain lines, his arias and duets. All this bulky external lumber hid an obsession for self-exposure far more profound than Strindberg's.'

Michael Meyer, on the other hand, rated *Hedda Gabler* one of the most economically written of all great plays, which Bergman cut as though it were a film. Much of the humour, said the increasingly humourless Meyer, went out of the window. So, for that matter, did the windows.

The stage was a red vault with a screen down the middle. On one side, the text was enacted while, on the other, the actors, primarily Hedda, explored unspoken emotions. Bryden assumed that this interpretation was based on the Freudian case history of Emilie Bardach, the elegant, repressed Viennese Ibsen had met and flirted with on a Tyrolean holiday in 1899. And he thought that this admittedly brilliant but non-naturalistic treatment deprived the play of its mystery and Maggie of the opportunity to exploit her gift for lacing her games in polite society with scornful artificiality. Irving Wardle, too, considered the device distracting, though Maggie

Smith's reactions, he said, like those of Gertrud Fridh, were 'powerful and stylistically beautiful'.

For others, myself included, the performance, given without an interval, was revelatory, a long rehearsal for the suicide Hedda executed in full view of both herself and the audience (the actress usually leaves the stage). When the producer Michael Codron went to see it, a woman seated behind him turned to her companion as Maggie picked up the gun and whispered, 'Now does she do it, or does she chicken out?'

The issue was in the balance while Maggie's Hedda turned again and again to the mirror, vainly seeking to unlock the puzzle of her existence by contemplating her troublesome physical reality. Finally she peered accusingly into the glass for the last time and continued peering as she pulled the trigger.

Bergman's opinion of Hedda was that she was a creature of complete vanity. He told Robert of a lady critic in Stockholm who was madly in love with a theatre director and who, when the director ran off with another woman, was found lying in bed having cut her throat, with an open razor in one hand and a mirror in the other.

The First Night was distinguished by the presence of Tennessee Williams sitting in a box, pretty far gone, laughing loudly at all the wrong moments. He alone seemed oblivious to the fact that the play, as *Time* magazine put it, had been removed from the sitting room into the psyche. It was clear that Judge Brack's fondness for the back entrance in Tesman's house was an unconscious reference to sodomy. The emasculation of Loevborg was underlined in the account of the bullet lodging in his pelvic region.

Olivier's original casting idea was for Robert to play Tesman, and Jeremy Brett Loevborg. But Robert persuaded him to reverse the roles. Instead of a beautiful Byronic wreck, Robert's Loevborg was a convincingly passionate creation, a memorable addition to the Stephens gallery of plausibly flawed writers.

As Anthony Curtis noted in the *Financial Times*, he was not the usual weak intellectual, 'but a man of coarse and brutal strength and strong sexuality, out of D. H. Lawrence rather than Gissing. One really does believe that he might have a great prophetic book in him.'

There was a deliberate contrast between the predominant public image of Hedda and her pre-play manifestation in a white shift, shoulders bared, smoking a cigarette and shuddering with disgust, her thin, blanched face subject to spasms of tearing torture. With her severe centre parting, high forehead, tapering fingers and heavily corseted costume, Maggie's stark physical appearance was a puritanical complement to her Jean Brodie disguise. She was so highly charged and pent-up, you felt she might explode if touched, and only the slightest facial movement betrayed the intensity of Hedda's welling emotion.

Harold Hobson concluded that Hedda had been profitably deprived of sympathy and that her performance was so generally terrifying that, when she nearly ripped out Mrs Elvsted's hair, he jumped out of his seat. Considering that Hobson was severely crippled and had to be hoisted between chromium-plated wheelchair and plush velvet *fauteuils* for most of his working life, the accolade was great indeed. We must assume that Maggie's Hedda, as far as he was concerned, was truly miraculous.

The *Evening Standard* drama panel agreed: on 25 January 1971, Maggie received the Best Actress award for the second time. It was handed over by Bergman, but not Ingmar – Ingrid. John Gielgud and Ralph Richardson were joint Best Actors for their performances in David Storey's *Home*.

Whenever leading actors of the day were discussed, Maggie and Robert, but especially Maggie, were now mentioned. The great director Tyrone Guthrie, in a book on acting published at this time, said, 'I certainly do not expect to coach or teach actors to play their parts. It would obviously be wild if I were to give lessons to Maggie Smith on how to make a line sound witty, or to suggest inflections to Sir John Gielgud.' The film mogul Daryl F. Zanuck, thinking of teaming Maggie with George C. Scott, termed them 'the greatest living actress and actor in the world'.

A week after Alice Ghostley had collected the *Jean Brodie* Oscar on her behalf, Maggie had a couple of days free to attend the Tony Awards ceremony in New York. She and Robert flew the Atlantic and presented a special award to Alfred Lunt and Lynn Fontanne. A direct succession was implied. But the next few years saw the alliance crumble and Maggie's career take a few wrong turnings. She was past Jean Brodie's prime, and well into her own as Mrs Sullen and Hedda.

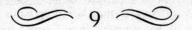

9

Pain within Private Lives

I THINK very few people are completely normal really, deep down in their private lives. It all depends on a combination of circumstances. If all the various cosmic thingummys fuse at the same moment, and the right spark is struck, there's no knowing what one mightn't do. That was the trouble with Elyot and me, we were like two violent acids bubbling about in a nasty little matrimonial bottle.'

Thus Amanda sums up the situation in Noël Coward's *Private Lives*, the last play in which Maggie and Robert appeared as a partnership. The tragic dilemma of two people who love each other too much to be able to live together was horribly appropriate. In real life, the simulacrum of their on-stage liaison, Maggie and Robert just ran out of steam. But 'deep down' there was always a scar left by the sparks of the fusion.

After *Jean Brodie*, Robert was keen to press home the advantages of working with the film's producer, Robert Fryer, who was in charge of the Ahmanson Theater in Los Angeles and host to the National on their successful visit with *Three Sisters* and *The Beaux' Stratagem*. A producing company was formed of Bobby, Maggie and Bobby – BMB – but the only fruit was a production in Los Angeles of Coward's *Design for Living*, in which the Lunts and Noël Coward had first made up what the play's standard prig calls 'a disgusting three-sided erotic hotch-potch'.

The idea had been hatched during *Hedda Gabler* at the Cambridge, where it had been decided that John Moffatt, who was Judge Brack, would play Leo to Maggie's Gilda and Robert's Otto. American Equity kicked up a fuss and, in spite of receiving a three-page cable from Coward himself on the matter, denied Moffatt permission. Denholm Elliott, who already had a green card, played Leo instead.

Also in the cast, as the prig, Ernest, was Roderick Cook, who had known Maggie since Oxford revue days and appeared with her and Kenneth Williams in *Share My Lettuce*. The director was the ever-faithful Peter Wood, whom Robert usually translated as 'Pierre Bois'.

Once again Maggie and Robert rented a house on the beach front at Malibu, a forty-five-minute drive from the Ahmanson. Wood stayed out there after dinner one night and travelled into rehearsal with them the following morning in the Rolls which Fryer sent each day to collect them. It was driven by Fryer's assistant, an orphan from Bristol, whom the director, himself a West Countryman, knew very well.

Wood sat up front making animated conversation. Suddenly, in a voice Wood had never heard before, Maggie said, 'Would you mind *not* talking.' The process of concentration had already begun. Wood cites this not as an instance of grandeur or pretension, but of a perfectly simple, professional request. Silence was mandatory.

The production broke all box-office records during its seven-week run, and Maggie's 'ankle work' was widely approved: she wore an ivory-white satin sheath, cut on the cross, and sat on an enormous sofa, facing the front, sending semaphore signals with one leg dangled over the other. Robert made an impressive second-act entrance in a white camel-hair coat. But the reports were mixed on the impact made by the central trio, 'the three amoral, glib and over-articulate creatures, who cannot help themselves,' as Coward called them.

The unease in the off-stage marriage was unwittingly touched on by a Californian admirer, Mrs Jeannette Warnken, who wrote a letter which Maggie found hilarious and had posted on the notice board of the Ahmanson:

Your performance . . . is exuberant, delightful, flawless and frightening . . . I am concerned about your health. Anyone with a keen eye and sincere interest worries that YOU WILL NOT MAKE IT THROUGH THE RUN (Damn this typewriter, those capitals were unintentional). How exasperating it must be for you to be working with your charming chubby cherub of a husband who seems to rollick through his part without the slightest bit of tension. You are an enchanting and capable pair, but please do not attempt to keep up with him physically. Do take a REST after this run and have your face done . . . You are the greatest actress of our time. Please take care of yourself. We of the great mass audience depend upon you for our dreams.

The two Bobbies wanted to take *Design for Living* to Broadway, but Maggie insisted on coming to London and playing in repertory with another production, to be directed by Zeffirelli. The proposed play was Goldoni's *The Housekeeper* and the producer was going to be Eddie Kulukundis, the vast and genial scion of a Greek shipping family whose enthusiasm for theatre was never quite matched by his artistic acumen.

Zeffirelli planned to infest the stage with crowds of villagers and donkey-drawn carts. The air would be heavy with cod Venetian accents, garlic and horse manure. Not surprisingly, Robert went slightly off his rocker at this stage, and the entire BMB project was abandoned.

Binkie Beaumont was miffed that Robert and Maggie had gone to Kulukundis and not to him. Maggie had been his last real West End star and he had watched jealously from his office at the top of the Globe in Shaftesbury Avenue as the

National, with Maggie and Robert, cornered the market in handsome classical revivals. In some ways, he had been outflanked at his own game, and it did not soothe his resentment that he was appointed to the NT's board. His career as top dog on the Avenue had been in serious decline since the middle 1960s. The new boys there, notably Peter Bridge and Michael Codron, had taken over.

By the end of 1973, both Binkie Beaumont and Noël Coward would be dead. So the plan to revive *Private Lives*, directed by John Gielgud, starring Maggie and Robert, would be seen in retrospect as Binkie's last West End throw. It opened at the Queen's on 21 September 1972, and, according to close friends, was part of a desperate final attempt by Maggie to keep her marriage, and Robert himself, on the rails.

Ten years later, John Gielgud wrote to B. A. Young confessing that he had heard rumours that Maggie was 'difficult', but that he found the experience a pleasure. She was, he said, 'a dreamgirl to rehearse. I never thought Robert at all rightly cast, and their marriage was running down in a big way, though neither of them showed when they were working that they were in the middle of emotional problems. She is a fanatic about rehearsals, always so full of new touches of invention that I found it difficult to decide which were the best to keep in.'

Gielgud's misgivings over Robert as Elyot were largely dispelled in a performance which dug deeper into the part than anyone thought possible. The overall effect was that he seemed not to be playing against Coward, but mining the text for even more intimations of mortality than are already there. A blasted intruder in the salon, rather like his Loevborg, Robert's Elyot caught both the savage hedonism of the character's proposals, and also the last gasp quality of his life with Maggie:

'Let's blow trumpets and squeakers, and enjoy the party as much as we can, like very small, quite idiotic schoolchildren.

Let's savour the delight of the moment. Come and kiss me, darling, before your body rots, and worms pop in and out of your eye sockets.'

Confronted with the bullish, unpredictable quality of this extraordinary performance, it was little wonder that Maggie's Amanda stiffened into a frantic bundle of signals. The wide divergence of reaction – among audiences as well as critics – demonstrated how very thin was the line she trod between style and caricature.

Maggie nonetheless looked stunning as an auburn-wigged, Marcel-waved Amanda, dressed first in flared pencil skirt and later in floral red pyjamas. The clothes were designed by another Shaftesbury Avenue legend, Beatrice Dawson, and the elegant curvilinear period setting was the work of Anthony Powell, a quondam protégé of Gielgud and an Oscar-winning designer for movies, who was to become one of Maggie's closest allies in this awkward period of her life.

Elyot is defined in the play as Amanda's first real love, a man who drinks and knocks her about and to whom only the worst part of her is attracted. Rarely can the pain of a disintegrating relationship have found such a poignant and direct artistic expression. 'Snap, snap, snap, like a little adder,' jeers Elyot; 'Adders don't snap; they sting,' scoffs Amanda. Robert snapped and Maggie stung.

The strain of the private life finally took its toll on *Private Lives*, and the reviews, though for the most part highly favourable (the idea that the whole shebang was a critical disaster is entirely mythical), contained two attacks, by Jack Tinker, who had recently joined the *Daily Mail*, and Harold Hobson, of such concentrated vitriol that they were later said to account for Maggie's subsequent departure to Canada. There is only the slightest element of partial truth in this.

Tinker accused Gielgud of allowing Maggie her head, or worse, her hands. She had, he averred, hands of sand which got into everything. Hobson was even more casually destructive, suggesting that the youthful promise he had spotted in Michael Meyer's *The Ortolan* eighteen years earlier had been entirely traduced by experience: 'There was once a time, at the Old Hall in Marston, near Oxford, when Margaret Smith could make the heart stop for a moment with a forlorn word, a crushed gesture. In *Private Lives* she is merely a compendium of grimaces, an anthology of little squeaks, a catalogue of double takes.'

The problem with Maggie had come to a head: you either found her weaponry of gestures and reactions wildly funny, a comprehensive guide to the nervous system which fuelled them, or you did not. And you did not even have to be For or Against. You could be For one day, Against the next, as critics whimsically proved down the years. The general rule, though, is that the mechanics of Maggie's acting, which are spontaneous and unrivalled, work best when she is relaxed and connecting fully with her emotional interior.

This was certainly not the case in *Private Lives*, though the production as a whole had the considerable merit of confounding cosy Cowardian expectations and Gielgud's gentlemanly attempts to impose order. It was a bit of a riot, and swung around enormously during the run. After the First Night, Coward went backstage and wagged his finger at Maggie, telling her off for overdoing it: 'You've got very common indeed. You're almost as common as Gertie.' Maggie told Alan Bennett that to be compared with Gertrude Lawrence, if only for overdoing it, seemed such a compliment that she instantly mended her ways.

Maggie was mightily relieved when, at the end of the year, Kenneth Williams moved into the Globe next door, in a comedy written for him by Charles Laurence, *My Fat Friend*. In spite of a difficult rehearsal period, the play had gone well and Maggie, who read other people's reviews even if she never read her own, left a note at the stage door: 'I've never seen such a wonderful crop of good notices. You may have been away from the theatre for a long time but you've certainly come back with a bang!'

They had supper together the following night and harked back to their occupation of these same theatres ten years previously, when Williams was still in the Shaffer double bill and Maggie was in *Mary Mary*. Williams said that God intended such things. It was 'the divine nature of special affections'. This unusually sombre conversation continued with Maggie declaring: 'It was all so carefree then, wasn't it? But the awful thing about success is that it gets harder every time, not easier. When we were young, arrogance blinded us to the pitfalls.'

Because of Williams, Maggie agreed to make her one and only appearance to date on a television chat show, hosted by Michael Parkinson on BBC TV on 17 February 1973. The first guest on this intriguing occasion was George Best, the brilliant but dissolute Manchester United and Northern Ireland soccer player who had just announced his retirement from the game. He admitted to Parkinson that he was irresponsible with his talent and not sure if he felt any loyalty to his audience.

Maggie, of course, is just the opposite. Best left and Parkinson brought on Sir John Betjeman, the Poet Laureate, who listed what he most liked in girls: freckles, turned-up noses, wide-apart blue-grey eyes, sulky lips and a hint of latent power. Still Maggie waited in the wings, while Parkinson said that she had a voice like a strangulated dove. She thought he had said 'a strangulated duck'.

Maggie appears in elegant black from top to toe, looking drawn and nervous to start with but loosening up as the interview proceeds. She quotes Pamela Brown's remark about the audience being stage-struck and how things get 'more and more difficult' the longer you go on. A couple of laboured clips from *Travels With My Aunt* do little to lighten the atmosphere. She answers the 'who influenced you' question with Ingmar Bergman and William Gaskill, which completely silences the studio audience. Luckily she adds the name of Parkinson's final guest, Kenneth Williams.

Williams comes on and takes over, delivering a rebarbative tirade against critics (trotting out the old Brendan Behan crack about eunuchs in a harem who watch it every night but can't do it themselves), making an exception for the enthusiastic profiles of Rex Reed. Maggie sticks up a little for critics who are serious, but is washed away on a tide of Williams rhetoric about hideous modern architecture and trades unionists who go on strike and inconvenience their fellow citizens. Parkinson scoffs at Williams's equation of himself as a successful actor doing something he enjoys with an underpaid workman on an assembly line who is bored to death.

It is all good sparky stuff, notably free of anything resembling a plug for the actors' respective West End shows, which Betjeman gapes at from the sidelines before coming back in to talk about his own days as a film critic and why he likes actors very much: 'Because they are givers, not takers.'

A really splendid programme – miles better than anything passing for a chat show on British television today – ends with Maggie and Williams reciting an early Betjeman poem, 'Death in Leamington', Maggie leading off with the first quatrain: 'She died in the upstairs bedroom, by the light of the evening star; That shone through a plate-glass window, from over Leamington Spa.'

Maggie had done little television work altogether since the early days of her career: just two 'Plays of the Month' for the BBC which she recorded before *Private Lives* opened: *The Merchant of Venice* and Shaw's *The Millionairess*. Portia was clearly not her role and Maggie found no way round the triumphal priggishness of the *Merchant* court scenes. Cedric

Messina's production was set in pastoral landscapes where men wore tights and prominent cod-pieces, especially in the case of Christopher Gable's anaemic Bassanio. Frank Finlay was a squinting, foxy Shylock in a pill-box hat and a big bushy beard, and Charles Gray a somewhat sinister and queenly Antonio. John Moffatt delivered a strikingly understated popinjay of a Prince of Arragon, vanity displaced in his tearful, touching adieu in the casket scene: 'Did I deserve no more than a fool's head?'

Maggie later told Alan Bennett that, at the time, Robert was having an affair with the make-up girl on *The Merchant*, so, as far as she was concerned, the quality of mercy was pretty strained. Her Portia submitted rather sulkily to her father's conditions of marriage, mocked the suitors inordinately and was implacably cruel in driving home the letter of the law. You sense, though, that Maggie did not love Portia enough to play her very well.

She was far more temperamentally suited to Shaw's Epifania Fitzfassen who, like Portia, is bound by a parental rule: any suitor for this woman worth £30 million must succeed in converting £150 into £50,000 within six months. The comedy eventually leads her to an Egyptian doctor (played by Tom Baker in dark pancake and a red fez) who has kept a clinic for penniless Mohammedan refugees. Under the rush and silliness of this technically engrossing performance, Maggie shot a bolt of profound loneliness. The final effect is one of helter-skelter skittishness subdued in scenes of limpid radiance.

Cedric Messina assembled a fine array of supporting talent: Peter Barkworth as the solicitor Sagamore, James Villiers as Epifania's first husband (Villiers added distinction to the boring Victor in *Private Lives*) and Charles Gray as a barking city slicker. Nancy Banks-Smith was seduced in the *Guardian*: 'From the hurlyburly of Epifania's entry, lashing her silver foxes like a tail, to the peace of the last scene when her doctor listened entranced to the slow sledgehammer of her pulse, it was mainly Maggie Smith singing Shaw. And that's well worth an hour and a half of anybody's life.'

An attempt to repeat the success of *Jean Brodie* in George Cukor's film of *Travels With My Aunt*, though not without its admirers, was a considerable failure, and further evidence that Maggie's career had peaked and not yet found a new direction. Robert Fryer had set it up with Maggie and the *Brodie* screenwriter Jay Presson Allen (with contributions from Hugh Wheeler) two years previously, but Maggie had rejected the idea.

The property then went the way of Cukor and Katharine Hepburn, and Alec McCowen was hired to play Henry Pulling. McCowen had done a read-through thinking he was being auditioned, and at the end of it, Hepburn turned to him and said, 'How was I?' He was at first expected to address his Aunt Augusta as 'Mumsy', Hollywood's notion of how English boys spoke to their mothers. Hepburn was never happy with the script and started rewriting it herself. She was eventually fired by MGM for insisting on a longer schedule than the allotted fourteen weeks.

Robert Fryer persuaded Maggie, against her will, to take over, and Robert was ironically cast as Visconti, the only man who ever really cared for Aunt Augusta and the first and only love of her life. The film took as long to shoot as Hepburn had forecast, chiefly because of Maggie's laborious make-up each day.

Alec McCowen recognised that she was not in the best of spirits, because of the problems with Robert: 'She was only eating one meal a week, and that was a little smoked salmon or consommé or something. She fainted on the set one day, and yet this extraordinary energy came out. Cukor should have been a little more controlled, but he simply fell in love with her. Every time she did something, he loved it.'

McCowen has no idea where Maggie's performance came from in these conditions. It was George Cukor's forty-ninth film. Aged seventy-two, he instantly admitted Maggie to his private pantheon of favourite ladies he had directed – Garbo in *Camille*, Audrey Hepburn in *My Fair Lady*, Judy Garland in *A Star is Born* and Katharine Hepburn *passim*. 'She is resourceful, inventive, and she has mystery and power. Mystery in a woman is terribly important,' he told David Lewin in the *Daily Mail*.

One mystery was how Maggie, her face lined for the role like an old map of the Indies, managed to evoke comparisons with a Modigliani drawing, La Goulue in Lautrec's poster, and, as George Melly said in the *Observer*, 'a Beardsley lady or one of those wicked old trouts in the novels of Ronald Firbank'.

Like some bizarre preparation for the other Aunt Augusta, Wilde's Lady Bracknell, Maggie sweeps through a survey of her own colourful past, dragging her impressionable 'nephew' in tow and reliving her affair with Visconti in some rather glutinous flashback scenes (in which, incidentally, Maggie, her flowing ginger hair restored, eyes sparkling, effortlessly manages to look like an achingly attractive pubescent schoolgirl).

Graham Greene's wonderful storyline, to say nothing of his superb comic dialogue, is entirely traduced and de-energised, and the unresolved ending, in which a future way of life is to be decided on the slow-motion toss of a coin which freezes in the last frame, is both idiotic and insensitive. The script, it now turns out, was mostly what Katharine Hepburn had written while holding everybody up. Jay Presson Allen told Cukor's latest biographer that one big speech was hers, and that there was nothing of Hugh Wheeler's: 'It was Kate's script.'

There are handsome location shots, especially in Paris in the George V Hotel and the buffet of the Gare de Lyon. And

McCowen as Henry is superb, crusty and dry as an old biscuit. But, as George Melly said, the central quality of Greene's heroine, her irresistible charm, is missing. Maggie manages a few shafts of sudden emotion, but this is very much a performance most memorable for its make-up. And even that has the occasional, unfortunate effect of making Maggie resemble a male drag artist.

Much better, but less widely recognised, is her performance in the film she made just before *Travels*, Alan J. Pakula's *Love and Pain and the Whole Damn Thing*. This curious project, scripted by Alvin Sargent, was one of many follow-ups to the 1970 weepie *Love Story*, which portrayed romance vitiated by the fatal cancer of Ali McGraw.

In *Love and Pain*, Maggie played Lilah Fisher, a lonely spinster from Bournemouth who is dying of an unspecified incurable disease and who discovers passion on a Spanish holiday with the much younger Timothy Bottoms. Bottoms, following up his notable début in Peter Bogdanovich's *The Last Picture Show*, was also 'crippled' in his role – by parental expectations, asthma and his own innate sensitivity. And Pakula was hot stuff after providing quirkily enjoyable vehicles for Liza Minnelli in *The Sterile Cuckoo* and Jane Fonda in *Klute*.

The result was not a smash, nothing like, but the film deserves to be better known, if only for Maggie's performance. Here are the first outlines of the mature studies in emotional disintegration of the 1980s. One scene in particular prefigures *The Lonely Passion of Judith Hearne* in its glum, suicidal alone-in-a-hotel-bedroom despair. Maggie has collapsed again with her mystery illness, scrawled 'Adios' on the mirror and finished off the brandy, no doubt with a whispered toast of 'Bottoms up'.

Earlier, Maggie has managed to shake off a few inhibitions at a flamenco club. Bottoms misreads the signals and jumps on her lustily when they return to the hotel. Rejected, he goes

next door and tearfully smashes his fist through the partition.
Maggie goes into his room, cleans up his hand and starts
thawing out a little herself. However unlikely this situation
seems at first, the playing of it is very beautiful, funny and
tender. When she gets out of bed, Maggie executes what the
New Yorker described as the first sexual pratfall by a girl in a
movie. She trips over her own panties.

The couple separate themselves from the coach-party tour
and take off with a trailer through some well-photographed
countryside around Madrid, Segovia and La Mancha. But the
story is badly controlled and the mawkishness of the last few
reels nearly intolerable. At least, after Aunt Agatha, we can
see Maggie's eyes, skin and freckles, and also her legs, which
are too often taken for granted. Her wardrobe is by Germinal
Rangel, the Toulouse-based couturier who had first dressed her
in the televised *On Approval*. He also provided her costumes in
Travels.

Maggie's progress from unfulfilled spinster to radiant bride
astride a Spanish donkey is expertly charted in a performance
coming straight down the camera with no hint of coyness or
artificiality. Vincent Canby of the *New York Times*, who had
disliked her intensely in *Travels*, thought she was 'magnifi-
cently funny', while Dilys Powell in the *Sunday Times* said
Maggie presented 'passion, shame, hysteria and a momentary
disintegration which are the more telling for being muted,
almost miniature.'

With her marriage under threat, there suddenly seemed a
danger that aimlessness would overtake her career. She
unexpectedly agreed to play Peter Pan at the Coliseum for the
1973 Christmas season. Captain Hook was not played by
Robert – who would have been ideal – but by the Irish TV
comedian Dave Allen, whose projection over the orchestra pit
left something to be desired. Allen was an old friend of both
Robert and Maggie, and was at that time still married to the

actress Judith Stott, Maggie's example at the Oxford High School.

Accounts of Robert Helpmann's production vary a great deal, but Christopher Downes, who was dressing Maggie, recalls one matinée she played barefoot, with a dreadful hangover, and the special silence she won with her query to the audience on the subject of their faith in fairies. Lauren Bacall was in the stalls with her child, and so was Peter Eyre, the actor. Of that one performance, Eyre said to Downes, 'I think this is not the performance of the year, but the performance of the decade.'

Michael Billington was impressed by Maggie's Peter: 'Like Dorothy Tutin before her, she rescues the role from thigh-slapping archness and presents us with a complex manic-depressive trying to ward off internal demons by surrounding herself with young people. Desperation is never far away as she talks of the barred maternal window or asks us if we do really believe in fairies; and, alone in the House of Trees at the end, her Peter becomes a potentially tragic Tennessee Williams hero living off memories and music in a warm climate.'

The weather had changed. Peter Hall had taken over from Olivier at the National Theatre, and the Old Vic company had been altered and overhauled in the new master's likeness in preparation for the move to the South Bank in the mid-1970s. Binkie Beaumont and Noël Coward had died. But Maggie herself was no back number. In a *Times* survey of the 'top of the pops' people of 1973, the British high-profile élite of sixty men and sixty women included, on the distaff side, Edith Evans at number fourteen and Maggie 'when playing the Master' at number thirty-one. Vanessa Redgrave just scraped in at number fifty-seven.

Maggie needed a new West End break. A play was commissioned from Charles Laurence, whose play for Kenneth

Williams had been a big hit. The result was *Snap* (originally 'Clap'), a loose reworking of Schnitzler's *La Ronde* in which everyone received venereal disease thanks to Maggie's character, Connie Hudson. It was awful. Peter Dunlop was informed by his wife that he was so drunk on the First Night that he was incapable of speaking to anyone. Clever ploy.

Christopher Downes maintains that audiences howled with laughter during the previews, but the critics descended like a ton of bricks and killed off all expectations. The producer, Michael White, is reputed to have asked Maggie whom she would like as a director, to which she languidly replied, 'I dunno, Ingmar Bergman or Bill Gaskill.' Gaskill she got, and he says today that *Snap* is the one piece of work in his long career of which he is thoroughly ashamed.

It opened at the Vaudeville in March 1974. In the programme biography, Maggie listed her favourite role as Mrs Sullen, her favourite food as oysters, her favourite music as applause and Bach, her favourite sport as watching Wimbledon and her ambition 'to dance and sing and keep on working'.

General critical uproar ensued over cheap tricks, mannerisms, prostitution of her high-class skills and an alleged inability to distinguish between rubbish and true comedy. Maggie gave it the works, jumbling her knees and elbows, falling over her own ankles as readily, said Alan Brien, as she collided with her own syntax. But the effort was unworthy of the play, which sank like a stone the more frenetically Maggie tried to administer the kiss of life.

This débâcle coincided exactly with the final, inevitable breakup with Robert. What had gone wrong between them? Their relationship, forged in the white heat of the National Theatre's inception, had been sustained by physical attraction and common purpose at work. Maggie had gone to the National as a West End star, Robert as a leading representative of the new intellectual theatre. Maggie took artistic respectability from her association with Robert; he assumed that her stardom and glamour would rub off on him.

This happened for a while, but the mistake Robert made was to assume that Hollywood stardom would automatically follow. Admittedly he was unlucky. But he never attained the eminence on screen of his wife, nor did he win an Oscar, and William Gaskill bluntly declares that, when the balance sheet is totted up, Maggie is the greater and more resilient performer.

Robert's understandable inability to accept this was a major factor in driving the couple apart. Temperamentally, too, they were a mismatch. Maggie's idea of fun is to shut the door against the world, immerse herself in a couple of good books, a hot bath and the bedroom comforts of an early night. Robert likes noise, people, flowing cups and piled-high plates, and as much social brouhaha as can be mustered.

In early 1969, Robert had been signed up by Billy Wilder to make *The Private Life of Sherlock Holmes*, a film that was going to do for Robert's international career what *Jean Brodie* had done for Maggie's. He was convinced that it was going to be his 'great statement', like Peter O'Toole's in *Lawrence of Arabia* or Albert Finney's in *Tom Jones*. Wilder assured him that the film would make him a star.

He was upset that, on the occasion of his 'one big chance', Maggie promptly moved down to Tigbourne Court for five months, with children and two nannies, leaving him to rattle around and fend for himself in Queen's Elm Square during the six-month filming. He asked her to read the script, which Wilder had written with his regular and distinguished collaborator, I. A. L. Diamond. Robert says that she couldn't care less about it.

To be fair to Maggie, she had plenty on her own plate at this time, organising her work on *The Country Wife* at Chichester, coping with the disappointment of Olivier's rebuff and caring for the baby. And Tigbourne was only half an hour's drive from Chichester. She and Robert were committed to return to the National for Gaskill's production of *The Beaux' Stratagem*, and Maggie regarded the Chichester jaunt as a means of limbering up.

Robert's view of this period is understandably tarnished by the fact that *The Private Life of Sherlock Holmes* (with Colin Blakely, his old Royal Court sparring partner, as Watson) was a disaster. The script fell below expectations, the acting misfired and Wilder's direction, for once, was wayward and cumbersome. Seeds of resentment were sown which yielded poisonous fruit. Robert took the failure of this film very badly and his behaviour became increasingly erratic. He was also prone to fits of violence. But only furniture was at risk with Robert around, never life or limb.

Design for Living in Los Angeles was an attempt to sustain the great success Maggie and Robert enjoyed in *The Beaux' Stratagem* and *Hedda Gabler* in 1970, but the writing was already on the wall. During this period, Peter Wood, who was directing them, reckons that Robert's various little compensatory infidelities and peccadillos were becoming intolerable to Maggie.

But his behaviour was not all that unreasonable given the pain of so many dreams evaporating. Robert always flirted and dallied, sometimes drank too much and was generally at his best, his most attractive and also his most dangerous, when he was having a good time. He is, in every way, as Wood says, 'an adorable rogue'.

The relationship became a trial of strength, and Maggie was never unduly bothered, at least on the surface, about showing how strong she could be. She felt deeply that marriage was for life, for children and for loyalty between the protagonists, however much the career took over. And so did her parents. Meg and Nat got wind of trouble brewing and began to suspect

that their worst misgivings about Robert were likely to be fulfilled, especially when he exacerbated the situation beyond
redemption by conducting his affairs around town with
Antonia Fraser and Vanessa Redgrave in the full public glare
of the gossip columns.

Maggie's husband in *Snap* was played by Barrie Ingham,
who had appeared with her in Beverley's *Strip the Willow*. It
was hardly surprising, therefore, that Beverley should re-enter
Maggie's life at this point. He had tracked Maggie from a
distance and had often spoken to her parents in Oxford. Nat
was always convinced that Maggie would one day end up
married to Beverley.

Beverley had also kept in touch through the proxy of Kenneth Williams. He certainly knew that the marriage was in
trouble. Early in 1972 he had rented a converted farmhouse
at Seillans in the Var, in the South of France, and Williams
had travelled across to stay in a nearby pension for a few days,
to talk over old times and have dinner in St Tropez.

Beverley returned to London in 1973 to work on the Tommy
Steele musical, *Hans Andersen*. Beverley sensed that now was
the time Maggie needed him most of all. He called backstage
at the Vaudeville, ostensibly to greet Ingham, but really
to catch up with Maggie. Over a period of several days,
Maggie told him the whole saga of her marriage to Robert, the
children and how her silently enraged parents were sitting
at home in Oxford muttering 'I told you so' to each other,
and to her.

With the failure of *Snap*, there was renewed talk of taking
Private Lives to Los Angeles, Toronto and New York, though
not with Robert. Audiences would have to make do with just
one of the 'New Lunts'; John Standing, who had taken over
from Robert at the Queen's (playing opposite Jill Bennett, who
had replaced Maggie), would be hired to play Elyot. Beverley
convinced Maggie that this was the right thing to do, just as

he had persuaded her in 1963 to accept Olivier's invitation to join the National.

Maggie, much to John Gielgud's amazement, insisted on three weeks' re-rehearsal before going to America, and the company moved into the vast expanse of Drury Lane, rattling out Coward's brittle prose in the incongruous shadow of the set for the Billy Liar musical, *Billy*, in which Michael Crawford was enjoying a huge success.

Gielgud, an inveterate film-goer, had of course been to see *Travels With My Aunt* since he had last crossed swords with Maggie at the Queen's. One day in rehearsal he dropped one of his celebrated bricks when he interrupted a scene to give an impulsive note: 'Oh, don't do it like that, Maggie, don't screw your face up. You look like that terrible old woman you played in that dreadful film . . . Oh no, I didn't mean *Travels With My Aunt*.'

Gielgud remembers her working furiously even after he had left Drury Lane at about tea-time to prepare for his own nightly stage performance as Shakespeare in Edward Bond's *Bingo* at the Royal Court. It was odd that, once again, Maggie should be playing a comedy about returning to a first love.

Beverley is far from boring, but he has more of Victor's solidity than of Elyot's raffishness, though he certainly shares Elyot's enthusiasm for travel. *Private Lives*, a crucially symbolic play in Maggie's life and career, was now an almost inverted paradigm of her situation. She had lived through the rough and tumble of life with Elyot (Robert Stephens), but was returning to the calm and safety of her sensible Victor character (Beverley Cross).

Maggie set off on her American tour with her sons. Christopher was now seven, Toby five. Divorce papers were issued between Maggie and Robert, and between Beverley and his second wife, Gayden Collins.

The minute she arrived at the Ahmanson Theater in Los

Angeles, where *Private Lives* played from the second week of October 1974, Maggie started experimenting with Coward and Amanda Prynne. Shutting out the pain of the break-up with Robert went hand in hand with stripping down the engine of her comedy technique.

She admitted privately that the harsher critics had been right about her performance in London. She had settled into automatic and then shot into overdrive when seduced by the audience. That was always the most dangerous seduction. John Gielgud had written to B. A. Young, in comparing her with Gertrude Lawrence, whom he had seen in the original production, that 'her main trouble lies in her inexhaustible vitality and invention (much like Miss Lawrence) and a good (or bad) audience is inclined to go to her head.' The only real corruption Maggie has ever suffered is that meted out by an enthusiastic crowd in the stalls.

The Victor and Sybil in London, James Villiers and Polly Adams, were replaced by the Americans Remak Ramsay and Nikki Flacks. The set designer Anthony Powell travelled to Los Angeles where, at one of the previews, Powell says, the play suddenly leapt to life: 'She threw away everything she had done in the past and played it as though it were Ibsen or Strindberg, pushing everything as far as she could. She tested it for all that poignancy of two people who cannot either live with, or without, each other, and it was unbelievable. I'd never seen anything like it in my life. The audience was spellbound.'

At the same time, according to Powell, she refined some of the London performance and knitted the two versions together. But on the First Night in the Ahmanson she chickened out and reverted to the old trickery, settling for the easy laughs. 'I went round in the interval and she just burst into tears and said, "Don't say a word. This is one of the most horrible moments of my life; I know what I should be doing and I can't do it." But within a week or so she was back on the track, working at the role as she had been before.'

Dan Sullivan of the *Los Angeles Times* had given the First Night performance a polite, respectable review, but heard from a friend of the subsequent transformation. He returned to the Ahmanson in the last week of the run and delivered an unequivocal rave, saying that Maggie's Amanda was now more human, more genuinely mixed up and not at all the study in external flamboyance he had first seen.

The production moved on to Chicago, Boston and Denver, and then visited the huge Royal Alexandra Theatre in Toronto just prior to the five-week engagement in New York. Gielgud was at last free to see what she was up to. He arrived from London for a matinée in Toronto and thought her acting was 'absolutely perfect'. The critic of the *Toronto Star*, Urjo Kareda, who had seen the performance in London, said that Maggie had now found something else, a new, faintly perceptible murmur of apprehension.

Maggie returned to New York for the first time since *New Faces* and was applauded as a more than worthy Broadway successor to the Amandas of Gertrude Lawrence, Tallulah Bankhead and Tammy Grimes. Clive Barnes in the *New York Times* declared that the London reviews had either been libellous or that Maggie had transformed herself. The outrageous triple take she executed on seeing Elyot on the balcony for the first time had been retained, followed by the hilarious crumbling spin across the stage. But, as Jack Kroll said in *Newsweek*, you also got a sense of heartbreak in this first act for which the four-square reliability of Victor was real compensation.

In Coward's play, Amanda and Elyot have been married for three years and divorced for five. Maggie and Robert had been married for the same total of eight years, with an almost identical period of separation within the marriage. Their divorce went through in April 1975, just after Maggie returned from

New York. And on 23 August she and Beverley were at last married in Guildford registry office. There were no guests apart from Alistair and Shān, their son Angus, and Christopher and Toby. Maggie wore a beige trouser-suit.

Important plans for a new life had been laid one fateful day in Toronto when Robin Phillips, newly appointed as artistic director of the Stratford Festival in Ontario, sent Maggie a telegram which read simply, 'If you want to escape for a weekend I'll come and collect you.'

Beverley had flown out to Chicago to join Maggie and the boys after the opening of *Hans Andersen* in London. They said they would love a weekend away from the touring grind, so Phillips asked one of his board members at Stratford, Barbara Ivey, if they could borrow her comfortable holiday cabin on Lake Huron for the weekend. Joe Mandel, Phillips's friend and partner, collected Maggie and Beverley in Toronto and drove to Stratford to collect Phillips. The party drove on for another hour to the cabin.

Robin Phillips recalls that Maggie was wrapped in mink, delighted to be free and 'absolutely hysterical'. After a good night's sleep, they all went for a long walk. It was an exceptionally cold winter. Only when the ice melted in the following spring did Phillips realise that Maggie had in fact been walking on the lake. Over the weekend, Phillips drove Maggie and Beverley back into Stratford and showed them over the theatre and around the town. They looked in on a rehearsal.

At some point on the second or third day, Beverley said to Phillips, 'You know, I think if you asked Maggie, she would be quite interested in coming here to do something.' The conversation turned to Cleopatra and Millamant. And the next stage in Maggie's professional life was agreed on the spot. She would return to Canada in a year's time and join Robin Phillips in his second season at Stratford. By then she would be married to Beverley and she could start over, with a clean sheet.

Robert's divorce from Maggie was much more of a defeat
for him than it was for her. He had envisaged a royal progress
through the National, the West End, Broadway and Hollywood. He wanted to be a star very much more than she did,
and she was one anyway. He was merely a very fine actor,
one of the finest.

After the London run of *Private Lives*, it was his turn to
retreat to Tigbourne, which he now says he always hated, and
to play a season at Chichester as Trigorin in *The Seagull*,
directed by Jonathan Miller. The production was revived in
1974 in an interrelated Freudian season at Greenwich, the
Chekhov presented alongside Ibsen's *Ghosts* (Robert as Pastor
Manders) and *Hamlet* (Robert as Claudius). It was excellent
work, but it was not the Big Time. All hopes were now pinned
on a 1975 Anthony Shaffer commercial thriller, *Murderer*.
Unhappily, this proved to be yet another disaster and not, as
intended, the new *Sleuth*. This, after the failure of *Sherlock
Holmes*, was a second body blow of ferocious impact. Robert
was sent reeling around the ring, having lost his wife, his
foothold at the National, his chance of film stardom and now
his promise of a compensatory financial windfall in the West
End theatre.

He reacted with a terrible wildness and for a short time
became socially impossible and virtually unemployable.
Luckily, during *Murderer*, Robert had fallen in love with the
talented actress Patricia Quinn (best known for her appearance
in the stage and film versions of *The Rocky Horror Show*).
They forged a relatively secure domestic relationship which
has lasted right through to the 1990s and has been Robert's
salvation.

In the post-Maggie years, Robert has had his professional
ups and downs, with some good seasons at the National
Theatre under Peter Hall and several notable television and

film appearances. But, for many years, it seemed that his unrivalled gift for projecting a sense of tragic waste would never encompass the heights. However, in 1991, and just turned sixty, he made a remarkable return to the top flight at Stratford-upon-Avon as both Falstaff and Julius Caesar. And, two years later, he at last played King Lear, also at Stratford. He had been invited to join the RSC by that company's new artistic director, Adrian Noble, who, as a schoolboy in Chichester, had undergone a Pauline conversion to the idea of a career in the theatre thanks to Robert's performance in *The Royal Hunt of the Sun*.

Lovable, unpredictable, noisy and in many ways reprehensible, Robert remains a true vagabond of the British stage, but one whose real glory was in a distant Camelot, first at the early Royal Court and later at the Olivier National, in harness with the woman he could neither live with for ever nor quite stop loving. He was out of the hunt, but he would always be Elyot Chase:

'You're looking very lovely, you know, in this damned moonlight. Your skin is clear and cool, and your eyes are shining, and you're growing lovelier and lovelier every second as I look at you. You don't hold any mystery for me, darling, do you mind? There isn't a particle of you that I don't know, remember and want.'

Entr'acte:
Maggie and the Soul of Wit

CERTAIN actresses are renowned for their wit and very few come wittier than Maggie Smith. It is not so much that she deals in polished, highly quotable aphorisms, as did Mrs Patrick Campbell, say, or Coral Browne. With Maggie, it is her slightly jaundiced and highly critical way of looking at the world that both makes her funny and characterises her acting.

She cannot *help* being funny. Harold Clurman once said she *thinks* funny. Her funniness is a condition of her existence in a way that marks her out from all leading contemporaries. Glenda Jackson and Vanessa Redgrave are not even remotely funny, except sometimes when acting in comedy. Judi Dench giggles a lot, *can* be funny in a high-spirited fashion and is loved by everyone. Maggie is just funny, wherever she is.

She enjoys nothing more, when in the right mood and perhaps with a glass of champagne to hand, than a good calumniating gossip. 'Laying people out to filth,' she used to call it when opening the file on friends and foes with her sons' nanny Christine Miller.

The waspishness of her nicknames for colleagues is invariably tinged with a precise germ of observation. Thus, Michael Blakemore is either 'the wily Aussie' or 'Crocodile Blakemore'; Vanessa Redgrave 'the red snapper'; Patrick Mower, who played opposite her in London in *Night and*

Day, 'the lawn-mower', with a drawling emphasis on the 'lawn'; Peter Shaffer 'Ruby'; Brian Bedford simply 'the Duchess', as in the Duchess of Bedford; and Michael Palin, with whom no fault can be found, even more simply, 'the saint'.

Like Coral Browne and John Gielgud, Maggie is widely imitated in other people's conversations, but remains entirely inimitable. Gielgud impersonations always suggest that the actor is ever so grand, which is the one thing he is not. No one, of course, is a better mimic of everyone else than Maggie herself.

Again, like Coral Browne, and indeed another demon perfectionist with a devoted cult following, the late Patience Collier, Maggie thrives in the company of homosexuals. This may have something to do with the elimination of sexual tension in the relationship or the fact that theatrical gays are often funnier and more fun to be with than their straight counterparts. But she has always needed close and confidential gay friends.

Kenneth Williams was Maggie's closest friend in her early days. He recounted how, when they were going round Fortnum's together, Maggie was aghast at the prices in the lingerie department. 'Seven guineas for a bra?' she exploded. 'Cheaper to have your tits off!'

Another Williams story has survived many reworkings. When Williams was cast as the young boy in Robert Bolt's *Gentle Jack*, Edith Evans was outraged. In her most extravagantly baroque and fluting of voices, she complained to the management, 'But you can't have him, he's got such a peculiar voice.' This pot and kettle story was recirculated when Maggie was said to have expostulated in a similar manner on hearing that Geraldine McEwan, another husky specialist in the loaded coloration of vowel sounds, was to succeed her in the London cast of *Lettice and Lovage*.

When Maggie went to New York with *Lettice*, an

all-dancing, all-singing black entertainment, *Queen Esther and her Gospel Singers*, moved briefly into the Longacre, the theatre which backed on to her own. She was furious at having her backstage peace and calm shattered by the frantic, noisy and ecstatic Praise-the-Lording going on next door.

Executives of the Shubert organisation, who owned both theatres, were summoned to a matinée performance. After much rubbing of hands and beating of chests, they came up with what they hoped would be a satisfactory solution. Apologising for not having thought of it before, they said that they had some wonderful thick black velours which they could string around the back wall of both theatres, thus insulating Maggie and Co against the invasive Glory-hallelulah-ing of Queen Esther and her exultant congregation.

Maggie went off for a break and returned to the theatre for her evening performance. The company manager met her with the good news: 'I think you'll be very pleased, Dame Maggie. We've hung all the blacks.' Maggie threw him a severe riposte: 'Well, I don't think there was any need to go *that* far.'

There are two versions of a jovial altercation with Ronald Harwood, author of *Interpreters*, in which Maggie appeared with Edward Fox. Even her closest friends have to judge very carefully when is the right moment to call backstage and visit Maggie. Harwood was impervious to such niceties and was always popping into the dressing rooms of the Queen's to jolly along the actors in a play that had not been a resounding success. In addition, Fox and Maggie, not the most compatible of co-stars, were hardly speaking to each other.

Eventually, Maggie had had enough and when Harwood put his head round her door yet again, he promptly had it bitten off. 'Hello, Ronnie,' enquired Maggie coldly, 'and what are you up to now?' 'Struggling with a new play, darling,' Harwood replied. Maggie paused and inspected her nails. 'Aren't we all?' she devastatingly twanged.

The other version suggests that Harwood replied to Maggie's question with 'Trying to finish a new play, darling.' To which Maggie impatiently snapped, 'Try finishing this one first.'

The hasty three-week filming of *Othello* at Shepperton Studios in 1965 entailed a lot of rushing about for Maggie, who was appearing at the time in *Miss Julie* and *Black Comedy* at Chichester. She was flown by helicopter between the theatre and the studios and was met on the first day of this arrangement by the director, Stuart Burge, who had gone out to give her some rehearsal notes. As Maggie emerged in a tangle from beneath the whirring blades, she exclaimed to Burge: 'Christ, I never thought I'd look down in between my crotch and see Guildford.'

One of Maggie's latest films is *Sister Act*, an unpromising-sounding remake of Billy Wilder's masterpiece *Some Like It Hot* in which Maggie plays a Mother Superior and Whoopi Goldberg a nightclub singer who has witnessed a murder and is taking refuge in the convent disguised as an inmate. She's a nun on the run.

On location in Reno, the actors experienced some difficulty with the narrative logic, or lack of it, in the script. The Pope was supposed to have sent a message to his subordinates, but it was not clear how the plot line could have accommodated his intervention with any plausibility. How could His Holiness have contacted the underlings? 'By fax vobiscum, I presume,' offered Maggie from the sidelines.

Whenever Maggie bumps into Alec McCowen, she makes him do his 'turtle routine', for reasons which are now lost in the mists of time but have something to do with the fact that McCowen has an old joke in his repertoire in which he impersonates a turtle. 'Hello, turtle,' Maggie says, and off he goes, doing his turtle business, bubbling his cheeks and clawing the air in doggy-paddle-cum-breast-stroke movements. Does this palaver dignify, you may ask, one of our most eminent senior actors, a CBE and, what is more, a native of Tunbridge Wells? 'Oh, Alec's always been about twelve,' Maggie chortles.

Her long-serving dresser, Christopher Downes, is a great collector of Maggie's famous barbs and asides, and immodestly enjoys one involving himself at a busy party. Downes was deep in conversation with another guest who was asking, 'Yes, Christopher, but what do you actually *do*?' At that precise moment, Maggie was wafting past with a tray and threw her voice back over her shoulder: 'He saves people's lives.'

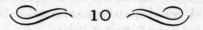

10

Canada Home and Dry

THAT weekend discussion at Lake Huron with Robin Phillips did indeed prove the basis of Maggie's first season at the Stratford Festival, Ontario. She signed up to play Millamant and Cleopatra, and she added her second look at Masha in *Three Sisters* and a vignette as Mistress Overdone, the noisy bawd in *Measure for Measure*.

She arrived to join rehearsals in the trim, quiet and prosperous festival town on 1 March 1976 in the middle of a violent storm. She would return for three more seasons, avoiding the worst winter weather by making films in Hollywood, to complete what many colleagues and critics would hail as her regeneration.

A qualifying opinion often expressed of this supposed exile was that nobody saw her work there except a few London critics and a lot of lucky Canadians. But London is often less of a theatrical world centre than its practitioners and critics admit. The greatest summer theatre festival in North America is not just a magnet for visitors from all over Canada. It attracts, at its best, keen attention in New York and sends reverberations right through the continent.

This was certainly the case in the Phillips years of 1975 to 1980. Maggie was Queen Guinevere in her second Camelot, a golden era indeed comparable in some ways to the Olivier years at the Old Vic, though without the acting in depth or the intellectual spine provided by Tynan. In Brian Bedford, the company's outstanding actor, Maggie linked up with one of her most trusted leading men, her Lancelot. And in Robin Phillips, King Arthur, she had found one of her most crucially influential and sympathetic directors.

Maggie was at last married to the man she began to say she should have married in the first place: 'My Bev. Nice, my Bev, isn't he?' The house in Queen's Elm Square was kept on but rented out, and would remain so until 1986 when the boys were old enough, and only too eager, to colonise it. For now, Christopher and Toby, aged nine and seven, were enrolled in a Stratford school.

The traumatic accumulation of Maggie's unhappy London experiences – marital collapse, rejection by the National, strain and controversy in *Private Lives*, critical disaster in *Snap* – would be cleansed by the concentrated process of work in a permanent ensemble on challenging roles no one had offered her at home. In Canada, Phillips says, Maggie felt relieved of 'the demons and pressures that haunt and taunt'.

Bedford, a perceptive Yorkshireman of working-class background who had made his career mostly on the other side of the Atlantic since going to New York in John Gielgud's production of Peter Shaffer's *Five Finger Exercise* in 1959, offers one of the most striking diagnoses of the 'Maggie' condition. He says that, for her, just the journey from breakfast-time to lights out each day is very difficult and fraught with problems: 'She's not at all affected, you know. I often think that her blood is of a different temperature to the rest of us. And that must be the Scottish side. I've always suspected that the chilliness, the rather bleak "Highlands of Scotland" element in Maggie comes from her mother.'

Maggie's parents were relieved that she was reunited with Beverley. They understood him in a way they did not understand Robert. Beverley had a *bona fide* association with the

University and often mulled over the old days in Balliol with Nat, much to the old man's delight. Nat liked nothing more than to relish his association with the medical and academic life of the city, and Beverley knew how to show a lively interest.

Throughout what became known as the period of separation from Maggie, Beverley had kept in touch with her parents. Robert was not someone to whom they felt they could safely entrust their daughter. He didn't fuss and guard her in the way they knew Beverley had, would and wanted to. From the moment Beverley achieved his life's aim of marrying Maggie, he exchanged his former domestic life completely for hers. For Nat, especially, Beverley was another son. Beverley returned the compliment: he saw much less of his own two daughters and committed himself wholeheartedly, and without a moment's hesitation, to becoming 'Dad' for Christopher and Toby.

Maggie asked Christine Miller, who had left Penelope Gilliatt's employ in 1975 and had been working in New York, to join them as child-minder, shopping companion, cook and general help-mate. She got on well with Beverley. She stayed for two and a half years and laughed a great deal for most of them.

And she adored the boys: 'Toby was a bit more what I'd call ballsy; he was wonderful when he was little, a real boy, very naughty. He got stuck in there straight away, went fishing with his mates and did all the "boy things". Chris was a little more ethereal, more reflective, more stay-at-home.'

When Maggie went on tour with *Private Lives*, the boys had been sent to a school in Los Angeles where most of the children were 'kids of posh lawyers'. They hated it. The fresh air, lack of pressure and informality of Stratford were as welcome to them as was the whole change of pace and climate to their mother.

The new family was billeted in a rambling 1894 three-storey house on Cambria Street. Built in red brick and Queen Anne style, with an odd little black decorative spire, the house was the work of Thomas Trow, a well-known local architect whose granddaughter, Eva McCutcheon, rented it out to the festival. Maggie and Beverley liked the house – it had a very large kitchen and dining area and a beautiful sitting room – but it was slightly too big for their purposes. In subsequent seasons they rented a more compact and practicable white clapboard house on Norman Street, previously occupied by Jessica Tandy and Hume Cronyn.

Mrs McCutcheon kept one cupboard in the attic of 220 Cambria Street locked, saying it contained precious mementos for her grandchildren. This attic was a large room, ideal for the boys to romp and run around in with their friends. Late one night, after a certain amount of running and romping had been perpetrated, Maggie and Christine returned from the theatre to find the lights on and the forbidden cupboard half-open on its chain.

Curious to see what treasures the cupboard contained, Maggie got down on her knees and rummaged around with her long spindly arms. She brought out first a tiny toy house covered in pebbles, looked at Christine and said, 'Ooo-er,' then produced some tiny gardening tools, a little window box and a mangled shoe. For some reason, the accidental discovery of these worthless signs of dwarfish domesticity – not at all the silverware or jewellery they expected to find – caused the two women to collapse in gales of uncontrollable laughter. They were only subdued by an angry, Malvolio-like intervention by Beverley in his dressing-gown.

In Stratford, such an event counts as a dramatic highlight. Compared to Stratford, Ontario, sleepy old Stratford-upon-Avon is a seething metropolitan centre. Both Stratfords are dedicated in the summer months, and increasingly the early winter ones, to a festival of drama based on the works of Shake-speare.

In the middle of the prosperous south-western Ontario farm-lands, in a town most renowned for being a glorified railway junction, this is more unexpected, obviously, than in the town of Shakespeare's birth. The idea of following the English example, but using that example to forge a national classical theatre of Canada, was hatched by a remarkably imaginative and persistent Stratford-born journalist called Tom Patterson.

The quiet, determined, bespectacled and altogether unlikely man who inspired Canada's most prestigious cultural insti-tution was, according to the Canadian critic and Stratford historian Martin Knelman, 'less interested in the aesthetics of Elizabethan theatre than in finding economic salvation for a town that was losing its chief industry – a repair centre for railway steam engines.'

Patterson's 'impossible dream' was launched in the spring of 1952, when he wrote to the Irish director Tyrone Guthrie, who had worked for the Canadian Broadcasting Company in his youth, inviting him to supervise a festival in 1953. The standing joke was that Patterson, who had only seen one play in his entire life, knew he wanted Guthrie but did not really know who he was until he looked him up in the local library's *Who's Who*.

He was instantly less of a joke when he caught his big fish and pulled the entire financial and political community of Stratford behind him. On 13 July 1953, the venture took off, locally and internationally, with Alec Guinness and Irene Worth leading the new festival company in *Richard III*.

They performed in a large canvas tent on the riverside site where the theatre, designed at Guthrie's insistence on a thrust-stage principle by Tanya Moiseiwitsch, would open four years later. All the money was raised on subscription, appeal and donation. The Festival Theatre combined the thrust stage with

a wrap-around auditorium similar to that of a Greek amphi-
theatre, with seating for 1,800 people.

A second festival venue was acquired and refurbished during
the 1960s: the downtown Avon Theatre, an imposing vaudeville house seating 1,100 people. And a third arena, the winter
home of the Stratford Badminton Club on Lakeside Drive, was
added in 1971 as a forcing house of workshop and experimental
productions. This venue, with seating for 500, initially called
the Third Stage, was renamed the Tom Patterson Theatre in
1991.

By the time the actors occupied the pillared and porticoed
thrust stage in 1957, Guthrie had moved on and the artistic
directorship was in the hands of the British director Michael
Langham, who both consolidated the festival's reputation and
nurtured many important native careers. He was succeeded in
1968 by the more controversial, and less successful, Jean Gascon, a French Canadian who started his régime in harness
with a Canadian administrator, William Wylie, who died, and
a fellow Canadian director, John Hirsch, with whom he
rapidly fell out. The general impression was that the exciting,
heady days of the festival's birth had been lost in a routine and
slightly predictable repertory, and that Gascon's stilted efforts
at more adventurous productions inevitably proved disastrous.

When Robin Phillips arrived in 1975, a new impetus was
sought and a new impetus was certainly found. The 1953
festival was a six-week season of forty-two performances playing
to 68,000 people and grossing $206,000 Canadian at the box
office. In Phillips's first season in 1975, a twenty-one-week
season of 362 performances played to 437,000 people and took
$2.6 million. Maggie's impact in 1976 was immediate: in a
twenty-two-week season of 338 performances, the overall
attendance jumped to 518,000 and the box office gross to $3.7
million.

In 1975, the government grants amounted to about twenty

per cent of the total income of $3.7 million Canadian. Five years later, when Phillips left an operation which had more than doubled its income to $8.3 million, those government grants, an almost standstill figure, constituted just ten per cent.

The nearest equivalent in Britain to the Stratford Festival Theatre is the Chichester Festival Theatre, which was conceived partly in response to Tom Patterson's adventure, with a similar mobilisation of private money and local involvement at business and management levels. Chichester's theatre, which opened in 1962, and where Maggie had worked in Olivier's National company, also has a thrust stage but one that is not nearly as effectively designed.

The Stratford stage is surprisingly small and seems at first limited in its potential. In fact, its simplicity allows for endless variations in the actor's relationship with the audience, which is clustered around the acting area – no spectator is more than sixty-five feet from the stage – in a much more intimate and successful way than at Chichester.

The main attraction to the Stratford visitor at festival time is the predominant air of holiday high spirits emanating from the river and the theatre. There are delightful walks through the woods and along the bankside, and the richness and variety of the domestic architecture – streets of sturdy brick houses and clapboard villas set among perfectly manicured lawns – are considerable compensation for the somewhat deadening respectability and almost shocking cleanliness of the town.

The Festival Theatre is just a few minutes' walk from the centre, surrounded by greenery and adjacent to a public baseball pitch where theatre patrons can prepare for fictional heroic encounters by witnessing a few minutes of the real thing: a schoolboy match is in progress on most summer evenings. Flags are flown and a brass anthem played by musicians before each performance. There are crowded bars, hot-dog and sandwich counters, a bustling bookshop and a pleasant air of delight at the fact that anything cultural is happening at all in so seductively bland and untroubled a setting.

Phillips was surprised to find that Maggie was more 'ready for escape' than he had thought, and detected a determination to rethink not only her art, but also her life: 'I don't actually believe that England has ever seen *that* Maggie, the one we had for six years. She found new muscles and toughness. Her voice became an incredible cello, no longer a violin.'

At the same time, Phillips was under continual attack from the nationalist faction who resented the import of British stars, and indeed his own presence as a British director entrusted with the future of the Canadian classical theatre. The private salvation of Maggie's acting career was bound up in a wider maelstrom of the debate about the festival's identity. These tensions had been endemic to the enterprise from the very beginning. But Phillips was a charismatic and aggressive personality who unwittingly fanned the flames of the dispute to a new level of intensity. There were orchestrated campaigns against him in the press, and private hate mail, too.

Phillips is a complex, impulsive and obsessive character who had failed to ingratiate himself with the Royal Shakespeare Company (for whom he directed a famously outrageous *Two Gentlemen of Verona* in 1970, set by a swimming pool) and the National Theatre. In London, he had most recently presented a striking selection of productions at the Greenwich Theatre, with glossy, eye-catching designs by Daphne Dare (who came with him to Canada) and notable performances by a string of outstanding actresses: Elisabeth Bergner, Joan Plowright, Penelope Keith, Mia Farrow, Geraldine McEwan and Lynn Redgrave.

He seized the biggest opportunity of his career so far with both hands, and his invitation to Maggie was a masterstroke. As a result of her coming to Stratford, Brian Bedford agreed to join the company for three years from 1977. Phillips's work-rate was phenomenal, and his ability to generate extremes of loyalty and exasperation among colleagues and journalists almost unrivalled. In general, and on balance, he created a perfervid atmosphere of expectation and excitement.

It is probably still too early to assess the overall state of Canadian theatre, especially as the French-speaking, multi-cultural contribution as represented by the work of such important figures as the playwright Michel Tremblay and the brilliant young Quebecois director Robert Lepage is only now beginning to make itself felt, both at home and abroad. Canadians themselves have been writing plays only for twenty years or so.

In the mid-1960s, there were just two regional theatres apart from the Stratford Festival and the nearby Shaw Festival at Niagara-on-the-Lake (the latter was launched in 1962). In Toronto, outside of the main houses, there was no fringe or supplementary theatre venue at all; today, there are fifty small theatres.

As the critic Martin Knelman wrote, Canadian actors become stars by not staying in Canada, and he cited the careers of Donald Sutherland, Genevieve Bujold, Christopher Plummer and John Colicos. To them you could add Hume Cronyn (who, with his London-born wife Jessica Tandy, was a frequent festival star), Kate Reid and the late Colleen Dewhurst.

In this rapidly changing theatrical environment, fraught as much with burgeoning patriotic pride as with its attendant parochial cringe, the commitment of the Stratford Festival to the idea of a classical company has been of rock-like importance.

In Guthrie's first company, Douglas Campbell was generally recognised as the leading native member. Other impressive classical careers have been carved on home Stratford ground by William Hutt, Martha Henry, Roberta Maxwell and Douglas Rain. But nationalist malcontents could sourly note the fact that, in Maggie's first season, her two leading men were both British: Jeremy Brett was Mirabell and Keith Baxter, Antony (although the latter was, admittedly, a last-minute replacement for John Colicos).

The paying customers, of course, did not worry too much about these niceties. And Maggie herself was both immune to the wrangling, almost impervious to it, and wildly popular within the acting company. As far as they were concerned, she brought them full houses to play to; she was demonstrably a great performer; and she worked as hard as, and probably harder than, anyone else.

Richard Monette, a native Canadian actor who had lately returned from working abroad (he was in the London production of *Oh! Calcutta!*) and who was just coming into his own, says that this combination of box-office success, magic and technical discipline was 'very important in sustaining a classical company for that long'. Monette, now back at Stratford as a director, voices the general consensus of opinion about that 'golden era': 'Everybody adored Robin and Maggie. Maggie paid the ticket for all the young Canadian actors, and everyone got a piece of the pie.'

Another key witness to this period is Ronald Bryden, who, after serving his stint on the *Observer*, had joined the RSC as a play adviser to Trevor Nunn. Bryden had been educated in Toronto (before going on to Cambridge University) and had returned in the mid-1970s, after his RSC attachment, as head of the Graduate Centre for the Study of Drama in the University.

He says that while it is obviously not true that Robin 'turned Maggie into a great actress by bullying her out of her mannerisms', he certainly removed what Phillips himself calls 'that nasal thing' from her voice and all superfluous flutterings from her wrists.

Bryden had been instrumental in Phillips' appointment.

'We think of those years as a Camelot. Nothing as good, certainly, has happened there since.' Even so, Bryden sounds a convincing note of dispassionate objectivity when he looks back and tries to sum up Robin Phillips' work:

'I think it was brilliant, some of the finest theatre I saw in my life. But there was always a kind of sleight of hand involved in it, because of the nature of the casts he was working with. After Maggie, Brian Bedford and Canada's one great home-grown actress, Martha Henry [who was born in America], he was working with a middle level of character stalwarts who would have seemed slightly over-parted in the Old Vic of the 1950s, and below them a ruck of young Canadians of uneven natural talent and almost uniformly inadequate training. With enormously careful casting and direction, he could assemble these disparate materials into gorgeous arrangements, but you were always aware that his bouquets were artfully surrounding orchids with wild flowers.'

London critics were flown over by the Canadian authorities to report back on the new régime and their encomiums would have looked slightly more suspect, perhaps, had they not chimed with what most of the Canadian and New York critics thought as well. There was a concerted campaign to restore Maggie to her pinnacle. Also, as Bryden shrewdly remarks, the London critics had become more accustomed in the mid-1970s to the prevalent austerity of most British classical productions, certainly at the RSC. The Stratford lushness came as a surprise, and possibly a relief.

The Way of the World and *Antony and Cleopatra* opened within two days of each other at the start of June. The hidden eddies of insecurity in the Congreve comedy were spotted by Walter Kerr, whose account in the *New York Times* suggested that Millamant's prattling was a defensive measure and that she was the most vulnerable character on the stage.

The tone of her proviso in the marriage-contract scene with

Mirabell was altered utterly, said Kerr, with not a flick of her
heavy-lidded eyes and an insistence on 'one small, ordinary,
unmistakably human need: the barest minimum of privacy'.
She brought the scene to a heart-stopping standstill, says Phillips, just as she would in the Chichester revival directed by
William Gaskill in 1984.

Maggie's Cleopatra was one of her more unexpected performances, though Bryden reckoned that Phillips was wrong
to batten on to a suggestion of Keith Baxter that the two protagonists, rather like Elizabeth Taylor and Richard Burton, were
no longer in love with each other but keen to sustain their
public image. There was no direct physical comparison with
Taylor: Maggie wore a long red wig and a succession of simple
kaftans.

B. A. Young reported that she was 'not visually voluptuous,
but wiry and active' and that there was not an inflexion or
gesture that was not fresh and personal. Caryl Brahms opined
in the *Guardian* that Maggie's Cleopatra was placed at that
stage 'where incandescence flowers into a steadier flame' and
that she was particularly touching when, reconciled with the
stricken warrior, she 'like some compassionate dragonfly,
drooped her azure wings to cradle her dying mate.'

Many of the Stratford productions of the past fifteen years
have been preserved on video for archival purposes. These
records of actual performances, shot in black and white on a
still camera at the back of the auditorium, are by no means
fully reliable guides to the shows themselves, least of all to the
detailed physical and facial work of the actors. However, in
studying them, one can breathe the atmosphere of a production and, especially, sample its vocal qualities.

The *Antony* video, one of the earliest in the archive, is a
bit of a blizzard to inspect. But you do hear the general unaffec-
ted purity of Maggie's delivery and, having learned of the
demise of Antony's paragon of a wife, the wonderful laugh she

wins on '*Can* Fulvia die?' There is sob-bolstered anguish on 'Oh, withered is the garland of the war.' In calling for her crown and owning up to those immortal longings, Maggie, now 'fire and air', picks up the slack and consigns her other elements to baser life. Her embrace of death is lightly, almost ecstatically, phrased and is the more moving for being so.

Richard Monette, playing Lucio in *Measure*, used to walk off the stage as she went on. 'She used to say, "How's the house, Richard?" and I would say, "Dreadful, I didn't hear a titter." All she then did was cross from stage right to stage left. She managed to get an entrance round, three of the hugest laughs I've ever heard and an exit round. And as she passed me, she'd say, "I don't think they're so bad, Richard." She could see where the audience was and simply conjure their reaction. Every time. This alchemy is hard-gained through experience and technique. And of course, with her, there is the recognition factor. But it is also evidence of inbred comic genius.'

And in *Three Sisters*, directed by John Hirsch, Maggie recycled her beloved Masha in a company at least the equal of the National's: Martha Henry was Olga and Marti Maraden Irina, with Keith Baxter as Vershinin. Nicholas Pennell, an English actor who had made his name in the second BBC television version of *The Forsyte Saga* alongside Eric Porter, Kenneth More and Nyree Dawn Porter, had been a Stratford Festival regular since 1972. He rated this *Three Sisters* the best he had ever seen, and Maggie herself wanted to know where John Hirsch had been all her life. She never worked with him again and one cannot rule out the possibility that Phillips – who considered the production 'semaphored', with emotions worn on the actors' sleeves – saw to it that she did not.

So greatly did Maggie enjoy this Stratford season that some observers sensed that she might emigrate to Canada entirely. She turned down a West End opportunity to star in Neil

Simon's *Plaza Suite* (she made the film, titled *California Suite*, two years later) because of the commitment she had already made to a second Stratford season, where Phillips had promised her Rosalind and Judith Bliss in *Hay Fever*. She had already become a founding member of Canadian Actors' Equity, which had declared its independence from the American organisation.

She watched some of the archival videos of Brian Bedford's work in the 1975 season, when he had played Angelo in *Measure for Measure* and Malvolio. Bedford was returning to Stratford to play Richard III, Jaques in *As You Like It* and, Maggie willing, her opposite number in Molnar's *The Guardsman*, which was scheduled for a December opening at the Ahmanson in Los Angeles before joining the Stratford season in the Avon Theatre at the beginning of June. Maggie was willing. Little Toby asked her what was she going to play in *The Guardsman*. She said, 'The Actress,' to which he replied, 'But I thought you were one of those already.'

Trying to arrive at the heart of what Maggie achieved in Stratford, Phillips states categorically that she has two talents, as a clown and as an actress in both comedy and tragedy. 'The first talent is beyond imagining in its skill and technique; I don't know about it, but I can watch and admire it. The other persona, the actress, is the one I've always worked with.' Phillips had seen the clown element starting to play in the Toronto *Private Lives* and did not like the cross-over of the two talents.

Personal taste comes into all this. Gielgud felt the Toronto performance to be almost perfect. And it would be impossible to pretend that Maggie's work in Canada was instantly, or ever totally, purified of those inflexional idiosyncrasies and gestural extravagances that are part of her registered weaponry and instinctive comic personality.

But the tendency was for Maggie to work through her technique to the outer limit of her potential as an actress, and not just be satisfied with what came easiest to her, the automatic vaudeville of the clown side of her talent. In the high-style, high-tension comedies of Molnar and Coward (*Hay Fever* in 1977, *Private Lives* for the last time, with feeling, in 1978), Maggie put her new resolutions to their severest test.

Maggie and Brian Bedford assumed the Lunt roles in *The Guardsman*, a basically silly play in which the Actor, cognisant of the Actress's energetic cultivation of lovers before their wedding, investigates his new wife's fidelity after six months of marriage by disguising himself as the supposed man of her dreams, a romantically impetuous Russian officer in full military regalia. The ruse is finally exposed, but not before the audience has to decide at what point the Actress, like Falstaff in the Gadshill escapade, recognises her sparring partner and justifies her protest that she knew it was him all along.

By all accounts, the comedy rattled rather noisily around the Ahmanson. Phillips was not impressed. Peter Wood, who watched from the stalls, was horrified to find that Maggie and Bedford were flashing their considerable techniques at the audience like knives. On her fifth outing to the Ahmanson, Maggie still found the big theatre hard work.

Just how thin was the line between good and bad habits is clear from the video, on which Maggie seems to play both the sentimental heart of the comedy and its outer flourishes with characteristic panache. The conveying of deep feeling with light and glancing technique is best illustrated when she begs her husband to 'Come here, you fool,' while pumping her arms towards him and seeming to signal the opposite instruction altogether.

Christine Miller counts this one of the most heavenly scenes in Maggie's Canadian career. She says she felt that everyone in the audience was prepared to get up and run into her arms. Michael Billington, on the other hand, compared her to 'a tic-tac man at Epsom Downs on a particularly busy day. If she did half as much, she would be twice as funny.'

Ronald Bryden said that, in the hands of Maggie and Brian Bedford, a pre-Sarajevo comedy laced with armagnac like some ornate belle-époque dessert became a Hungarian forerunner of Pinter's *The Lover*: a wittily searching study of a woman's need for freedom in marriage: 'When she tears through the confession to her husband that she's seen a better Romeo than his "in a stock company in Schmatz", she snatches his self-esteem from him with the speed and grace of a pelican seizing a basking sardine. And in the last act, reading in aloof boredom while her husband drones on about money, she brings down the house with her disgusted discovery that her fingers are absently helping with his sums – she has declined into a wife.'

Maggie's Judith Bliss finally emerged from its impatient chrysalis in September. She entered through the French windows and went straight behind a sofa, where she stood like a restless heron arranging some flowers and putting them on a piano. When she finally moved round in front of the sofa, the audience noticed for the first time that she was wearing her garden wellies.

This speed and constant element of physical surprise galvanised the production. At the first hint of her husband's philandering, she seems to swoop down the staircase in a single motion. And, on the video, something very peculiar but extraordinary is going on in the tea scene. Maggie is downstage in her floppy hat, checking through the contents of every single sandwich on the silver stand. The audience is convulsed with laughter for minutes on end.

Where Edith Evans was dotty and vague, Maggie was distracted, yes, but acid and sharp. She was a portrait not of woolly vagueness but of rampant vanity, and also a credible object of young Sandy's sexual desire, however casual. There's a way in which she delivers the line 'I've been pruning the calceolarias' that is almost the final explanation for everything, and the last word on it.

Myra Arundel raises hardly a titter on 'This haddock is disgusting.' The central, manipulative consciousness of the comedy is indisputably Maggie's Judith, with her menacing control of the charades and her string of bitchy prophecies thinly disguised as helpful advice ('Men don't grow old like women, as you'll find out to your cost in a year or two, Myra').

In the following summer, Maggie was ready for her third and final assault on Amanda Prynne, having fine-tuned her working relationship and personal friendship with Bedford. 'By the time we got there, we really did love and hate each other, which was just right,' her partner confessed. Bedford had played Elyot as a RADA student directed by his contemporary Albert Finney, and again on Broadway opposite Tammy Grimes in 1969. This time, Bedford says, 'we did it very seriously, less of a comedy of manners and more like Chekhov. It seemed very real to us.'

SIBYL (*rushing after him*): Elyot, where are you going?
ELYOT: Canada.

The tart exchange implying a random and inappropriate choice of escape route was extremely funny, especially in self-conscious Canada. Maggie told the *Toronto Sunday Sun* that there would be no more triple takes, as there had been when she played it with Robert Stephens:

'Seriously, now, if that really happened, if someone you had loved walked in unexpectedly, you wouldn't do a triple take, would you? . . . Mind you, if my first husband walked in right now, I'd feel very, *very* odd. But it doesn't require a triple take, does it . . . I mean, he might get one. I mean, he would certainly get one if he walked in right now. But it's not quite the answer, is it? If you know what I mean.'

Instead of bounding across the stage like a headless chicken when Elyot appeared on the adjacent balcony, Maggie merely executed a svelte double take and leaned back on her chair. Her gestures, as Bryden had noted in the Molnar, had acquired the refinement and perfect elegance of a Japanese print. One hand is forever fluttering to her forehead or the nape of her neck. The effect is beautiful and not irritating.

When she tells Victor that 'Men are transparent, like glass', her right arm shoots straight up in the air, slightly crooked, and shoots straight down again, as if rapidly closing a blind. The gesture punctuates the line itself and conveys, in the quickest of flashes, an extraordinary complexity of descriptive thought: contempt, spelling out the obvious for a backward listener (i.e., Victor), the sheet of glass, a literally penetrating observation, a joke, an assertion of superiority.

At the same time, Nicholas Pennell, who played Victor, felt that Maggie allowed for enough resonance in their relationship to suggest there might have been something in it in the first place. And the second-act quarrel is preceded by the hilarious sequence of Maggie trying to get comfortable on the sofa, adjusting her limbs, jostling, lying down and moving agitatedly about for a full two minutes.

'To use a Maggie phrase,' says Bedford, 'there is nothing to discuss about those arms. There is nothing like them and I don't think there ever has been.' Bedford's Elyot was hailed by Jay Carr in the *Detroit News* as a brilliant black diamond of a performance, generous and solidly motivated. The emotional undertow was not as pronounced as it was with Robert Stephens, but the style combined truth with polish.

Maggie was good for Bedford because of the demands she made on him: 'In *Private Lives*, I always used to go into her dressing room during the half and she was usually very low.

One day she was sitting with the mascara brush just gazing into the mirror. "How are you, darling?" I said. "Oh, darling," she replied, "one is nothing, off!" And of course the phrase has entered our repertoire.' Along with 'ghastly', 'richocheting around', and 'deranged'.

Back in Oxford, just as *The Guardsman* was about to open in Los Angeles, Meg suffered a cerebral haemorrhage in the front room of 55 Church Hill Road. She had always enjoyed good health, apart from the recurrent minor affliction of sinusitis. Nat had gone upstairs to write a letter and she called him down to the front sitting room, said she was tired, put her arms around his neck and collapsed. She lay for seven weeks in a coma in the Radcliffe Infirmary before passing on, in a freezing cold January, at the age of eighty.

Nat was grateful that Meg never recovered from the stroke. She would have been a helpless invalid, a vegetable. But he was devastated. A month before he died himself, fifteen years later, he tearfully pointed out that nothing much had changed in the house since that day:

'I've kept up the repairs. But the furnishings and the photographs of Margaret, all of that, has never been changed. And I never will. If I changed that, I'm going to change the vision that's been built up over the years. It would have been lovely for Meg to know that Margaret had become a Dame.'

Maggie was by no means indifferent to her mother's collapse, but having been assured by Nat that there was nothing to be done while she was in the coma, and that obviously she could not communicate with anyone, Maggie felt obliged to continue in *The Guardsman* at the Ahmanson.

During this period, she had taken serious stock of her own health and had been to a Chinese hypnotist in Stratford in order to give up smoking between the first two Stratford seasons. In California, where she was filming, she visited a psychic nutritionist, Eileen Poole, whom Bedford had recommended to her. She spent a lot of time 'shrinking into elevators' to avoid guests who mistook her for Vanessa Redgrave.

Maggie also spent more time not explaining herself than was her wont. She told Gina Mallett, the sharp critic on the *Toronto Star*, who monitored the Phillips régime as carefully as anyone, that she only felt real on stage: 'I don't like myself very much. I'd much rather be someone else.'

When Meg had eventually died, Maggie had been unable to return to England for the funeral, unwilling to break her overriding commitment to the public and the management at the Ahmanson. *The Way of the World* from the 1975 season had initially been booked, but the expense of such a large-cast show was prohibitive. Phillips, Maggie and Brian Bedford had agreed to fill the schedule with the Molnar. 'What could I do?' exclaimed Maggie to Gina Mallett. 'One can't just chuck a show.'

Even as a girl, Maggie had never been close to her mother. In adult life, she remained even more distant. And no one – Robert, the boys, Beverley, her parents, dead or alive – took precedence over her professional duties, as she saw them. This was never a matter of choice or decision as far as she was concerned, but of simple fact. She did feel deeply the loss endured by Nat. Still, she did not return to Oxford for a good few years.

After two years in Los Angeles and two years in Canada, Chris and Toby now returned to Surrey and Tigbourne Court, where Alistair and Shān Smith took charge. They were enrolled at a local prep school and spent most of their time at home in their aunt and uncle's side of the house.

Years later, Christopher said that, while he enjoyed 'the brilliant gardens' of Tigbourne, he was 'freaked out' by spending most of his time living in one half of the 'Gothic pile' and looking through the windows into his own house. Toby, too, found this 'quite unpleasant'. The prep school had an 'incredibly religious headmaster', and the boys found themselves seriously behind the rest of the school because they had not learned any Latin or French in Canada.

Christine Miller had outlived her usefulness, though not her capacity for friendship. Beverley had more time to deal with the domestic arrangements as well as his own writing and paperwork, and the boys had gone. Maggie was in the middle of some of the most taxing roles of her career. Christine slipped away to work as a secretary and house-minder for members of the *Monty Python* team.

Today, Christine Stotesbury (née Miller) is married to a graphic designer and runs his office. She always felt that Maggie was much closer to Nat than to Meg: 'Meg wasn't a very soft person and she had some strange, old-fashioned ideas about discipline. I once took the boys to Oxford and left them there for a few days. She seemed to me just like a very stern, staid old lady.'

Toby remembers Granny Meg as 'always knitting. She terrified the life out of Nat, who liked his drop of whisky at night. He'd creep around the house avoiding her like the plague and pouring out his toddy.' The boys thought of her as 'quite warm, really'.

She had not seemed warm to Maggie, but at least she could no longer advise her daughter to complete a secretarial course as a safeguard against the possibility of failure in show business. But Maggie's career had baffled Meg. She took little pride in it and probably never understood what she had done to deserve such a peculiar and unconventionally successful little girl.

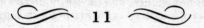

11

In the Forest of Arden

Wɪᴛʜ the boys safely tucked up in Surrey and Nat pot-
tering around happily in Oxford, Maggie settled in at
Stratford feeling reasonably content, or as near to that condition as she would ever be. Beverley told Gina Mallett that
the only serious worry in life was luggage, and Maggie, flitting
between England, Hollywood and Stratford, added, 'I don't
honestly know where home is. We're nomadic. It is odd, but
it doesn't worry me very much. I guess I'll go where the work
is. It's a marvellous new kind of life.'

Britain was denied not only some of her greatest performances, but also some of the best Shakespearean productions of
the decade. Few critics had seen the equal, for instance, of
Robin Phillips's production of *Richard III* with Bedford as
Crookback (Maggie played Queen Elizabeth). Ronald Bryden
said that, on that evidence, Phillips was fit to join the inner
ring of great directors – Peter Brook, Peter Hall, Ingmar Bergman, Roger Planchon and Jerzy Grotowski – capable of orches-
trating a disparate group of actors into an entity.

Margaret Tyzack had also joined the company, replacing
Kate Reid, who was ill, to play the Countess in *All's Well
That Ends Well*, Queen Margaret in *Richard III*, and Mrs
Alving in Ibsen's *Ghosts* (in which she scored an unequivocal
triumph).

Maggie's high, light comedy was rightly seen within the

proscenium Avon Theatre, but all the major Shakespearean work was on the Festival thrust stage. Phillips had concocted an imaginative and intuitive response to Maggie's personality. He knew that Cleopatra was the first of the Ptolemies to bother to speak a variety of languages, as did Elizabeth I. He felt that, in Maggie, there was an extraordinary link with past times and she came to be closely identified for him with something Garry O'Connor refers to in his recent biography of Shakespeare, the poet's ontological instability.

'During a totally lively, modern conversation, you can see right through her skin to almost every period back through time. Her skin is very thin, translucent, and you become aware of those strange medieval eyes, eyes of the palest blue, watery, liquid, limpid. Her skeleton actually represents English history. I do think of everything about those Elizabethan miniatures of Hilliard when I look at her.'

The 1977 season, Robin's third, Maggie's second, and the twenty-fifth anniversary of the Stratford Festival, coincided with the Silver Jubilee of Queen Elizabeth II. Phillips revived his 1976 A *Midsummer Night's Dream* with Maggie succeeding Jessica Tandy as both Hippolyta and Titania.

She was, in fact, those characters as dreamed by Elizabeth I, and the production opened with Bottom's Dream sung on tape by Hippolyta attired as Gloriana herself, in gold and black with a wig of startling crimson ringlets. Not so much Bottom's Dream as Gloriana's trip, mused Michael Billington: the queen saw herself not only as Titania and Hippolyta, but also as Helena, as played by Martha Henry.

Maggie's articulation of Titania's 'These are the forgeries of jealousy' speech, delivered standing stock still, her arms extended, was reckoned magical by all; its devastating simplicity and masterful phrasing and control are apparent on the video. Referring to the Indian boy, the bone of contention between Titania and Oberon, she reveals that his mother, 'being mortal', of that boy did die. It is a moment lit with sudden pathos, similar to the moment in *Much Ado* where Maggie's Beatrice invoked the pain her mother endured in childbirth.

Gloriana also commandeered the 'lunatic, the lover and the poet' speech of Theseus in Act Five as a sort of explanation of her intervention in such 'shaping fantasies'. Robin confesses he was unable to have Maggie on the stage as Elizabeth-cum-Hippolyta and not allow her mind to encompass that speech:

'She is in tune with Shakespeare, as she is with both sexes. Which is why I think of her as a creature. There are things which she hasn't learned, but which she simply *knows*. She knows about the Elizabethans, and she knows how to speak Congreve, and lots of other things that you can't possibly know from having gone to Cambridge.'

She knew, too, how to stand still and not move her hands. For all its imperfections, the video of *Macbeth* shows Maggie in her long black wig and floor-length black dress standing centre stage, pencil-thin and sleek, hands by her side, calling on spirits to unsex her here and take her milk for gall.

As Bryden says, she, not Macbeth, was 'the great imaginer' in this production – 'I feel the future in the instant' – rhapsodically ahead of the game and in for a penny, in for a pound. She moves her right hand to her left breast on 'I have given suck and know how tender 'tis to love the babe that milks me.' (Maggie always considered it cruelly ironic that she, who has splendid large breasts, had experienced difficulty producing milk for her own sons.) The hand scythes down again on 'dash'd the brains out.'

Maggie had arrived late from Hollywood for rehearsals (*California Suite* was overrunning), so her Macbeth, Douglas Rain, had rehearsed for several weeks, and worked out his own performance, with a stand-in. The result was unevenness and uncertainty all round, but Maggie made sure she took care of herself.

She had asked Coral Browne for advice. 'It's a fucker, darling,' Miss Browne had soothingly replied, 'and all I can say is keep your eyes open in the sleepwalking scene. For some reason, it rivets the fuckers.'

Thus reassured, Maggie did precisely that and glides hauntingly through the scene in a long white nightgown, reaching out for only the second time in her performance (the first is on 'Full of scorpions is your mind') on her quadruple 'Come' when she hears the echo of the knocking at the gate.

Richard Eder of the *New York Times* thought that this final wandering speech, 'rubbing her hands, recalling her action in a broken voice and reaching for the husband who has moved into a separate nightmare', was 'pure grief'. But the production divided critics and audiences alike. Ronald Bryden was more enthusiastic than most: 'It is hard and dark as onyx, austerely unfamiliar, jumping over time and expectation like a bad dream. But few *Macbeths* can have looked deeper into Shakespeare's inferno.'

After the dead-of-night murder of Banquo and the escape of Fleance, there was delivered one of Phillips's most spectacular coups, Bernard Levin recalls, as the lights came up almost immediately on the banquet – 'tables, glasses, everything. They must have done it in fifteen seconds and there was no noise at all. It was astounding, and a complete gasp went up from the audience.' Maggie told Levin later that she knew nothing of how it was done, was totally in the dark and had to be led to her place for the scene.

No such guesswork attended her Rosalind, one of the roles about which Maggie had rightly felt proprietorial for many years. It seemed absurd that she should have had to wait until the age of forty-three to play it, older even than was Edith Evans, the other most famous 'over-age' Rosalind (Dame

Edith played the part aged thirty-eight, and then again aged forty-nine).

Phillips set the comedy in the late eighteenth century, the period of George III, and Robin Fraser Paye's design was of a single large gnarled oak tree on a grassy knoll, the actors dressed in big hats, flowered skirts, bustles and riding breeches. The stage shimmered like a watercolour painting of Thomas Rowlandson.

As You Like It opened in August 1977, but most of the critical approval was clustered around the revival in June 1978. Watching the video, you can hear the audience falling in love with Rosalind, just as she had fallen in love, and with a younger man. As with her Millamant, the performance is perfectly balanced on that razor's edge between tears and laughter, with the underlying urgency of a woman energetically seizing her last chance for love. And of course the speed and wittiness of Rosalind's interventions in the forest were exactly matched by Maggie's qualities as an actress, and her physical beauty was compounded by a strange, ethereal sadness.

David William, the English director who worked regularly at Stratford over the years and became artistic director in 1990, left her a note: 'I have never seen the falling in love and then the being in love given such depth and detail.' Peter Shaffer, too, was bewitched, to put it mildly: 'I thought you were entirely beautiful and entirely extraordinary and wonderful and indeed unforgettable . . . You are simply blazing like a comet these days.'

Orlando was played by a blond, fresh-faced and well-built Canadian actor called Jack Wetherall. Brian Bedford chipped in with a darkly confidential Jaques, punctuating his 'Seven Ages of Man' speech with some wonderful pauses. The rest of the performances look, frankly, a bit dodgy, but the balancing and pacing obviously carried the night and day.

Looking back on Maggie's Rosalind, Ronald Bryden is reminded of Hans Andersen's mermaid, 'walking on knives to be near her prince'. And Levin is even more convinced today that this was one of the definitive performances of his lifetime. He detected the fuller music of her marvellous voice and approvingly observed that, although she had rid herself of the old vocal mannerisms, she could still go knock-kneed at the slightest provocation. Levin was never outdone on the effect of Rosalind's adieu: 'She spoke the epilogue like a chime of golden bells. But what she looked like as she did so I cannot tell you; for I saw it through eyes curtained with tears of joy.'

Robin Phillips felt that the clown tendency in Maggie's Rosalind had been exorcised in a particular morning of rehearsal when they were considering the Rosalind/Ganymede protestation of how turbulently *she* would be in love: 'more jealous of thee than a Barbary cock-pigeon over his hen, more clamorous than a parrot against rain, more new-fangled than an ape, more giddy in my desires than a monkey.'

Encouraging Maggie to be more serious, Robin suggested that she should first of all make it as funny as possible. She improvised an entire menagerie and monkey-house, squawking and swinging around the tree that was the single feature of the set.

The entire company was laid out on the floor with laughter and Robin breathlessly commented on how remarkable had been the evocation of the tree where no tree stood: 'Everybody stopped and looked at an empty rehearsal room with a blank wall. They stared at a space where she had just been halfway up a tree and swinging in its branches. To this day, I cannot tell you how she did it, how she swung from those branches without leaving the ground. I don't understand it, but she did it. We all saw her in the tree. I called a coffee break and people dispersed in stunned silence.'

On resuming rehearsal, Phillips took the scene in the other

direction, towards the pain of the disguise and protection, and, because of what had gone before, 'Maggie was able to do that in a remarkable and very moving way. And of course that was finally in the production.'

Maggie's idea of social life was, and is, extremely limited, so she did not feel particularly deprived in Stratford. If a performance had not gone well, or even if it had, she would philosophically inform Brian Bedford that there was nothing for it but 'to get untimely ripped', and quantities of champagne or white wine were duly consumed. Cold meats and the occasional cooked goose were laid out for friends at home after the shows.

Nicholas Pennell recalls one lively evening in the large kitchen in Cambria Street when Bernard Hopkins, an extrovert member of the acting company, was calling everyone 'she', and a conversation at one end of the table with Beverley was cut across by Maggie savagely intervening from the other, 'Will you please *not* call my husband Mavis.'

The centre of social life, such as it was, in Stratford, was the Church restaurant, which Robin's partner Joe Mandel had opened, retaining the spacious ecclesiastical open-plan interior, the Gothic windows and the stained glass, and painting the walls in a restful coffee colour. The food was excellent, the prices beyond the pay packets of the humbler company members.

Maggie and Robin, Beverley and Joe would always sit at the first table on the left by the front door, and this area became known by other festival personnel as 'bomb alley'. The assumption was that it was wired for sound and microphoned to pick up any passing gossip or unofficial information.

The Church remains, to this day, even without Mandel and Phillips in situ, a pleasant bolthole, now with salmon décor and an informal annexe upstairs called the Belfry, which opened in 1983. The Church passed into new ownership in

1988 and is still loyally patronised by Stratford actors and audiences alike, though the food is not generally counted to be as good as it was during 'Camelot'.

Robin says that he never really socialised with Maggie at all. He had dinner at Cambria Street just once, during the first year. 'Our relationship through work is probably deeper and closer than any has ever been, but it is entirely work, work as *we* think of work, a very intimate relationship.'

After their time in Stratford, Maggie visited Robin and Joe on the farm they had bought in Ontario. She and Robin were looking through the window at the lakes and fields, the chipmunks and the squirrels in the feeder. And the birds. Talk had turned to yellowhammers and speckled tits. Suddenly Maggie said, 'There's a yellow screwdriver.'

Robin, an English country boy, knew rather less about Canadian bird varieties than about the robins and chaffinches in his native Haslemere, and had certainly never seen such a creature. He wanted to see it, looked hard, couldn't, and became furious.

Finally, he saw what Maggie was agitatedly pointing out: a workman's tool for putting in screws, lying on the garden path. Phillips says that they could not speak for three hours afterwards and were so helpless with laughter that they had to go off on separate walks to relieve the agony.

Soon afterwards, Robin came to England to direct a rock opera about Joan of Arc at the Birmingham Rep. He checked into his hotel room and went to the bathroom. On the towel rail, resting on the towel, was a tiny, yellow screwdriver. It had somehow been pressed against the wall and had become stuck to the towel. At first, he believed Maggie had arranged for it to be left there. But she hadn't.

'That whole story is a perfect example of our six years together. In many respects, life *happens* to Maggie. And I think that's to do with her being connected to all those periods, right back through the Victorians to the Elizabethans and the Ptolemies. I think she is a creature, an animal, in a sense. I don't mean she's not human. But she has senses that are more than human. In humour, certainly. She can respond to something that perhaps only squirrels would sense in the air. And I think that comedy, travelling around in the atmosphere, finds out her. Absolutely finds out her.

'I remember our time in Stratford in the way one remembers childhood summers. They were immensely hot and golden, those days, and the boys would get suntanned and Maggie would whizz home for dinner before coming back to the theatre.'

During *As You Like It*, when she was off stage, Maggie used to walk through the park because Robin had suggested that it would be a good idea to remain in contact with the trees. People would sometimes stop and stare when they came across her in costume, apparently nowhere near the theatre. But she always was. And she walked, every Rosalind day, through the trees.

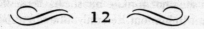

12

Star Billing in Hollywood

THE Canadian adventure was to a large extent subsidised by three Hollywood movies Maggie made, none of them masterpieces, but all guaranteed to maintain her international profile and keep her in good screen company. As she restored herself as a stage actress, so she underpinned her screen status.

Two of the three films involved Neil Simon, whose revue sketch Maggie had performed in *New Faces* at the start of her career; two featured David Niven, who became a good friend of Maggie and Beverley; and one of them won Maggie her second Oscar.

The wackiest was *Murder By Death*, which was Neil Simon's first original script for the cinema (most of his screenplays are adapted from his own stage hits). The director, another débutant, was Robert Moore, responsible for Broadway's first commercial gay play, Mart Crowley's *The Boys in the Band*, and for Simon's musical (with a score by Burt Bacharach) *Promises, Promises*, itself adapted from an earlier movie, *The Apartment*.

Murder By Death is a witty attempt at a parody of a murder mystery in which send-ups of fictional detectives are summoned to 'a dinner and a murder' at a fog-bound manor in California. The host is Truman Capote, making his acting début as the sinister connoisseur, Lionel Twain, abetted by a deaf and dumb cook, played by Nancy Walker, and by a blind, inscrutable butler (Alec Guinness). The butler's name is Bensonmum, confusedly thought to be Benson by the ma'am who enquires after it. Guinness can then say that, no ma'am, the name is not Benson, ma'am, but Bensonmum, ma'am.

Each of the five detectives has a motive to murder the host. Elsa Lanchester is Jessica Marbles (distantly related to Agatha Christie's Miss Marple) and has been jilted by him. Peter Sellers as Sidney Wang is a glorious steal of Charlie Chan, and also Lionel's resentful stepson. Peter Falk as Sam Diamond is a near-miss for Dashiell Hammett's Sam Spade, whom Lionel has unbelievably picked up in a gay bar and can therefore manipulate. James Coco, plump and jumpy, is Milo Perrier, approximating to Hercule Poirot and tragically deprived by Lionel of his pet poodle. And David Niven and Maggie are Dick and Dora Charleston (as opposed to Nick and Nora Charles in Hammett's *The Thin Man*), heavily in debt to the old rogue.

The delicious barminess of the script and the expertise of the acting from such a blissfully ideal group of performers never quite coagulates into screen magic. Maggie has her moments, as do they all, and she looks ravishing in a low-cut white dinner gown. She and Niven are billeted in Wang's wing of the manor and, darting an appalled look at the blind butler, Maggie half-mutters to Niven, 'Don't let him park the car, Dickie.'

Similarly, Capote, who propels himself around the dining room in a wheelchair and at one point whizzes rapidly backwards out of sight, prompts Maggie to comment, half-interestedly, 'I hope he knows how to stop that thing.'

The dénouement hinges on the removal of a face-mask and a riddle of double identity, after the detectives, with the exception of Peter Sellers, appear to have been bumped off.

The 'real' Poirot appears in the pear-shape of Peter Ustinov in *Death on the Nile*, where Maggie picks up the thread not only with her old sparring partner in *Hot Millions*, but also with Niven, the costume designer Anthony Powell, who deservedly won an Oscar for his work on this film, and Jack Cardiff, whose superb cinematography is one of the best elements of John Guillermin's somewhat leisurely overall direction.

The movie was a sequel to the hugely successful *Murder on the Orient Express*, in which Albert Finney had concocted his version of Poirot – strenuously bizarre, less urbane than Ustinov, at least as memorable – for Sidney Lumet. It had a screenplay by Anthony Shaffer, Peter's twin brother and author of *Sleuth* and the unhappy Robert Stephens vehicle, *Murderer*, with music by Fellini's regular composer, Nino ('The Glass Mountain') Rota; sumptuous Egyptian locations in the first half; lush on-board period interiors (the year was 1937) in the second; and a cast list including Mia Farrow, Angela Lansbury, Jane Birkin, Jon Finch as an incongruous Marxist in a beret, and a hopeful new heart-throb, now a fixture in American television soaps, Simon MacCorkindale.

Whereas in Stratford, Ontario, Maggie was an inspirational cog in the wheel, here she was merely one of several extraordinary spokes. The film spooled round and she did her stuff. She played Miss Bowers, a severe travelling companion, masseuse and secretary to a rich widow, Mrs van Schuyler. This would not be all that significant had Mrs van Schuyler not been played by Bette Davis, enshrined in a series of exotic costumes and complicated headpieces like a glittering lizard encased in a mummy's tomb.

Within the limitations of the film's dramatic potential, this double act, played almost as a shadow duel to the chummily conspiratorial 'old pals' act of Ustinov and Niven, looks like one of the great cinematic liaisons of the day. In their scenes together, you sit watching an old legend slugging it out with a new pretender. And one leaves the film rather regretting that we do not follow Maggie and Miss Davis on their next expedition to the Gobi desert; Maggie receives news of this plan with all the enthusiasm of someone being sentenced to death.

The story's murder victim is a grotesquely rich honeymoon girl, Linnet Ridgeway, played by the beautiful and now-forgotten Lois Chiles, whose father ruined Miss Bowers's family on his ascent to the financial summit and thereby doomed Maggie to a life of grumbling servitude.

Mrs van Schuyler's holiday on the Nile is rife with the possibility of fall-out: Davis slaps Maggie down with a warning to keep a civil tongue in her head or she'll be out of a job, to which Maggie scathingly replies: 'This town is filled with rich old widows willing to pay for a little grovelling and a body massage . . . You go ahead and fire me!'

By the time they clamber aboard the steamer at Alexandria, the double act is bristling with an air of uneasy truce. Maggie confides to the captain that 'the roasting afternoon sun will do wonders for those jaundiced jowls of hers', while Davis acidly apologises for Maggie 'accidentally' barging into Lois Chiles with the excuse that she once went fifteen rounds with Jack Dempsey.

Shaffer's script glints and ripples along like this for well over two hours, but the second half of the film is fatally devoted to awkward flashbacks following up each possible enactment of the murder and an extended resolution, again using flashbacks, only more excitingly, of what actually happened.

Maggie and Bette Davis slip tantalisingly away, but not before Maggie makes the most of one heavily inflected hint at her spiritual condition. Consoling Mia Farrow after yet another surprise revelation, she conveys the whole history of her character by confessing that 'It's been my experience that men are least attracted to women who treat them well.'

This sexual defensiveness, compounded with a deep sense

of injury, is a common trait in many of Maggie's performances. The prickliness, combined with vulnerability, is a distinctive element in a great many of her heroines, and is rather obviously exploited in *California Suite*, where Maggie plays the actress Diana Barrie, vaguely anticipating the receipt of an Oscar for her performance in a movie she thoroughly despises.

That Maggie herself went on to win an Oscar, as Best Supporting Actress, is an irony that was never lost on her. Nor, indeed, was it lost on her loyal father. Nat was reported in the *Oxford Mail* as saying that he was delighted, but surprised, as 'the film itself was somewhat bitty.'

As with the murder films, *California Suite* was constructed on the '*Grand Hotel* and fill the screen with stars' principle. Simon adapted his four short 1976 Broadway plays to show five couples simultaneously checking into the Beverly Hills Hotel for different reasons.

Jane Fonda is a divorced career journalist locked in a child-custody battle with Alan Alda. Walter Matthau has arrived ahead of Elaine May for his nephew's barmitzvah and is assigned a prostitute as a gift for the night by his brother. Bill Cosby and Richard Pryor as a couple of accident-prone doctors are on vacation from Chicago with their wives (they crash the car en route to a Japanese restaurant). And Maggie is in town for the Oscars with her wayward bisexual husband, Michael Caine, who sells antiques and purchases young men.

The black foursome mess up their room and fall over on the tennis court, thus earning the scorn of Pauline Kael in the *New Yorker*, who found their representation (and the Jewish scenario of Matthau and Elaine May) insulting and offensive. Cosby and Pryor, said Kael, were transformed by the whitened décor of the movie into 'tar babies'.

My own view is that Kael is rather scraping the barrel here to justify the structural deficiencies in Herbert Ross's direction; audiences today, thanks largely to performers exactly like

Cosby and Pryor, are increasingly colour-blind and able to laugh at absurd antics regardless of the protagonists' skin tint. The sequences, in retrospect, look groundbreakingly insensitive to the very objections Kael raises. More convincing is Kael's complaint that the stage-bound nature of the material denies us a ringside seat at the most crucial part of Maggie's story, her moment of non-triumph at the Academy Awards.

Michael Caine, one year older than Maggie and busy in movies since 1956, remembers *California Suite* as 'a very enjoyable film'. But Herbert Ross continually badgered Maggie for not, in his opinion, doing enough. 'I thought you were supposed to be funny,' he would yell at her, an approach which did not go down all that well, especially as Maggie was determined not to make a meal of a script heaving with quite enough coarseness already. 'As a result,' says Caine, 'she spent a lot of time on the set in floods of tears.'

Caine could have worked with Maggie on *The Private Ear* and *The Public Eye*, but he denies any knowledge of having been first-choice casting as the besotted music-lover in the first play. Just one year after that Shaffer double-bill, as Maggie forged her classical reputation at the Old Vic, Caine embarked on his great series of career-shaping mid-1960s movies, *Zulu*, *The Ipcress File* and *Alfie*. He became a dedicated film star in a way that few British actors have since the war and has noticeably failed to dissipate his talent in the style of Richard Burton, Richard Harris or Peter O'Toole. Caine has remained a committed and hard-working professional all his life, just as Maggie has divided a similar effort between stage and screen.

Caine's chemistry with Maggie in *California Suite* is just right, in spite of the mawkish romanticism of a script which requires Maggie to pull her errant husband down on top of her in bed and, in what Kael describes as 'one of the most degrading of all scenes: a woman pleading with a man – who does not desire her – to make love to her,' requests servicing:

'Screw the Academy Awards, screw the Oscars, screw me, Sidney, please . . .'

Caine wears his role of an automatic filling station with dignified levity. Maggie despises him because he has used her celebrity to mark his dance card. She finds him so doing at the end of the tawdry ceremony and, after an evening of ups and downs, crunchingly invites him to continue the motion.

Back at the hotel, Maggie cleans her teeth in the nude. As she slips on her nightgown, we catch a single, fleeting glimpse of her full left bosom in profile. 'Never again,' exclaims Walter Matthau after the prostitute passes out on him after consuming a bottle of tequila. You can imagine Maggie muttering the same phrase through clenched teeth along the corridor as Ross bullies her patiently through the bedroom scene with Caine.

The final straw for Diana Barrie is that the film with which she has failed to win an Oscar is being shown on the flight back to London after the junket. Caine says that Ray Stark, the film's producer, was so taken with the characters he and Maggie played that he promised to get Neil Simon to write a sequel for them alone. This has never materialised, though the partnership of these two specialists in the undercutting throwaway department could be, as they say in the political arena, 'a dream ticket'.

Caine and Maggie liked each other a lot. Both hail from the wrong side of the tracks, both have a devastating sense of humour and neither tolerates very much of the bullshitting hyperbole and self-importance that surrounds their industry. Caine, the ultimate screen professional, plays every scene knowing exactly where the director has placed his cameras. He was enthralled by Maggie's indifference to such technical niceties, noting how all her concentration was channelled into the details of the performance itself.

The rest she left entirely in the lap of a director who, for some reason, had decided that the best way of handling her was to reduce her to tears. Caine jovially offered Maggie cold comfort: 'As long as they're on your back, that's all right because they're not on mine.' Caine had a good time. He said that acting with Maggie was like attending a one-woman masterclass on comic technique; he would gladly enrol again – 'as long as they provide plenty of handkerchiefs.'

Pauline Kael said that Maggie performs in this movie like a professional who is used to doing the dramatist's job for him. Frank Rich, writing in *Time* magazine, thought that Maggie gave her best screen performance to date: 'Alternately buoyant and defeated, youthful and ageing, she transforms a potentially campy character into a woman of great complexity and beauty . . . Caine sets off Smith's brittle wit with soothing tenderness. Together these actors prove that a marriage of convenience can be a dynamic emotional affair. They also demonstrate that Simon, when he puts his mind to it, can be a worthy American heir to Noël Coward.'

The critical reception was generally more enthusiastic in America than in Britain. Maybe this was because Diana Barrie had triumphed in triviality, bitten the bullet and sold out to Yankee showbiz; she had spent eight years with the National, appearing in Pinter, Shaw and Shakespeare, and had finally been nominated for an Oscar because of her work on 'a nauseating little comedy'.

America staked its final claim on British talent in the bestowal of its ultimate accolade. In *California Suite*, Maggie articulates the dilemma of the great actress in search of a proper reward in the face of personal disappointments. For all its faults, the film most entertainingly and memorably recounts the price of that struggle in the too-fleeting partnership of two of our greatest post-war British screen stars, Maggie Smith and Michael Caine.

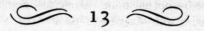

13

Farewell to Camelot

WITH Maggie seemingly lost to Robin Phillips in Stratford and the film moguls in Hollywood, offers of work in the London theatre had temporarily dried up. But when Tom Stoppard completed *Night and Day*, his 1978 West End comedy about freedom, journalism and politics, one of the first actresses considered for the role of Ruth Carson, bored wife of a mining engineer based in a fictitious African country, was Maggie Smith.

It is something of a rough irony that Maggie's agent, Peter Dunlop, was not impressed with the play and returned it to Stoppard's agent without passing it on. Maggie certainly never read it until the opportunity arose to take the play to Broadway and she prepared for her third New York appearance on condition that she could perform the role in London first. This she did, in July 1979, taking over from Diana Rigg, who had scored a big personal success when the play opened in the previous November.

As things worked out, *Night and Day* only ran a couple of months in New York at the end of 1979, and Maggie was therefore free, having missed the 1979 festival, to return to Stratford for Robin Phillips' last season; from there she fortuitously made a resounding London comeback as Virginia Woolf in a tailor-made vehicle by Edna O'Brien.

As usual in Maggie's career, everything fell into place

without anything much having been planned. She was as strangely resigned as ever to her obsessional calling, her fate. Nothing much had changed in that respect, as she told Fiona Lewis of the *New York Times* before opening on Broadway: 'Acting is what I do. One is nervous, every single time, to go on a stage at all. But it's the only way I've lived. I've never been in a position to question it. It is my work.'

The background to the action of *Night and Day* is a rebellion against a dictatorial president. The press corps covering the story includes the tough nut Dick Wagner, a boastful and competitive 'fireman' ('I go to fires. I don't file prose. I file facts'), and the idealistic young freelance Jacob Milne, who has scooped Wagner in his own paper and is threatening to scoop him again with a presidential interview.

The journalists' rivalry extends also to Ruth, in whose house the action is set. She has had an affair with Wagner in London, but Milne now strikes her as metal more attractive. Ruth herself has rather languid views on the ethical debate on journalism in the play ('I'm with you on the free press. It's the newspapers I can't stand').

Peter Wood was once again her director, and he cites one day of rehearsal where Maggie gave her greatest performance. At the start of Act Two, Ruth comes from behind a tree after a rather strange, unsettling scene with the younger journalist; Ruth, naked (in the guise of her double), walks across the stage and into the house, and Maggie walks round the tree:

'She had this ability to communicate that what we had just seen was a fantasy, but that was way down her list of priorities. What Maggie offered was a woman appalled by the force of her own sexual fantasy, unsteadied by it, so that when she came round the tree, she shook it away. Then she wondered if it *had* been real, and her hand came up to her face, and slowly she began to take a humorous attitude towards her own fantasising.

'This was simply the most dazzling display. She did it on that morning in rehearsal, then she lost it, got it back, lost it again, and by the time we got to New York she had laid her hands on it very precisely. It triggered an immensely complex audience reaction: a rapt silence, followed by this magnetic power, the slow realisation that they'd been hoodwinked by the dramatist . . . It was miraculous how Maggie handled the house and finally persuaded them into an extraordinary, rueful laughter.'

That, says Wood categorically, and the scene she rehearsed with Olivier in the first act of *The Master Builder*, were the two greatest moments he has ever known in the theatre. Maggie opened with Patrick Mower as Wagner and Edward de Souza as her husband, at the Phoenix.

She made much more of Ruth's inner turmoil, in contrast to the devastatingly cool, self-possessed and glacial version of Diana Rigg. As Michael Billington noted, Maggie's Ruth was a nervy, vulnerable expatriate sending out periodic cries for help which were totally ignored. In this way Maggie got closer, one felt, to the tension Stoppard sought between the character's pronouncements and, a subtle distinction, her speaking thoughts.

Stoppard had evened up some of the arguments about the press and wrote in a topical gag which referred to the protracted strike at Times Newspapers in the struggle between the unions and the management leading up to the installation of new technology and the reduction of manning levels required by the new proprietor, Rupert Murdoch. Ruth was asked if the papers were flown in and she replied, 'I don't think so; we're still getting *The Times*.'

During this summer, Kenneth Tynan, despite suffering horribly from emphysema, was beginning work on a *New Yorker* profile of Maggie, although his friend and researcher, Ernie Eban, had been trying to persuade him to turn his attention instead to Bob Dylan.

Tynan lunched Maggie twice in L'Etoile, his favourite London restaurant, during June. When he went along to see *Night and Day*, he scrawled on his programme a reference to Maggie's long upper lip and 'some of the finest fingers in the business', noting that she distinguished ('where Rigg didn't') between the private thoughts and normal dialogue of a play in which she entangled herself like a vine. Tynan's profile never progressed beyond a few dozen small pages of spidery jottings; he died, aged fifty-three, in July 1980 in hospital in Santa Monica.

When *Night and Day* opened at the Kennedy Center in Washington in October 1979, the response was enthusiastic and the play sold out for six weeks. Joseph Maher, the Irish actor who was playing Maggie's husband, Geoffrey Carson, was convinced that New York was going to be 'colossal'. Tom Stoppard was elated by the performance and gave Maggie an enamel 'head girl' badge. He felt as blessed in her performance as he had been in Diana Rigg's:

'When it comes to humour, comedy on any level, Maggie perhaps has no rival. She can get more out of a phrase, sometimes a single word, than any playwright has a right to expect. She manages to inhabit a character totally while simultaneously standing outside the characterisation and making her own ironic commentary. This is an "impossible" trick, like being in two places at once.'

Dick Wagner was played by a perfectly competent actor, Frank Converse, but, by the time the show reached New York, he had been replaced by Paul Hecht. Maggie refused to comment on whether she had had Converse fired; Converse sued for the rest of his salary on his run-of-the-play contract.

The producer Michael Codron reported to Maggie's dressing room in Washington and she said, talking into the make-up mirror, 'I'll say this for you, Michael, you sure can pick'em!' Codron believes that he has never recovered from the Converse affair as far as Maggie is concerned.

Maggie's name was above the title outside the ANTA, now the Virginia, on 53rd Street. (ANTA was an acronym for the American National Theater Academy, original home of the Guild Theater.) As Ted Kalem said in *Time* magazine, 'playing the ANTA stage is like pitching a tent in the Sahara.' Maggie did not like it, and she did not like her dressing room, either. She had it painted and recarpeted and continued moaning about it in an interview with Rex Reed in the *Daily News*. She complained that she had to wash her hair at home each day as the sink at the ANTA 'didn't work'. Reed recorded the exasperated reaction of the theatre owner:

'That woman has made so many impossible demands that she's becoming damned tiresome. Nothing seems to satisfy her. We recarpeted, relighted, repainted, and reshampooed the theater and it's still not enough. She even wanted the aisles changed. Helen Hayes, Kate Hepburn, Raymond Massey, Julie Harris – all occupied that same dressing room and never complained. Alfred Lunt and Lynn Fontanne even occupied it together, at the same time. No complaints about the sink.'

One of Edward Albee's plays, *The Lady from Dubuque*, had recently opened on Broadway, and the title amused Maggie. Each night, Joseph Maher was touched to find Maggie standing in the wings holding a jacket for his very quick change and ready to assist in a rapid adjustment of his cravat. The job should have been that of a very fat, camp dresser who was working on the show, and over dinner one night Maher commented on her unnecessary kindness. 'Well,' said Maggie airily, 'we couldn't have the lady from Dubuque doing it for you, could we?'

Another well-travelled anecdote attaches to one of the monologues, when Maggie had to say quietly to her confused self, 'Run, run, you stupid bitch.' She inserted the slightest of pauses after the first 'run' and, at one matinée, a deaf lady near the front loudly enquired of her neighbour, 'What did she say?' Maggie quickly continued, a little more forcefully, 'Run, you stupid bitch,' which the deaf lady took in quite the wrong spirit.

Maggie and Beverley were borrowing Ruth Gordon and Garson Kanin's house in Turtle Bay and often supped after the show in Gallagher's Steak House opposite the ANTA, usually with Joseph Maher, who became a close friend and devoted Maggie-watcher.

Like Alec McCowen, Maher has a good ear for the distinctive quirkiness of Maggie's laser-like observations. One of the producers of *Night and Day* was the bustling, business-like Nell Nugent, and Maher remembers Maggie whispering *sotto voce* as she heaved into view one night, 'Oh dear, here comes Nell Nugent, mean as paint.'

There had been a notably intelligent review of the play in the *Washington Post* by John Lardner, but he feared for a piece that discussed issues, and not fathers, mothers and gastro-intestinal tracts. In New York, Walter Kerr excoriated 'an abstract talkathon' (while beginning to wonder if Stoppard was a true dramatist at all). Harold Clurman, who conceded that the play was probably Stoppard's first traditionally handled plot, but that it nonetheless lacked coherence, also hailed Maggie as 'the most skilful actress in all English-speaking comedy'.

Much later, Maggie explained the play's New York failure to Jack Tinker in terms that make very good sense: 'They simply couldn't comprehend why a woman would go out and have an affair just because she hadn't sewn Cash's tapes in her son's clothes when he went back to school. It may be a very *stupid* reason to have an affair. But there isn't a woman in England who wouldn't understand.'

Katharine Hepburn, when she visited backstage in her flat shoes and raincoat, told Maggie and Maher, 'The audience hates this play.' There was no way round it. One night, Maggie took her customary solo call in front of the cast, and two people stood up in the front stalls and offered a weak 'Bravo.' 'Oh dear,' Maggie muttered as she shuffled back into the line, 'deep sarcasm!'

Within a few months of opening, *Night and Day* closed. Maggie had received an Edna O'Brien script about Virginia Woolf, a writer she much admired and one who preyed on her subconscious. She had once told an interviewer that she wished she had a strong, large face like Virginia Woolf's: 'Mine is very, very small. Too small.'

The novelist had written the play with Eileen Atkins in mind, but Kenneth Tynan read it, suggested Maggie and made sure she received a copy of the script. Edna O'Brien did not know Maggie at this point, but she shared the same hairdresser, Patricia Millbourn, and the latter acted as another go-between. Robin Phillips liked the script and agreed that Maggie could do it at Stratford. It was to be a highlight of their last season together.

Things had gone slightly awry in Ontario. During rehearsals for *Private Lives*, Robin had been taken ill and Maggie was not planning to return for the 1979 season. Robin thought he had cancer and resigned his post from England, where he had gone for medical attention. He withdrew the resignation under pressure, and it was agreed that 1979 should be a sabbatical year and 1980 his final season. In the event, the opening 1979 production fell apart and Robin found himself back at the helm immediately, directing three productions.

In 1980, Robin was once again convinced he had cancer – his father died of the disease that year – and he was beset with symptoms of blood loss and acute lassitude. In the event, he recovered, but this period was rife with speculation as to who would succeed him.

In addition to Maggie's reunion with Brian Bedford, there was a *King Lear* starring Peter Ustinov. Five days after *Lear* opened, however, the Stratford board cancelled the proposed transfer to London and incurred a hefty lawsuit from an irate Ustinov (the claim was finally settled at a cost of $45,000 Canadian).

Phillips always hoped eventually to bring his best Stratford work to London, and the possibility of a showcase Canadian company led by Maggie, Brian Bedford and Ustinov was a dream full of possibilities, not least for Robin's career prospects on home territory.

This plan never quite worked out. The key to the chaos, according to some Stratford colleagues, was that Robin refused to take the *Lear* to London because three of his major supporting actors suddenly indicated they would not go. Robin may have become nervous, they say, of a weakened company, of shoring up a *Lear* tailored to Ustinov's severe limitations as a tragedian and of being butchered by the London critics.

Nonetheless, the 1980 season was a memorable last thrash. Maggie scored a sensational triumph as Virginia Woolf in the Avon, while she said farewell on the Festival stage with a second look at Beatrice, perhaps her final exorcism of the partnership with Robert Stephens, and a first, and so far only, Arkadina in Chekhov's *The Seagull* surrounded by her favourite sparring partner, Brian Bedford, as Trigorin; her golden Orlando, Jack Wetherall, as Konstantin; and a trio of Stratford's own biggest stars – William Hutt as Dorn, Roberta Maxwell as Nina and Pat Galloway as Masha.

Her Beatrice was a much more stately affair than the reading à la Zeffirelli at the Old Vic. She still punctuated the laughter on her mother's cry of childbirth but, on the video recording, 'Kill Claudio' elicits a huge laugh, albeit one mixed with shock and disbelief. Lavishly costumed by Robin Fraser Paye in the English Civil War period, Maggie and Bedford strike a handsome cavalier partnership that is most notable, perhaps, for its air of civility and relaxation. The edge and the bite have given way to an almost total luxuriance in the security of a comic partnership. Michael Billington thought they now sparked each other off like Tracy and Hepburn. With Maggie's maturity goes a richer, more gravelly voice and the almost imperceptible shading of tears into laughter, of exquisite pathos, that characterises all her work with Robin Phillips.

She was exactly the right age for Arkadina – forty-three going on thirty-two when her son's not around to contradict her – and she played the comic monster side of the character to the hilt. The silliness and volatility of Arkadina are apparent, but above all the impression you get is of an absolutely rampant stinginess.

Just as she used elements of her mother's Scottish Calvinism for Miss Brodie, one senses Maggie harking back, in a sub-conscious way, to Meg's well-intentioned but ferocious penny-pinching in Ilford and Oxford. Twice she declares, very firmly, to Sorin and to Konstantin, that she has no money. Finally, she's had enough and stuns the audience with one of the loudest and angriest explosions of her career: 'I'm an actress, not a banker!'

This meanness underpins the mercurial vanity of all she says and is marked savagely on her departure, when she sweeps away from the servants with 'Here's a ruble; it's for the three of you to share.'

But she kills incisively, too, on the simplest of remarks which are just slightly inflected to cause maximum damage. 'The garden *reeks* of sulphur; is that intentional?' she teasingly remarks, thus scuppering at a stroke her son's serious artistic aspirations and his faith in her judgement.

And when this Arkadina states that she'd rather be in a melodrama than perform the gibberish her son writes, you feel the full force of a blow delivered by an actress who really does identify with that remark and has always preferred to line up with the tried and tested as opposed to the difficult and risqué.

The backstage politicking was hotting up. While Robin had a repertory season planned for the Haymarket in London, in conjunction with the Birmingham Rep and Duncan Weldon's Triumph Theatre Productions, a 'Gang of Four', supported by Robin, was being manipulated into the Stratford succession.

This quartet comprised three Canadians – the actress Martha Henry, the director Peter Moss and Robin's literary manager, Urjo Kareda – and the British director, Pam Brighton, who had worked with Phillips in his Third Stage company, the 'bunker' operation he had initiated in the previous season.

But the British administrator Peter Stevens, who had been Peter Hall's chief lieutenant in the National Theatre's administration after Olivier, was also being wooed by the board. Stevens wanted the Gang of Four sacked and John Dexter (who talked of doing *Othello* with Christopher Plummer) installed as artistic supremo.

The wrangling led to accusations of duplicity by the board at a highly charged all-day company meeting, where the ebullient Canadian actor Richard Monette stood up and called the chairman a pig. The Gang of Four were fired, Peter Stevens was appointed and almost immediately dismissed, John Dexter had his work permit blocked, and the succession fell finally to the generally admired John Hirsch, of whom Robin had very little good to say.

In the early 1980s, when the theatre was hit by the deep economic recession, the estimated audience, as reflected in the production budgeting, slipped from eighty per cent to sixty-five per cent. By the end of 1984, the Phillips surplus was transformed to a three million Canadian dollar deficit, and there were serious overruns on expenses.

By 1985, still under John Hirsch, the festival's fortunes had begun to stabilise and Hirsch's successor, the English actor and director John Neville, supervised a three-year period during which a healthy financial surplus was achieved and Robin, to a minor degree, restored as a directorial force, on an occasional basis.

The current artistic director, David William, budgets for an audience of sixty per cent. The theatre's reputation now rests on a par with other big North American festivals in Seattle and Minneapolis, but these are days, perhaps, of consolidation rather than inspiration.

Robin was appointed artistic director of the Chichester Festival Theatre in 1988 but resigned almost immediately for reasons that have never been made clear. Today, he is artistic director of the Citadel Theatre in Edmonton, Alberta. He will probably never expel the Camelot era from his system, nor do you feel that he has ever really been able to tear himself away from Stratford. The whole period is as difficult for him to forget as it is sometimes painful to recall.

Undoubtedly, Robin must be credited with salvaging and re-launching Maggie's stage career. And although his plans to re-enter London in triumph, and with Triumph, were in tatters, *Virginia* and Maggie's performance would come to the Haymarket at the start of 1981. This event, more than the takeover in *Night and Day*, marked Maggie's official return to London.

Everyone sensed this. The first night audience at the Haymarket on 29 January 1981 included John Gielgud, Ingrid Bergman, Joan Plowright, John Osborne and Harold Pinter.

The play begins and ends with the words 'Something tremendous is about to happen,' a description of the one experience, death, that Virginia told Vita Sackville-West she would never describe. This paragraph was delivered by Maggie in a voice of quiet apprehension. At the end, her voice soared, exultant and golden. In between, we had an expressionistic distillation of what Virginia Woolf herself called 'moments of being'.

Throughout the 1970s, subsequent to Quentin Bell's Virginia Woolf biography, hardly a Sunday had passed, it seemed, without the publication in one of the newspapers of yet more revelations and secondary material about Virginia and the Bloomsbury set. Maggie's performance achieved the extraordinary feat of entering a plea for privacy on the writer's behalf.

Edna O'Brien's script did not refer to the everyday trials and tribulations of running the Hogarth Press, and contained not a whisper of the pamphleteering literary feminist. The social whirl of London and the Woolfs' country retreat at Rodmell were vague, unpopulated backgrounds against which Maggie registered disgusted shivers at all intrusions, a shuddering distaste for the physical life in general and for copulation in particular, and an impatient desire to be left alone. As Quentin Bell said of the novels, an audience actually heard Virginia Woolf thinking.

Virginia had received only seventeen performances in Stratford, but Michael Billington had caught one of them and declared this the best role written for a woman since Miss Brodie was in her prime. In London it was apparent that a great tragi-comic actress was restored in full bloom, and Jack Tinker's comment that Maggie's Virginia contrived to look 'as though she was indeed born with one skin too few to survive in this world' was surely prophetic of one or two self-lacerating performances to come.

In the *Evening Standard* report of how the judges decided on giving Maggie her third Best Actress prize, Bernard Levin said that her achievement in keeping him awake and interested in a play about Virginia Woolf was not to be underestimated. Years later, Levin had not altered his view of the morbid scribe: 'I hate Virginia Woolf more than anything in the world, bar *Pelléas and Mélisande*.'

The production was minimalist, with photographic images of the haunting branches at Rodmell and the streets of London projected on to an arrangement of scrims. There were no properties, and just two chairs. The whole presentation seemed designed to show how Maggie had stripped down her engine and reassembled the parts after giving them a good clean.

Nicholas Pennell was Leonard Woolf and Patricia Connolly Vita Sackville-West, the latter playing a fine scene culled from the book written in her honour, *Orlando*. O'Brien had distilled the entire play from the novels, the diaries and Quentin Bell's biography. She described the process of possession to Lucy Hughes-Hallett: 'The play came from inside me, but it is all Virginia. I worked like a sleepwalker, like a medium. It is a wedding for the two of us. For her, I hope, it is a resurrection.'

Pennell and Connolly had come to London from Canada with Maggie and Robin. A favourite haunt near the Haymarket was the Val Taro in Orange Street, an Italian restaurant immediately rechristened 'O rat lav' by Maggie reading the name backwards.

One night, there were flashing lights before the curtain rose, traced to a lady in the front circle wearing a dress heavily adorned with sequins. When told about it, Maggie asked, 'Is she hanging from the dome and revolving slowly?' But the sequins were not, it transpired, the real cause of the trouble. A light in the fridge in the downstairs bar had short-circuited all the auditorium lighting.

Nicholas Pennell remembers above all the relish with which Maggie acted: 'She'd say, "A rose is a rose is a rose . . . is it?" and she'd swivel round to me with those large eyes. It was never a question of whether she was going to get a laugh. Sure she was. But she was about to have the most delicious meal with it. It is a sheer joy playing with her. It's how I imagine downhill skiing must be: you know you're not going to stop once you're on the skis, and there's a helter-skelter sense of recurrent switchback. It is truly exhilarating.'

Jollity took a jolt halfway through the twelve-week run when Maggie's brother, Alistair, dropped dead of a heart attack one Sunday in Tigbourne Court. His demise, at the age of 52, was totally unexpected. He had no record of ill health. Ian was the twin who had been rejected for National Service in 1951 on health grounds.

Pennell called Maggie to sympathise, assuming that the Monday night performance would be cancelled. But she was determined to go on, and said she wanted 'to get concentrated'. Pennell and Patricia Connolly joined her in the theatre at about three o'clock and went through some physical stretching exercises for a couple of hours in the front-of-house area.

They returned to the dressing rooms through the darkened auditorium. Pennell recalls that, as they came up the stairs to the stage and went through the proscenium arch that divides reality from fiction, 'Maggie went, she absolutely went. Trish and I sat on the steps by the orchestra pit and held her while she had a big cry. Then she had a big laugh, and she'd always say afterwards, when we went up those stairs, "That's where I had my Waterloo."

'We then had to go out in the first act and I'm reading a letter, the first line of which is "I am so sorry to hear about your brother's death," and I didn't know what would happen. Those glacial blue eyes looked straight back at me as she gave the reply, "We don't talk about that in our family." It was a very weird moment. I think that, like most great artists, Maggie stores up all her experience and dredges through it later.'

Ian Smith, the surviving twin, thinks that Maggie has difficulty in expressing emotion and may sometimes give the impression that she does not care very much. She *did* care very much about Alistair's death, but she never transmitted what she felt to the family. The matter was simply not to be discussed.

Tigbourne Court, which had been bought for £37,000, was sold for £185,000. Shān, Alistair's widow, decided that she would not move with Maggie and Beverley, but that she'd be better off on her own. She found a very comfortable house in Milford, three or four miles from Tigbourne, with stables for her horse; she lives there still.

Alistair was so like Ian, says Shān, that their son, Angus, used to think that he had two fathers. Angus went into the City but decided at the end of the 1980s that show business was in his blood, too: he works as a location manager in a film production company.

Beverley found a well-concealed farmhouse in several acres at Fittleworth, near Pulborough, West Sussex. It was more manageable than Tigbourne, on two floors and not too big. The original farmhouse dated from the late fifteenth century and a farmer had added some rather fine Georgian extensions in the early nineteenth century. The place had fallen into disrepair until the prominent QC, Sir Peter Rawlinson, had acquired it from a dowager aunt and installed proper plumbing and other amenities. Maggie and Beverley moved in during 1981 and have lived there happily ever since.

The boys were enrolled at Seaford College, a minor public school situated on the downs between Petworth and Chichester which neither of them much enjoyed, though both proudly claim to have passed more O-Levels than their mother. Maggie had insisted on them knuckling down to their work. Christopher persisted into the sixth form and successfully took A-Levels in English, history and politics.

Toby was mightily relieved to be out of Tigbourne Court, liberated from its airiness and bigness, and its situation on an increasingly busy main road. 'Also, Surrey is such a boring county, with horrible places like Godalming. Sussex is really nice.'

In the 1980s, Maggie appeared in some very reputable films, but still the 'great film' eluded her. On the stage she brought only one of her Canadian performances to London – Millamant, in a new production by William Gaskill. The decade ended with the tumultuous commercial and critical success of her performance in *Lettice and Lovage*.

She would always remain imperishably funny. But perhaps those heart-stopping moments of doubt, insecurity and anguish as Stoppard's Ruth Carson and as Edna O'Brien's Virginia Woolf could be seen as indicators of some extraordinary non-classical tragic work to come, on both large screen and small.

Entr'acte:
The Honouring of Dame Maggie

I N May 1991, Maggie went to Hamburg to receive the Shakespeare Prize, one of Europe's most prestigious arts awards, worth DM30,000, about £10,000. An air of acute pain and resignation always surrounds the actress on these occasions. She finds them vaguely flattering but mostly embarrassing and, of course, slightly absurd. Beverley persuades her that participation is expected and probably good for her reputation, and she quietly goes along with his advice, though only partly convinced.

I travelled to Hamburg with Maggie and Beverley in order to observe at close quarters some reactions to public acclaim. The airport departure lounge was packed, but neither there nor at the boarding gate was Maggie the subject of stares or the slightest speculation. This confirmed my view that actors are only ever recognised in public if they make a song and dance about their celebrity, or indeed its price.

Olivier would come off the Old Vic stage as the raging, titanic Othello and walk down the Waterloo Road, squat, suited and bespectacled, as unrecognised and blandly unfamiliar as any bank under-manager. Maggie says, 'I'm never recognised in the street. I'm a sort of nothing, I think. I don't make any impression at all, really.'

Soon after the opening of *Lettice and Lovage* in London

she and Beverley went for dinner at the Café Royal with Peter
Dunlop and his wife, Verrall. There were crowds of people
on the pavement and an ostentatious limousine at kerbside.
Joan Collins was within. Maggie said to Dunlop that she
simply had to stand at the bottom of the stairs in the reception
hall and wait to catch a glimpse of the soap diva. She was
overruled, and Maggie's party sped through the throng, totally
unheeded, to find a taxi in Piccadilly.

On arriving in Hamburg we had gone to our separate hotels.
We met up at a reception given in the British Consulate in
the leafy residential area alongside the Alster lake. Maggie was
attired in her customary elegant black cocktail dress ('Thank
heavens for Jean Muir' is a recurring phrase), a picture of
discreet charm and taut graciousness. Rather more bubble and
high spirits were being provided by the young trainee theatre
designer whom Maggie had nominated as her attached student
beneficiary of the Shakespeare prize, Laura Peckham of the
Slade School of Art. The four of us – Maggie, Beverley, Laura
and I – finally escaped for dinner.

Maggie disconsolately pushed a piece of fish around her
plate and sipped modestly from a glass of mineral water. She
was tense almost to snapping point: 'You get involved in these
things and wonder why on earth you did.' At the adjoining
table, a couple were eating their way doggedly through one
course after another as if their lives depended on it. Maggie
shot them an acid glance and wondered, *sotto voce*, if they,
too, had won a prize for something.

The Shakespeare Prize, earmarked only for the British, is
stranger than most. It was initiated by a wealthy Hamburg corn
merchant, Alfred Toepfer, in 1937, as a practical expression
of his Anglophilia in a darkening political climate. The first
recipient was the composer Ralph Vaughan Williams, the
second the poet John Masefield.

Then came the war. The prize was only re-inaugurated in

1967 to coincide with the Queen's first official post-war visit to Germany. The recipient was Peter Hall, and the roll call of winners now constitutes an impressive array of internationally significant indigenous talent: the poet Philip Larkin, the singers Janet Baker and Gwyneth Jones, the novelists Iris Murdoch, Doris Lessing and Graham Greene, the painters Graham Sutherland and David Hockney, the playwrights Harold Pinter, Tom Stoppard and Peter Shaffer, the directors Peter Brook, John Dexter and John Schlesinger, the actors Paul Scofield and Alec Guinness. Maggie is the first actress to be honoured.

For a bright girl who performed indifferently at school, the gathering of academic honours must be a peculiar sensation. She opened her address in Hamburg with an almost stuttering disclaimer: 'It might be a relief to us all today if I were to be as brief as the evil Don John in *Much Ado About Nothing* . . . "I thank you. I am not of many words, but I thank you!"'

We were sitting in the great Gothic town hall, the Hamburg Rathaus ('Where the rats come from,' Maggie had whispered), bright May sunshine streaming through the windows. Suddenly, with that opening shot, it appeared to be all over. But Maggie, simply dressed yet again in black with a single rope of pearls, pushed her reading glasses further up her nose and glided smoothly into a résumé of her life among the Shakespearean comic heroines and 'any number of queens'.

After the ebullient academic encomium intoned by a local professor, Maggie's *aperçus* had the merit of both practicality and concision. Beatrice, she said, was 'a very pleasant evening' because the lady doesn't have all that much to say and most of it is in prose: 'The secret is that everybody else is always talking about *her*.' Rosalind, on the other hand, had a very great deal to say, and to do. 'Where a sentence will do for Beatrice, Rosalind prefers paragraphs. If Beatrice has

something of Noël Coward's Amanda, then Rosalind shares
Mr Stoppard's or Mr Shaffer's enthusiasm for verbosity.'

This identification of the witty, independent heroine in
English drama from Shakespeare, through the Restoration to
modern theatre, was as much a point worth making as a revelation of her character. As teasingly playful as Beatrice, as wilful,
androgynous and enigmatic as Viola – 'I am all the daughters
of my father's house; and all the brothers, too' – Maggie's
comic, romantic stage persona embraces the trenchant, dignified wit of Millamant and the melting, resourceful passion of
Rosalind.

She bade an official farewell to all these roles in Hamburg,
but not before pinning us to our seats with Millamant's great
proviso speech ('These articles subscribed, if I continue to
endure you a little longer, I may by degrees dwindle into a
wife') and moving us to tears with Rosalind's adieu:

'If I were a woman, I would kiss as many of you as had
beards that pleased me, complexions that liked me and breaths
that I defied not. And I am sure as many as have good beards,
or good faces, or sweet breaths, will for my kind offer, when
I make curtsy, bid me farewell.'

One feels that more probably came out of this ceremony
than on the first occasion Maggie was capped and gowned.
She received the honorary degree of Doctor of Letters at
St Andrews University in July 1971, and the citation by the
Dean of the Faculty of Arts blandly, and not altogether accurately, declared that 'Miss Smith comes from one of the most
talented, aspiring and successful communities in England –
the Oxford Scottish . . . What should be emphasised is the
intelligence and originality of her interpretations, which have
without question thrown new light on great plays.'

A second honorary doctorate was offered at Leicester University in 1972, but Maggie was unable to attend the ceremony
and so forfeited the honour. In November 1991, she was due

to receive a third D.Litt. from London University, but her working schedule again prevented her from attending the ceremony and receiving the honour.

Her four *Evening Standard* Best Actress Awards are for the Shaffer double bill, *Hedda Gabler*, *Virginia* and Millamant, a record that was only equalled by Vanessa Redgrave with her fourth Best Actress award for her performance as Isadora Duncan in Martin Sherman's *When She Danced* in 1991. Maggie's trophies are discreetly distributed around the main sitting room at Fittleworth: the two Oscars, two of the *Standard* statuettes as bookends, the Variety Club heart and the Banff (a Canadian festival town) metal sculpture with celluloid Rockies, which she received for her performance in Alan Bennett's *Bed Among the Lentils* on television.

With such acknowledgement goes a certain cachet that lands people on invitation lists at Buckingham Palace and Downing Street. On St Valentine's Day in February 1984, Maggie attended a luncheon at the palace and sat on the Duke of Edinburgh's left, and opposite Professor Bernard Williams, the Provost of King's College, Cambridge.

In July 1985 in Downing Street, Maggie sat opposite her old Oxford contemporary Michael Heseltine at a dinner given by the Prime Minister, Mrs Thatcher, in honour of Vice-President Bush of the United States. Other guests included Sir Terence Conran, Sir David Lean, Richard Branson and Tom Stoppard.

Four months later she and Beverley were back at Downing Street, again with Tom Stoppard, to honour the general secretary of the Hungarian Socialist Workers' Party. The guests this time included Robert Maxwell, the now drowned and disgraced newspaper magnate and entrepreneur, who astonished Maggie by the size of his appetite.

One cannot imagine Maggie actually enjoying any of these beanfeasts. She takes more pleasure in the peripheral aspects of such jaunts, the mishaps and sillinesses. When she was nominated for the Oscar as Best Supporting Actress in *California Suite*, she stayed in the Beverly Hills Hotel, where the film itself was set, with her friend and hairdresser Patricia Millbourn.

In the film, the Jane Fonda character describes Hollywood as 'like Paradise with a lobotomy'. Diana Barrie (Maggie) doesn't understand why she's attending the Oscars ceremony: 'Glenda Jackson never comes, and she's nominated every goddamn year!'

The spooky reality of her and Patricia's experience was echoed in its celluloid representation. On screen, Diana Barrie says, 'No woman can look good at five in the afternoon – except possibly Tatum O'Neal!' Maggie and Patricia did indeed have to be ready and all dressed up in the middle of the afternoon. And, as in the film, champagne and caviar had been sent up to the room. Or rather, round to their allotted cottage in the hotel grounds well away from the central brouhaha. They stood under a lamp-post waiting for their lift; in the film, Maggie sweeps imperiously through the front entrance through a riot of fans and photographers ('Christ, the royal treatment!').

Patricia Millbourn recalls that Maggie had prepared nothing to say in the event of winning the Oscar and that, when she won, she duly said it. Jane Fonda, ironically nominated as Best Actress on another movie, *Coming Home*, *did* have something to say when she picked up her prize. She made a speech about the millions of handicapped people whose plight she had considered in a movie dealing with a paraplegic veteran of the Vietnam War. All Maggie really had to say was, 'I didn't think I had a hope in hell.' She was only the third actress ever to win in both the Best Actress and the Best Supporting Actress categories, following the fine examples of Ingrid Bergman and Helen Hayes.

California Suite is in part about not winning an Oscar, but the ceremony is not depicted. Instead, Maggie's actress acidly remarks on the general decline in the standard of face-lifts and hair-transplants, and the fact that a prize has duly gone to 'Miss Teeth and No Talent'. The words could have been taken out of her own mouth.

After the real-life ceremony, a big, informal party was thrown as usual by the agent Swifty Lazar and Irene Selznik, but Maggie found herself herded towards the official reception for the winners. She was terrified of not knowing anyone there, so she slipped away to find friends, including Patricia, at the alternative bash. 'I hope you don't mind me coming to this one instead,' she said to Miss Selznik. 'Oh no,' replied the hostess, 'it's perfectly all right, because you won!'

At the Tony Awards for *Lettice*, her co-star Margaret Tyzack was certain that Maggie would win the Best Actress. Tyzack herself was a surprise winner in the Best Supporting slot, and remembers verbatim the acceptance speech she made: 'Peter Shaffer's written a wonderful play and I wish I had his eloquence in order to thank him and our marvellous director, Michael Blakemore, our producers, and, above all, Dame Maggie, whose inspired idea it was that I should play this part. I thank them, I thank you, the Tony voters.'

Maggie has not a clue as to what she said when she was announced. She had not been in the best of health. She stood up and bumped her leg against the chair, executing an extravagant, laugh-winning double take on the offending obstruction, just as she had when rushing into an Oxford classroom thirty-five years previously.

A letter from Downing Street dated 10 November 1989 had informed her that the Prime Minister was submitting her name as a Dame Commander of the British Empire, DBE. She accepted the honour as diffidently as she accepted the plaudits in Hamburg eighteen months later.

Maggie's flamboyant withdrawal from the celebrity circuit
is the most constantly refreshing aspect of her fame. Her background taught her good manners and an abhorrence of vulgarity in public and private affairs. Her correctly sceptical view
of the world and its humorously self-serving endeavours keeps
her immune to the blandishments and invitations of the television chat shows and well away from all clubs and restaurants
patronised by the fashionable media folk, the literati and their
attendant sycophants and hangers-on.

There were few of such creatures in evidence in Hamburg.
Maggie would not have known anyone there from Adam. But
she had treated the event as if it were a First Night at the Old
Vic. She had gone to bed early to study the script Beverley
had provided. She left the rostrum in a flat spin of anxiety
and embarrassment, shrugging off all proffered greeting and
congratulation with a blank indifference and an acceleration
towards the exit door. She had melted as Rosalind but frozen
over as Maggie.

At lunch in the cellars of the Rathaus, she was the toast of
the assembly, but she assumed nothing in her occupation of
the central table. She was neither pleased, nor displeased,
with what was said and what was eaten. Herr Toepfer, aged
ninety-seven, the host and originator of the prize, rose creakily
on his pins to discharge a few well-chosen platitudes and
elicited a somewhat dirty gurgle of laughter from the object of
his attentions when he referred to Beverley as 'Mister Smith'.

A great artist had been honoured. But as far as she was
concerned, the sooner we all got home, and on with the next
job of work, the better. It is a great paradox, and one particularly appropriate to Maggie, that, in a profession whose
members thrive on applause and recognition from the darkened auditorium, the impersonal void, the formalised and spe-
cific channels of that appreciation can seem so threatening
and insincere.

As an actress, she demands attention, but also protection against the social symptoms of that attention. Her liberty, of which we in Hamburg had demanded an unfair share, must remain as precious an agreement between herself and her audience as it must remain between Millamant and her betrothed Mirabell:

'Liberty to pay and receive visits from whom I please; to write and receive letters, without interrogatories or wry faces on your part; to wear what I please; and choose conversation with regard only to my own taste; to have no obligation upon me to converse with wits that I don't like, because they are your acquaintance; or to be intimate with fools, because they may be your relations. Come to dinner when I please, dine in my dressing room when I'm out of humour, without giving a reason. To have my closet inviolate, to be sole empress of my tea-table, which you must never presume to approach without first asking leave. And lastly, wherever I am, you shall always knock at the door before you come in.'

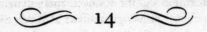

14

Best of British

ONE of the distinctive features of Maggie's film career in the 1980s was that she appeared in movies that had more appeal for her than for the accountants in her agent's office. In her time at Fraser and Dunlop, Jimmy Fraser handled the film contracts and Peter Dunlop the theatre business. However, their influence on what she actually *did* was minimal.

Dunlop retired in 1980, shortly after the mix-up over *Night and Day*; in July 1981 Maggie announced in *Variety* that her sole worldwide representation was now handled by James Sharkey at Fraser and Dunlop. Or rather, Sharkey made the announcement, which featured a photograph of Maggie in *The Guardsman* at her most impishly soignée: hair up, eyes soft and sparkling, full lower lip, a jewelled halter.

Sharkey is possibly the most widely respected and brilliant of all actors' agents. But Maggie didn't take much notice of him, either. By 1984 she had joined Laurence 'Lol' Evans, chairman of International Creative Management and Olivier's general manager at the Old Vic in the 1940s. Evans is the most senior and distinguished of all the ten-per-centers. His all-star cast included Olivier, Rex Harrison, John Mills, Albert Finney and Peter Hall.

Maggie was even more of a mystery to Evans and, in the serene, secure twilight of his career, he happily went along with anything she wanted to do. By the end of 1991, Evans, too, had become a back number as he was eased into a consultative retirement and the younger, more dynamic Duncan Heath took charge of Maggie's affairs at ICM. She summed up by commenting, 'Nothing ever seemed quite right after Peter Dunlop.'

Maggie was increasingly attracted to smaller budget, reputable ventures in preference to the international blockbuster projects that left her little chance to get her teeth into a good part. On both stage and screen she can be squeamish about bad language, and in this respect is unprepared to betray either the propriety of her lower-middle-class upbringing or the genuine instinct she has for not alienating a broad popular audience.

Like all the great stars of old, she believes in exercising good taste wherever possible in matters of apparel, manners, public statements and morality. She can, of course, swear like a trooper when she's in the mood and behind closed doors.

When William Gaskill sent her a copy of Howard Barker's rewrite of *Women Beware Women*, she was aghast at the barrage of filthy language and explicit sexual discussion, and turned him down flat. She had also turned down his invitation to appear as a cannibalistic Queen Victoria in Edward Bond's *Early Morning*.

Similarly, when she was invited to impersonate Peggy Ramsay, the straight-talking agent of the dramatist Joe Orton in the film *Prick Up Your Ears*, her reaction to Alan Bennett's screenplay, which dealt in homosexual promiscuity and murder, was to retreat behind the excuse of not wanting to embarrass or upset her sons by appearing in such a film (the role was memorably taken by Vanessa Redgrave, though the agent's bird-like frailty and coruscating waspishness were really Maggie's forte).

But it would be wrong to claim that she was completely

unadventurous in her choices of material. After her final seven-month season in Stratford, Ontario, she had a week's holiday and then, typically, went straight to Paris with Beverley to join the Merchant/Ivory shoot of Jean Rhys's first novel, *Quartet*. Jean Rhys, a favourite novelist, was, like Virginia Woolf, someone whose every written word she had long since devoured.

Like her responses to most things, Maggie's response to literature is instinctive and intuitive. In drama, the challenge of Shakespeare and Congreve is inexhaustible because the writing demands the utmost technical concentration. It also offers the attractive challenge of playing women who assert their individuality in the face of social and marital constrictions. For similar reasons, Maggie has always found inspiration in the high stylists of the feminine consciousness: Woolf, Rhys, Jane Austen, Charlotte Brontë, E. F. Benson and many of the writers published or reissued these days by the distinctive and aptly named Virago Press.

There is a definite link in the 1980s between the spiritual nutrition Maggie found in her reading and the projects she undertook. The producer of *Quartet*, Ismail Merchant, the director James Ivory, and their regular screenwriter Ruth Prawer Jhabvala, were embarked on a series of literary adaptations on low budgets that found large audiences attracted to their visions of faithful and respectable nostalgia. Ivory is not a galvanic or deeply imaginative sort of director, but he does deliver pretty packages. As Pauline Kael has said, 'he's essentially a director who assembles the actors, arranges the bric-à-brac and calls for the camera.'

The autobiographical heroine, a doomed Creole waif played by Isabelle Adjani, is corrupted by the married partnership of the writer Hugh Heidler and the paintress Lois after her husband has been convicted of trafficking in stolen works of art. The Heidlers, played by Alan Bates and Maggie, had been modelled by Jean Rhys on her Parisian Svengali, Ford Madox Ford, and his wife Stella Bowen.

The setting was mostly Montparnasse in 1927, and the full period flavour was dutifully milked. There were stunning scenes set in their proper locations of Boeuf sur le Toit, a steely art-deco restaurant, and the virtually unchanged ballroom of the Hotel Pavillon, where Maggie glittered menacingly in a silver sheath dress, green eye make-up, and a silver skullcap.

Maggie had never worked with Alan Bates before, and the pairing, not since repeated, is a major factor in the film's attractive surface. There is something compulsively sinister in Bates's devious hedonism for which Maggie dutifully pimps, confiding to Adjani through clouds of cigarette smoke that her husband is not always 'nice' to her, and that she is accustomed to his extra-marital adventures.

Like all the Merchant/Ivory adaptations, however, the movie fed off the original by softening the novel and failing to match its essence with a transforming artistic identity of its own. It is also fatally careless with the story line, so that it is almost impossible to know exactly what happens at the end. There is no such confusion or ambiguity in Rhys's narrative. As a film, it leeched on literature and certainly imported, as Hilary Spurling suggested in the *New York Times*, 'an alien ambivalence, something altogether different from Jean Rhys's black and bitter clarity'.

The acting all-round was very good, with some delightful vignettes from British actors Sheila Gish, Anthony Higgins and Bernice Stegers, but Maggie walked off with the Best Actress prize in the *Evening Standard* Film Awards (for which the judges were Dilys Powell, Lady Marcia Falkender, Alexander Walker and Alan Brien) in an exceptional year for British movies. Other winners were *The French Lieutenant's Woman* (Best Film), Bob Hoskins making his decisive breakthrough in

The Long Good Friday, and Colin Welland's screenplay for *Chariots of Fire*.

After the bohemian quartet came a thoroughly mawkish 'ménage à trois' (at one point the film's working title), *Better Late Than Never*, written and directed by Bryan Forbes and a strong contender for Maggie's worst film.

The main point of interest is that it was also David Niven's last picture (he died in 1983), and the third he made with Maggie. Maggie liked Niven as much as anyone she ever worked with. He had, as is well known, an indomitable sense of fun and a great penchant for practical jokes. But in this film he is a drawn and haggard figure, a shadow of his former self. Beverley finds the film hard to sit through for this reason:

'During the shooting he was his usual charming and amusing self but, between takes, he would sit with me and confess how hideously tired he felt, and how he was finding great difficulty in even articulating the lines. But he seemed so relaxed and well when entertaining at his home on Cap Ferrat.'

Niven played Nick Carter, a seedy nightclub singer, 'England's soufflé of song', who is summoned to Monte Carlo by a lawyer (Lionel Jeffries) to compete for the guardianship of a ten-year-old girl, Bridget, who might or might not be his grand-daughter. The other contender is a huffing New York photographer, Charlie Dunbar, played by Art Carney.

Nick and Charlie used to share a girlfriend in Paris at the end of the Second World War, and that woman's daughter (Bridget's mother) has been drowned at sea. Maggie is the stern child-minder, Anderson, '*not* Mary Poppins', whom Nick and Bridget tease with such rollicking wheezes as blue soap, rubber eggs and whoopee cushions.

The issue of grand-paternity is resolved when Bridget is knocked down by a car and Art Carney's rare blood group is revealed as the one that matches Bridget's. After a tense wait in the hospital, Bridget is going to be okay. Maggie has her 'moment' of emotional release as she tells Nick and Charlie to go home before she bursts into tears and spoils her stern reputation – which she promptly does.

With Bridget claimed by Charlie, Nick returns to the cabaret circuit. But as he sings, sadly and badly, Coward's 'I Went To A Marvellous Party', Bridget and Charlie and Anderson leap out of the audience to plead with him to go home with them all . . .

The mechanics of the comedy are pretty hopeless and an overall air of shoddiness is not dispelled by some attractive locations in the South of France nor by the Niven character's bottom-chasing antics on the beach. He picks up an over-made-up pneumatic good-time girl called Sable who turns out, most unfortunately, to be an apprentice embalmer. Mixed in with the awful soundtrack by Henry Mancini and a charmless child actor, the film leaves a sour taste in the mouth.

After this aberration, Maggie's only two 'international' blockbusters of the 1980s – the mythical epic *Clash of the Titans* and a second Agatha Christie luxury-cast mystery insouciantly unravelled by Peter Ustinov's tunbelly Poirot, *Evil Under the Sun* – come as a considerable relief. Both have their merits.

The first was scripted by Beverley, who had not worked with or for Maggie since she appeared in *Strip the Willow* in 1960 (a projected Stratford collaboration on a Cross script about the Brontës, *Haworth*, had been scrapped at the time of Robin Phillips' first illness in 1978; the play was premièred, starring Polly James, at the Birmingham Rep in 1981). The second reunited Maggie with several of the *Death on the Nile* team: screenwriter Anthony Shaffer, Ustinov, Jane Birkin and her favourite costume designer, Anthony Powell.

In *Clash of the Titans* Maggie plays the goddess Thetis, mother of Perseus, and tetchy inamorata of Zeus. As the latter is played by Laurence Olivier, presiding over an idealised, antiseptic Olympus where the other white-gowned goddesses include Claire Bloom, Ursula Andress and Susan Fleetwood, the ancient Old Vic rivalry is lightly resumed.

Olivier had resolved never to act on a stage with Maggie again after *The Master Builder*, and Maggie's Thetis, albeit only in a reported incident, once again 'bests' the old boy: she recounts with relish how Zeus once disguised himself as a cuttlefish in an attempt to seduce her, but that she beat him at his own game by turning herself into a shark.

Beverley had taken spirited liberties with Greek mythology in racily retelling the Perseus legend. Perseus is obliged to return to Joppa and rescue Andromeda from a deformed suitor, Calibos; he must answer a riddle, capture and tame the last of the flying horses, Pegasus, and enter the temple of Medusa; there, after being attacked by snakes and a two-headed wolf, he cuts off Medusa's head and, with her eyes, petrifies the monster Kraken, whom Zeus has unchained from the ocean bed to ravish Andromeda and destroy Joppa. ('Great Zeus,' says Maggie, 'it is now the eve of the longest day'; 'Very well,' replies Olivier, 'release the Kraken!')

The last sequence owes something to the assault on Fay Wray and New York City by King Kong, and indeed this homage is intentionally perpetrated by the film's co-producer and special effects wizard, Ray Harryhausen, who was a protégé of King Kong's creator, Willis O'Brien. Harryhausen, in addition to creating the pterodactyl which carried off Raquel Welch in *One Million Years BC*, had provided the special effects for another Beverley Cross-scripted film, *Jason and the Argonauts*.

The influence of *Star Wars* could be seen, too, in Harryhausen's golden owl, a speaking mechanical android whose appeal to audiences was similar to that of R2D2 in the 1977 George Lucas fantasy. But the film really belongs to the general tradition of Hollywood escapist adventures, and Beverley had cast his net wide.

The hairy, sexually frustrated Calibos was obviously related to Shakespeare's Caliban, and the sea-monster Kraken had arrived from Norse mythology via Tennyson. There were also magical swords, enchanted shields, invisibility helmets, the belief in the overwhelming power of a kiss and even three blind witches, the grotesque Graeae, who share one single crystal eye; they were unrecognisably impersonated by Flora Robson, Freda Jackson and the Irish actress Anna Manahan. The good-looking Perseus was played by the muscular and engaging Harry Hamlin, and his pretty Andromeda was Judi Bowker.

Maggie meets her nemesis when the marriage of Perseus and Andromeda is anointed by Siân Phillips (playing Andromeda's mother, Cassiopeia): her statue crashes hilariously to the ground and breaks up while her gigantic face continues to mouth demands for the life of her daughter-in-law. At least Maggie could not complain in this scene that her head was too small.

The effects of the flying horse, the speaking owl and the disintegrating Kraken (Kraken's crackin' up) are indeed enjoyable, even if in long shot the bestiary now resembles those plastic animals one used to find in cereal packets.

Roger Ebert of the *Chicago Sun-Times* rated *Clash of the Titans* Harryhausen's masterwork, and MGM pushed the boat out. The promotional campaign was the company's most sustained since *Gone With the Wind* and the critics were in no mood to be captious. Dilys Powell found it 'charmingly unpretentious', Alan Brien acclaimed 'a magical holiday outing, at once splendid and incredible', while Thomas Quinn Curtis of the *International Herald Tribune* judged Beverley's script 'no tabloid cartoon strip' but an attractively smooth translation of classic literature to the screen.

Not much more of a performance was demanded of Maggie in *Evil Under the Sun*, and, as a result, she resorts to a lot of wrist-flapping as the cheerfully coarse-grained Daphne Castle, a royal ex-mistress and hotel proprietress, who is in love with the murdered woman's husband (Denis Quilley). Christie's 1941 novel had been moved by Shaffer back to the 1930s – thus justifying lavish holiday costumes and the songs of Cole Porter – and transported from Cornwall to a remote Tyrrhenian island. The principal location setting was Majorca, with its travel-brochure beaches, craggy cliffs, turquoise lagoons and sub-tropical gardens.

Quilley's doomed wife, the actress Arlena Marshall, played by Diana Rigg, represents a rivalry with Daphne going back to their days together as chorus girls: 'She could always throw her legs up in the air higher than any of us – and wider!' The twosome momentarily bury the hatchet in a squirm-inducing, badly sung rendition of Porter's 'You're the Tops'.

As Diana Rigg has already refused to appear in a show called 'It's Not Right and It's Not Fair' because, she says, it sounds like a black man's left leg, she receives no less than her just deserts when she is strangled on the beach. The incident is presaged by one scene *Variety* thought worthy of Luis Buñuel: Maggie is shocked on a walk through the lush landscape by the sight of a dead rabbit with worms crawling through its innards.

Maggie, understandably, is anxious to pin the murder on anyone but herself, and her performance improves slightly as she is quickened into anxiety by circumstances. But Diana Rigg is not the only stiff on board. The cast includes cardboard cut-outs by Sylvia Miles as an importunate producer (incongruously paired with James Mason) and Roddy McDowall as a campy showbiz columnist called Rex Brewster, reinforcing the idea that he is a pitifully dull facsimile of the real thing, Rex Reed, with a succession of lame and spiteful aphorisms.

Ustinov cumbersomely unravels the mystery in a narrative punctuated by flashbacks.

The movie was deemed inoffensive enough to be chosen as the Royal Film for 1982, the third time Maggie had been implicated in that command event (her other 'royal' films to date were *Jean Brodie* and *California Suite*, both considerably superior and more 'adult').

In concentrating on a now highly paid film career in between the seasons at Stratford, Maggie had not had time to take up any offers on television. She had not made any television appearances in Britain since going to Canada, but she now returned to the medium with a performance in a William Trevor story, dramatised by Bob Larbey, that is a crucial statement of poignant, funny isolation on the journey from Virginia Woolf to the fraught heroines of Brian Moore and Alan Bennett in *The Loneliness of Judith Hearne* and *Bed Among the Lentils*. She began to specialise in ladies on the brink, alone in their rooms and on the verge of some cataclysmic, menopausal break-down.

Essential to this is the cast of the actress's mind, which had always suggested that relations with the opposite sex were seriously overrated. Funny ladies – Beatrice Lillie, Ruth Gordon, Carol Burnett, Lucille Ball, Lily Tomlin – were traditionally slightly beyond the pale, freakish, sexually intimidating, even neutral. Maggie, with blazing individuality, combined their cavalier raucousness and low view of masculine rapacity with an aching physical plausibility, an obvious capacity for being attractive.

This unique admixture of spiritual hauteur and physical need set off some fascinating alarm bells in the gallery of characters she now began to create. In William Trevor's *Mrs Silly*, directed by James Cellan Jones for Granada TV as part of an 'All For Love' series, Florence Barlow is a divorced vicar's wife whose son, Michael, is wrenched from her by the expectations of a snobbish preparatory school which she visits like some pathetic intruder, clumsily mistaking the head-master's wife for the matron (the head was played by her old *Private Lives* spouse, James Villiers).

The production was filmed at the school on which Trevor modelled his story, Bilton Grange School near Rugby, and a hundred of the boys were pressed into service. Trevor had taught there, under his real name of T. W. Cox, in the early 1950s.

Beyond the school's cruelties and cross-currents, Michael's father has remarried an ambitious lady executive. The couple stay in the Grand Hotel near the school after the confirmation ceremony, and drop Florence off at the 'Sans Souci' boarding house. Florence has rabbited on too nervously at tea in the great hall and sent cups flying in all directions before falling over in her desperately vulgar feathery red hat. In the dormitory at night, Michael tearfully disowns his own mother as 'some kind of aunt'. Florence sits alone in her boarding-house bed-room, the red hat discarded on the single bed.

Maggie's remarkable performance as Florence both pre-figures and complements the more widely acclaimed interpret-ation of Susan, the vicar's wife, in *Bed Among the Lentils*. The overpowering sense of social ostracism is in both cases compounded by one of resilience and dignity in defeat, though Bennett provides an additional strain of sarcastic commentary.

The Trevor heroine is less complicated, but conceived on the tragic scale by dint of piercing observation and emotional truth. Physically, Maggie's Florence has the stark angularity of a Modigliani portrait and the chattering, incipiently out-of-control disposition of any inner-city bag-lady. The looming gulf between herself and her son is a dark pit into which she is starting to fall.

Richard Ingrams, the former editor of *Private Eye*, was at

that time writing a television review column in the *Spectator* famous for its general lack of enthusiasm. He broke the mould for Maggie:

'I can't remember any play which so well conveyed the awful consequences of the break-up of a marriage and the misery of a child caught between two homes . . . The star was of course Maggie Smith, who must now be the best actress we have. Her portrayal of a woman totally lost and on the verge of lunacy was exceptionally moving and in the great tradition of British acting.'

Another small-screen project, a co-production between the BBC and Hungarian television, was not nearly so memorable. *Lily in Love* was an unhappy rewrite by Frank Cucci of *The Guardsman*, directed by Karoly Makk and starring Maggie and Christopher Plummer as the married protagonists.

Plummer played an actor, Fitzroy Wynn, a Broadway has-been with unfulfilled ambitions to be a cinema heart-throb, while Maggie was Lily Wynn, an authoress whose next comedy screenplay, with a good-looking, sexy male leading role, was deemed unsuitable for her spouse. The Molnar conceit is reworked as a ruse by Fitz disguised not as a Russian guardsman, but as 'Roberto Terranova', an absurd blond Italian actor from Parma (a town famous for its hams) who seduces Lily on location in Budapest.

It is quite a controlled and attractive performance by Maggie, and she looks very beautiful and elegant. She seems, for purposes of minimal plausibility, to suggest that she knows Roberto is Fitz all along. But everything that is funny and ambiguous in the Molnar play is trampled in a crassly inappropriate script which sounds as though it is being made up on the spot.

In the Stratford, Ontario, production of the stage play, Maggie had tried out her French when offering Brian Bedford's guardsman some tea: 'Combien de . . . lumps?' (The joke is briefly extended in the exchange 'You are sighingk'; 'It meant nothingk.') Aiming for the same effect in a romantic garden scene, Maggie invites Plummer's prancing popinjay to 'Come and join me on . . . il bencho.'

The film, shown as part of a 'First Run' series on BBC2, also features Elke Sommer, and was originally called 'Playing for Keeps'. Maggie confessed to an interviewer that work on the set was complicated because she had trouble understanding what the director was saying. She referred to the film as 'the ghoulash' (and to her co-star as 'Christopher Bummer'): 'It was all slightly horrendous. You didn't know where you were half the time. Usually in the wrong place.'

The British film industry of the 1980s was for a time relaunched on a wave of investment and optimism unprecedented since the 1950s. Like all such hallucinations, it proved as temporary as it was briefly dazzling. The rise and fall of Goldcrest, the emergence of David Puttnam as an independent producer of real flair and the increasing investment raised by co-production with television companies were all significant elements in the boom.

When the tide finally recedes on this era in British moviemaking, Maggie will be seen to have been involved in at least two films of especial interest. They were both produced by HandMade Films, the company financed and run by ex-Beatle George Harrison and producer Denis O'Brien, which had been responsible for such exuberant British movies as the Pythons' mock-Biblical *Life of Brian*, Peter Nichols's *Privates on Parade* and Barrie Keeffe's *The Long Good Friday*.

The first, *The Missionary*, starring and written by Michael Palin, is not a total success, but is certainly, as David Robinson said in *The Times*, 'a superior comedy as British comedies go'; the second, *A Private Function*, also starring Michael Palin but written by Alan Bennett, is not only one of the funniest, and most nearly perfect, British films of the century, but also,

Right A shot in the dark. Maggie in her favourite production, Ingmar Bergman's *Hedda Gabler*, 1970 (*Zoë Dominic*)

Below Domestic friction: Robert and Maggie in the quarrel scene of Coward's *Private Lives*, 1972 (*Zoë Dominic*)

Relaxing on set with Alec
Guinness during the
filming of *Murder by Death*
(*Mel Traxel*)

Radiant, alluring and
serene in Molnar's
The Guardsman, 1976
(*Zoë Dominic*)

Her first Millamant. With Jeremy Brett in *The Way of the World*, Stratford 1976 (*Zoë Dominic*)

A lingering farewell to *Private Lives*, with her preferred leading
man at Stratford, Brian Bedford (*Zoë Dominic*)

Anxiously awaiting the Oscar ceremony with Michael Caine in
the film of Neil Simon's *California Suite* (*Columbia Pictures*)

Preparing for the next scene in *A Room with a View*. On location in Tuscany with James Ivory and Ismail Merchant

Maggie as the exotic Jocasta in Cocteau's *The Infernal Machine* at the Lyric, Hammersmith, 1986 (*Robert Workman*)

The two Tony winners: Maggie and Margaret Tyzack in Peter Shaffer's transatlantic hit *Lettice and Lovage* (*Zoë Dominic*)

A crisis of faith in *The Lonely Passion of Judith Hearne*
(© 1987 HandMade Films (E.J.) Partnership)

Supervising lunch in West Sussex with her sons Christopher
(left) and Toby (*Ian Cook, Time & Life*)

Star support from husband Beverley Cross, photographed by
Maggie Smith in San Francisco, 1991

Maggie as Lady Bracknell considers the 'profeel' of Cecily (Claire Skinner), Aldwych Theatre, March 1993 (*Catherine Ashmore*)

as Philip French said in the *Observer*, 'as authentic a picture of the darker side of post-War Britain as our cinema has given us'. I would be tempted to submit *A Private Function* as the best movie Maggie has appeared in.

It is entirely typical of her that she should have fallen in with two of our most irreverent and talented satirists, Palin and Bennett. Both are university wits, performers with no formal training or theatrical background, and influential humorists: Palin, in his *Monty Python* mode, sparring partner to John Cleese and Terry Jones, operates in the robustly surreal and funny-voice tradition of Lewis Carroll and *The Goon Show* of BBC Radio in the 1950s (which starred Spike Milligan, Harry Secombe and Peter Sellers); while Bennett, who made his name alongside Peter Cook, Jonathan Miller and Dudley Moore in the revue *Beyond the Fringe* in the early 1960s, had emerged as a substantial playwright, mixing the incisive Yorkshire wit of his social commentary with beautifully rhythmed verbal tapestries.

Neither had had any previous contact with Maggie. Richard Loncraine, the director of *The Missionary*, had asked Maggie to take part in a Gerald Durrell film which never got made, *My Family and Other Animals*, and she had expressed interest.

He sent her a copy of Palin's script for *The Missionary* and the two of them, Loncraine and Palin, went along to meet her at the Berkeley Hotel. Palin remembers being apprehensive because, as he says, he was still 'overawed by great names, and certainly theatrical great names; most of our work in *Monty Python* had been fairly self-contained up to that point. And we played all the women, too.'

It was the day after Maggie had received the *Evening Standard* award for *Virginia* and Palin says that while she was not exactly disparaging about this, she was palpably uninterested in such highly organised expressions of adulation.

She had a vodka and tonic and a chat. Palin and Loncraine were prepared to change the script, allow her to make her own schedules, and come in as late as she liked in a white Rolls Royce. They would have done anything to have her in the film. But Maggie, as usual, specified neither ifs nor buts. She simply said she would do it. Palin asked Michael Caine for some advice when acting with Maggie. Caine merely said, 'Watch her. She'll have that scene from under your feet.'

Maggie plays Lady Isabel Ames, the sexually frustrated wife of the richest man in England (a classically gruff and treasurable performance by Trevor Howard in one of his last films). She offers to finance an Edwardian home for prostitutes in the East End of London if the do-gooding cleric, played by Palin, will go to bed with her. When she visits the home and finds three of the fallen inmates romping lasciviously with the missionary, she withdraws her support and the girls are thrown out on the streets once more.

The priest is engaged to a girl (played by Phoebe Nicholls) who is afflicted with a perverse passion for filing cabinets. A rather messy plot separates these two, consigns Maggie to a bizarre shooting accident on the Scottish moors and sends Palin back to the East End, where Maggie joins him after the house of correction is closed down in 1907.

It is a lively but unsatisfactory film, made for a mere £1.5 million, a curious mish-mash of Shavian morality, merry facetiousness and class-conscious satire. It prompts loose comparison with the famous 1930s case of the Rector of Stiffkey, who disappeared each Monday morning from his Norfolk parish to consort with shop girls and prostitutes before returning in time for the following Sunday's services.

Just as the Stiffkey padre would solemnly inform his young ladies that God had no objection to sins of the body, only sins of the soul, so Palin embarks on his bedtime salvation duties with many a quotation from Saint Paul. Maggie looks marvellous in silks and brocades and fine hats and her acting is so good it nearly blows a hole in the mixed quality fabric of the film itself.

But for once the funniest scenes do not involve Maggie. At a large country house in Wiltshire – the location used was Longleat, home of the Marquess of Bath – Palin is received by a butler, played by Michael Hordern, who gets hopelessly lost down his own corridors. After a long, sombre, futile and increasingly hilarious tour of the labyrinthine property, entering wrong rooms, disturbing ancient layers of dust, turning wrong corners, the imperturbable Hordern finally shows Palin to the spot where they started and shuts him out with a conclusive slam of the front door.

For all its imperfections, Maggie much enjoyed working with Palin on *The Missionary* and was happy to join him again on *A Private Function*. Palin had interceded on Alan Bennett's behalf and they all had as jolly a time as it is possible to have on a film with Maggie Smith. It was mostly shot in Ilkley, in West Yorkshire, under the first-time direction of Malcolm Mowbray, whom Maggie would refer to alternately as 'Our great leader' and 'Moaner Mowbray'.

The film, like so many British films of this decade, has a period setting, on the eve of the 1947 royal wedding between Princess Elizabeth (who became Queen in 1952) and Prince Philip, later the Duke of Edinburgh. As Philip French inimitably observed, this same event had prompted two previous films: *Here Come the Huggetts*, in which Jack Warner and Kathleen Harrison had bedded down in the street for the night to catch a glimpse of the royal couple en route to Westminster Abbey; and *Royal Wedding*, an MGM musical in which Fred Astaire and Jane Powell romanced across the same weekend among the English aristos.

Bennett's Yorkshire community is a microcosm of post-war 'austerity' Britain rekindling the pecking order in social aspirations against a still restrictive background of food and petrol rationing and busy licensing authorities.

Palin is Gilbert Chilvers, a call-out chiropodist who uncovers a conspiracy to rear an unlicensed pig and slaughter it illegally for a civic banquet in celebration of the royal wedding. Maggie is Joyce, his ambitious wife, a piano teacher and cinema organist who wants her future to live up to her past; her father had a chain of dry cleaners and the family 'regularly used to take wine with the meal'.

Bennett, the Oxford-educated son of a Leeds butcher, is almost the perfect writer for Maggie: stylish, discreet, with a double purchase, affectionate and wry, on the everyday speech of ordinary people. His idiomatic style is perfectly matched by Maggie's scathingly risible determination to move up the social ladder. Taking afternoon tea in the Grand Hotel is her rightful milieu: 'This is where I belong; put me in a long dress and surround me with sophisticated people, and I'd bloom.'

Bennett stings and stabs, but in the gentlest possible way. Those 'sophisticated people' would be anything but. Litotes, the expression of an affirmative in which the negative is ironically implied, is a speciality of both this writer and this actress. And Maggie, as she showed in Stoppard's *Night and Day*, loves to perform, simultaneously and miraculously, both inside and outside a character, precisely *on* the line while reinforcing either its inherent contradiction or an objective critical slant.

This technique is sometimes mistaken for mere camp. Camp comes into it, certainly. But, like Lettice Douffet, we must remain enemies of 'the mere'. There is something essentially, almost primevally, funny, as well as genuinely subversive, in Maggie's comic shrugs of rueful and analytical scorn.

As Joyce, the Lady Macbeth of Ilkley, she wickedly encourages Palin's delightfully slow-witted Gilbert to steal and kill off the pig, thus thwarting the local bigwigs who have denied her husband a new clinic in the High Street parade of shops. She will deal with them from a position of supremacy: 'It's not just steak, Gilbert, it's status'; or, more to the point, 'It's not just pork, Gilbert, it's power!'

The other characters are written and acted with a positively Gogolian relish: Bill Paterson's sweatily dedicated food inspector, John Normington's lily-livered accountant, Tony Haygarth's cowering, blotchily complexioned farmer and Pete Postlethwaite's amorous butcher, who fondles the buttocks of his beloved 'war widow' with as much loving attention as he devotes to the porcine carcass on his professional slab.

Best of all is Denholm Elliott's intemperate doctor who deplores the spectre of a socialist Britain where 'scum' rise to the top and where, on the National Health Service, 'anyone can come and knock on my door and demand treatment.' He gives this country 'five years'.

Rex Reed missed the point by saying that *A Private Function* was the kind of film that could only be made by the British 'with their frumpy disdain for nostalgia, their kinky humour and their riotous bad taste'. But Reed is right in implying that, for America, *A Private Function* is almost a Foreign Film. Bennett is an intelligent satirist and a serious historian; the *lingua franca* of showbiz doesn't come into it, except obliquely.

The 'private function' is both the projected dinner party and a reference to the grim habits of the pig. The farmer has placed his illicit charge on a diet of shredded rats and garbage, thus causing severe incontinence and an unprecedented pungency of domestic aromas in Joyce's kitchen area.

Joyce's mother (the beatifically lobotomised Liz Smith), who lives in the same house, thinks that the furtive smuggling of the pig is something to do with getting her into an old people's home. 'I won't show her it,' says Maggie, 'she's seventy-four and it's past her bedtime.' Once Joyce has fixed her deal with the top brass, she turns with equal matter-of-factness to her

own private functions: 'Right, Gilbert, I think sexual inter-
course is in order.'

Several pigs were used in the shoot, but the main bulk of
bacon belonged to Betty, a cross-breed of the floppy-eared
Large White family and the prick-eared, more alert Tamworth
clan. The supplier was Intellectual Animals (UK), a company
specialising in clever beasts for film-makers. Maggie was so
impressed by Betty's talent and sensitivity that she said she
would always think twice in future before referring to any
colleague as 'that pig of an actor'.

The pig brought out the best in Maggie. One instance of
quick improvisatory thinking is treasured by Palin: 'As in all
the pig scenes, we rehearsed without the animal, which was
then brought in like a great operatic star, or Liz Taylor. There
would usually be endless takes into which the pig would sort
of be fitted.

'On this occasion, the pig, for some reason, unerringly did
what was required first time. She lumbered straight round the
room and stuck her head in the oven. Maggie was suddenly
trapped and only had the option of backing out of camera
shot. But she didn't. She put one hand on the oven, the other
on the table and executed this wonderful two-footed leap right
over the more than oven-ready pig. It's in character, it's in the
film and it's a brilliant moment.'

The pig is finally slaughtered while Maggie drowns out its
squeals with her piano-playing and the pageantry of England
is celebrated in a party in the sitting room. Maggie's
Joyce, succulently overdressed in a blue suit, declares, in a
line that laceratingly mocks generations of suburban gentility:
'I'm going to throw caution to the winds and have a sweet
sherry.'

As the film fades on the post-prandial dance, a smooching
Denholm Elliott places his hand on Maggie's bottom, her
features pucker into an expression of distaste that just stops

short of a reprimand and Palin salivates over another sweet little piggy.

Michael Palin remained in awe of his co-star: 'Terrifying is too strong a word. But she's formidable when crossed. There's an intensity of animosity sometimes, which comes out in her acting and which can be quite chilling. Maggie in a bad mood is clearly a few degrees worse than most people in a bad mood.'

Palin and his wife, Helen, subsequently drove down to visit Maggie and Beverley in Fittleworth, taking a vase they had bought for her in the Japanese shop in Covent Garden: 'The vase had lots of flowers with it, and paper blooms. As I gave it to Maggie, I realised the paper blooms were in fact very small price tags and, as we talked, Maggie idly picked off the tags, one by one, without causing any embarrassment. I remember thinking that this was a great actor at work!'

Alan Bennett says that Maggie was in a consistently good temper throughout the filming of A *Private Function*. 'I was there most of the time. I used to go and chat. I was what one of the actors, Jim Carter, called "continuity giggles". One of the things about Maggie is that she is more intelligent than most actresses, much quicker, and so she arrives at what she wants to do very quickly. She easily gets bored and one has to be careful of that. She can't resist a joke, but I don't think she's malevolent. I do find her frightening when I think of her career and the people she's worked with. The same is true of Judi Dench, but I'm not frightened of Judi Dench, simply because she wouldn't let you be. Maggie has a reserve which you never penetrate, really.'

The critical reaction to A *Private Function* was ecstatic on both sides of the Atlantic. Vincent Canby considered it 'the most high-hearted, stylish English film comedy since the Boulting Brothers and the golden age of English comedy' and Maggie 'ferociously funny' as Lady Macbeth's 'dainty, lower-middle-class spin-off'.

In the 1984 British Academy of Film and Television Awards (BAFTA), the film split the honours with David Puttnam's *The Killing Fields*, and Maggie was declared Best Actress, with the prizes in the supporting categories claimed by Denholm Elliott and Liz Smith.

A second film with Merchant/Ivory, *A Room With A View*, enjoyed enormous popularity but had considerably fewer teeth than the Bennett movie. Maggie was cast as Charlotte Bartlett, 'a terrible pain in the neck' and yet another chaperone, this time in charge of a somewhat bland Helena Bonham-Carter as Lucy Honeychurch, E. M. Forster's impressionable virgin who goes to Florence, sees a murder and is sumptuously kissed in a Tuscan cornfield by George Emerson, played by Julian Sands.

Both *The Missionary* and *A Private Function* had been relatively low-budget affairs, and so was *A Room With A View*, although, at £2.4 million, with an eight-week shoot and four weeks on location in Tuscany, it cost twice as much to make as *Quartet*. It was co-produced with Goldcrest and Channel Four. A revealing comparison is with David Lean's E. M. Forster film, *A Passage To India*, which cost £16 million.

A crack British cast included Maggie's old friend Judi Dench as Miss Lavish, the ubiquitous novelist; Daniel Day-Lewis as Lucy's diffident bookworm of a fiancé, Cecil Vyse; and Simon Callow as Mr Beebe, the rumbustious young vicar from Tunbridge Wells.

Denholm Elliott chipped in with another craftily understated performance, as George's father, and summed up the appeal of the project with delightful insouciance: 'You may not earn much money, and the lunches aren't exactly the greatest, but it is Forster, it is Maggie Smith and Judi Dench, and it is Florence. It's good upmarket stuff which I like to be associated with . . . usually, I play abortionists.'

Chronologically, the film picked up where *The Missionary*

left off, in 1907. And the Edwardian distance was maintained by a series of irritating chapter headings, faithful to Forster, but suggesting a lack of ideas about filmic adaptation. Pauline Kael felt that Helena Bonham-Carter was recessive and unradiant, depriving the movie of a centrifugal force; she certainly does not convey with any urgency the dilemma of a young girl torn between expressing her emotions and stifling them.

Yet, as Kael says, the actors around her create a whirring atmosphere, a comic hum, that makes the film completely watchable. Maggie, whose spinsterish Charlotte 'sees sins against propriety everywhere', visits the Honeychurches in deepest leafy Kent and does not have the correct change for the cab-driver. Lucy's young brother pays the driver, but Maggie, over-emphatically and in order not to seem as impoverished as she is, insists on 'a settling of accounts'. As Kael exclaims, 'it's like a Marx Brothers routine, with the glorious Smith fingers and wrists fumbling and flying in all directions.'

Maggie's line on the pathos of the character – 'In my small way I am a woman of the world' – is absolutely straight and uninflected. She goes for a walk through Florence with Judi Dench's novelist, the person to whom she finally betrays Lucy with a description of 'the kiss', several inches taller than her keen and precise friend ('no Baedeker'), head jutting and corkscrewing around like that of a startled chicken. She makes the expression of the romantic secret an inevitable, gushing release for her own bottled-up feelings and unfulfilled sexuality. Every glance is informed with a signal of despair, an excuse, a cry for help, a diversionary remark.

Even off camera, Maggie could be just as alarming, and just as funny. Simon Callow had hardly met her before they worked on the film. Ismail Merchant renewed their acquaintance in the foyer of the Excelsior Hotel in Florence before shooting started and promptly departed to make arrangements for lunch. Callow recalls that there was an awkward pause before Maggie, looking distractedly into the middle distance, said, 'I hope he won't be long. Fabia Drake's been sitting outside in that car for an hour and if she sits there any longer, she's going to turn into a monument.'

After Callow had, as he admits, gurgled fatuously at this remark, he became tongue-tied once again before making his biggest mistake of all – blurting out praise for her most recent performance. Maggie suddenly turned on a bowl of flowers which she said she found 'worrying' and walked off to see the venerable actress and save her from the accelerating process of monumentalisation.

Once again, Maggie picked up the BAFTA Best Actress award. Judi Dench was honoured in the supporting category and the film itself was named Best Film. A *Room With A View* made profits for its six major investors, but not enough to put a brake on the decline of Goldcrest, the once-shining hope of the 1980s film industry, which was now in almost terminal economic trouble.

Maggie's reputation, like that of all the fine actors she worked with, survived intact. She had imperceptibly adjusted to the new mixed-economy realities of film-making and was as much in demand as ever. These first few years of the 1980s were as busy as any in her career. For, as well as making eight or nine films in six years, she had been trying to find her way back on a London theatre scene very different from that which she had abandoned for Canada.

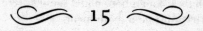

15

Coming in to Land

S ETTLING into the West Sussex farmhouse was a pleasurable chore for Maggie and Beverley after the upheavals of leaving Tigbourne Court and the nomadic existence spent shuttling between Stratford and Los Angeles. Maggie's sallies to the film studios were invariably conducted from home base in Fittleworth, with the boys reassuringly nearby at Seaford College and Maggie's father within easy reach in Oxford.

The most striking aspect of the house is its uncluttered, tasteful cosiness. It is a place to sink into and to hibernate inside. Maggie's bedroom has an unobstructed view of the surrounding fields, which made a more than welcome change from the busy main road that rushed by the bedroom at Tigbourne. On the landing outside hangs her treasured collection of Erté's original costume designs for the Lillian Gish silent movie version of *La Bohème* (Gish disliked them, so they were never used).

In the main sitting room, there are books everywhere, an almost complete collection of the distinctive Virago reprints of classic feminist novels, and the latest clutch of literary biographies in hardback. The trophies are strewn discreetly around. They serve as decorative props, not displays. There are some modest, pleasant landscape paintings. Not a trace of vulgarity or ostentation.

Some interesting posters in the study include one of a play billed for a performance on 4 September 1939, aborted by the outbreak of war, at a theatre in Eastbourne managed by Beverley's stepfather. Michael Caine and Robert Shaw in Beverley's first play, *One More River*, are framed on the mantelpiece. Another photograph, taken on Southend Pier, shows Beverley's mother, Eileen Dale, who died in February 1991. At a first glance, I took this likeness of a conspicuously pretty woman with elegant limbs, small frame, laughing eyes and porcelain features to be a photograph of Maggie. The resemblance is uncanny, though it had never before occurred to Beverley.

The duck pond has been converted into a small swimming pool. There are three listed barns on the property's couple of acres, an ancient bakehouse, an orchard which yields apples, plums, pears, mulberries and walnuts, awash with daffodils in the spring, and a vineyard which Maggie hates. According to Chris, the elder son, she just says it's 'useless', and refuses to elaborate further.

Beverley, however, oversees the entire plot with indiscriminate care and affection. His plans include converting the old bakery into a summer-house and acquiring a cider press to crush all the apples in the garden and save money at Christmas. His current home-produced tipple, a brew he dubs 'Old Methuselah', is a lethal mixture of mildewed garden berries, sugar and vodka, which he leaves to ferment for a couple of years.

This new home was a great comfort to Maggie at a time when it was not quite clear what direction her career would take. During her absence in Canada, everything had changed in the London theatre. Primarily, the National Theatre was no longer a close-knit caucus of actors and directors working briskly and intimately in ramshackle but friendly circumstances on one repertoire for the Old Vic stage, but a conglomerate of companies entombed in the concrete anonymity of the new building on the South Bank.

She was confused. She felt she did not belong anywhere, and that no one wanted her at the RSC (where she had no association) or the National and, as she told Sheridan Morley, although she did not at this point see herself as 'Dame Maggie', bravely battling on into her eighties, she did need someone like Olivier or Robin Phillips to tell her what to do next. 'I come back to a theatre which seems to have changed in some odd way during the years I was in Canada. Nobody seems to be in charge; just a lot of little groups all carrying on as best they can.'

One such little group, United British Artists, had received Maggie's blessing at the end of 1982. The alliance, announced by the entertainments mogul Lord Grade, constituted a peculiar and finally ineffectual bid to imitate the old Hollywood United Artists, which set its agenda according to the whims of a few all-powerful stars. The British theatre at the start of the 1980s was not remotely receptive to an attempt to reproduce the 1919 adventure launched by Mary Pickford, Charlie Chaplin, Douglas Fairbanks and D. W. Griffith. The board included Maggie, Diana Rigg, Glenda Jackson, John Hurt, Albert Finney and Peter Wood, and decided on more or less nothing.

The attempt at least had the value of acknowledging the situation: the two big national theatre companies had become impersonal monoliths; there was no natural home any more for the star leading actors of the day; a most enormous chasm had opened up – notwithstanding the works of Alan Ayckbourn – between the best contemporary playwrights and the most commercially viable actors; the spirit of adventure had been replaced by a struggle for survival; companies, except on the defiant fringe, were a thing of the past. In such an environment, a star like Maggie might look increasingly anomalous.

There was nothing for it but to test the water by taking a familiar plunge. Fittleworth, like Tigbourne, was within easy striking distance of the Chichester Festival Theatre. Just as Maggie had sprung free from disappointment at the National by giving her Margery Pinchwife there in 1969, so she relaunched herself in a home-grown British production in another Restoration classic, albeit one she had 'tried out' in Canada. She and William Gaskill took up where they had left off in 1974 (with *Snap*) in a sumptuous revival of *The Way of the World*.

The whole family, in fact, tuned in to the Sussex playhouse. Chris had done well at Seaford, but his plans for going to university were scuppered by the attractions of a student Assistant Stage Manager post he gained at Chichester in the early days of the theatre's supplementary venue in a tent.

There is one neat little coincidence here. This tent, a home for new plays and rare revivals, was entrusted by the Chichester supremo John Gale to the artistic supervision of a talented young director called Matthew Francis. Matthew Francis, who now runs the Greenwich Theatre in London, is really called Francis Matthews, but he had to invert his name because of the well-established British television actor who shares it. As has been noted, when Maggie started her professional career, also as an ASM, at the Oxford Playhouse, the company of actors there included this eminent and original Francis Matthews.

Beverley's playwriting career was also revived at Chichester. In the mid-1980s he titivated the old Fred Terry vehicle *The Scarlet Pimpernel*, directed with spectacular success by Nicholas Hytner, with a cast led by Donald Sinden (the production later transferred to Her Majesty's in London). Less happily, he adapted Goldoni's *La Locandiera* as *Miranda*, a vehicle for Penelope Keith at her most overweening in a slightly misfired analogue of Mrs Thatcher's Britain.

You never really know what Beverley might produce next. As young Toby says, 'He's an incredibly taciturn bugger,' and Chris is convinced that there are surprises in store: 'I think he's writing something pretty major.' There are potential diversions. Almost every year, apparently, Beverley receives an invitation, addressed to 'Mrs Beverley Cross', to mount the podium at the annual 'Women of the Year' shindig at the Savoy Hotel. Chris thinks he should accept one day, 'if only to frighten the life out of them'.

One of Maggie's major consolations in this period was her geographical and neighbourly closeness to Lord and Lady Olivier. 'Larry and Joan' had been living in nearby Steyning, as well as at Brighton, with their growing family since the middle 1960s. Maggie's rivalry with Joan Plowright and the edgy hostility with Sir Laurence were finally forgotten in these years of friendship and camaraderie. The truce was sealed by Plowright's appearance alongside Maggie in *The Way of the World*.

The contrast in the type of acting each expertly delivered was summarised for William Gaskill in their backstage preparations: 'If you went past Joan's dressing room, you heard her going through every line, from beginning to end. And as you went past Maggie's, you heard that wonderful record of Nellie Wallace's laughing song, which she played to put her in the mood.' Maggie returned to one of her greatest roles, and one with which she had begun her Canadian sojourn, or exile, Millamant. And Joan Plowright played Lady Wishfort, 'that old peeled wall, that famous antidote to desire'.

Understandably sensitive to her own approaching qualification for the senior roles, Maggie, in her fiftieth year, took furious umbrage at a programme biography which anticipated the half-century by several months. The entire print run had to be withdrawn at the last minute.

The Way of the World opened at Chichester on 1 August

1984. Maggie's Millamant was a gloriously emaciated, darting
figure, using her wit as a cover to insecurity. She had been
admired in *Night and Day* and in *Virginia*, but she had not
been seen in her full comic flow on the British stage for ten
years. The critical reaction reflected the sense of a starved
theatre-going public reconnecting with one of its favourite
icons.

Jack Tinker said she finally displaced Edith Evans in the
role. He was beside himself and 'once more at her feet'. Less
gymnastically, Nicholas de Jongh in the *Guardian* said her
'stupendous' performance would surely rank 'as one of the
great high-comedy achievements of the past three decades',
noting how she charted the independent girl's progress from
languid disdain conveyed from a great height, nose tilted sky-
ward, to reach in her wooing scene with Mirabell a tantalising
mixture of role playing and real feeling.

The production was London-bound (it opened at the Haymarket in November) and had been given the works by director
Gaskill. The design was by two of his old Royal Court associ-
ates – sets of oaken doors and evocative emblems by Hayden
Griffin and beautiful costumes of silks and quilts patterned
with stripes, butterflies and birds by Deirdre Clancy.

The kinship structure of a complex plot in which, as Anne
Barton reminded us in a programme note, 'everybody is a
half-brother, niece, mother, cousin or nephew of somebody
else', was cleanly exposed around the simple motivating main-
spring of the chase for Lady Wishfort's money. One also felt,
among all the couplings and liaisons, that this was a play about
three widows: Millamant, Lady Wishfort and Mrs Fainall.

This last role was powerfully played by Sheila Allen. The
casting throughout was formidable. As Irving Wardle remarked, 'Without departing from this director's austere prin-
ciples [it was] the kind of show that would have gladdened
the heart of Binkie Beaumont.' The company included Sara

Kestelman, Ian Hogg, Jane Carr, James Villiers and John Moffatt. Mirabell was taken by Michael Jayston, who had trouble making him either weighty or interesting. During the London run, Frank Barrie and Margaret Whiting replaced Hogg and Kestelman as, respectively, Fainall and Mrs Marwood.

Above all, Maggie embodied what Hazlitt called 'that peculiar flavour in the very words' of Congreve's comedy and, once again, she convinced us in the great proviso scene that she really did set important store by her dependence on solitude and morning thoughts. This jocund marriage of style and gravity typified the light and adult plangency of Gaskill's exemplary production.

And Maggie's brilliant and capricious creation, with wit her quick and deadly weapon, made her immune to all invasions. No one in the British theatre – and we have seen Millamants from Geraldine McEwan and Judi Dench – can rival her in this vein. She could flourish a remark to create havoc and then retreat quickly behind her fan, as Michael Billington said, like a soldier behind a redoubt. And the repulsion of the rustic Sir Wilfull with a cry of 'A walk?' was that of a woman dealing brusquely with an indecent proposal.

Seven years later, the *Sunday Telegraph* ran a series in which actors and other artists recalled 'A Night to Remember'. Susan Fleetwood, no mean actress herself and one who has played several 'Maggie' roles (Silvia, Rosalind, Beatrice, Arkadina), picked this Millamant as the most outstanding performance she had ever seen:

'I think Maggie Smith is an artist of the high wire, and to be that can cost a lot. She avoids the cosy, she takes the risk of being unsympathetic. And yet, even when she's spitting venom, one's heart is broken for her . . . When I see Maggie act, I always feel tremendously excited that I'm an actor too. She just makes me feel good about the job.'

John Moffatt rekindled the joy of working with Maggie: 'I'd

go on with her for the first entrance in the park and sometimes she'd say, "Moffatty Woffatty, surprise me." She liked to keep it all as fresh and flexible as possible. So I would say, *sotto voce*, "There's an awful lot of midges in St James's Park today," and we'd play that scene slapping midges, a great twinkle going on between us. It was subtle and the audience would not really notice. But the scene would be enlivened by this, and her own performance freshened.'

Moffatt also testifies that Maggie's Oxford enthusiasm for J. D. Salinger had not waned. If a matinée was looming for which neither of them felt at concert pitch, she would gee up Moffatt and her other colleagues by invoking the showbiz motto at the end of Salinger's *Franny and Zooey*, 'Let's do it for the Fat Lady.' The Fat Lady is in every audience, the one person out there who is really waiting for the performance as the highlight of her day and a balm to all woes. Maggie never cheats on a matinée; she always does it for the Fat Lady.

Having given Barker and Bond short shrift when approached by Gaskill, Maggie was always liable to feel with especial keenness the dearth of new West End plays for actresses of her age and calibre. But within a year, she was acting with John Moffatt once again, in *Interpreters*, a Cold War comedy designed as a vehicle for her and Edward Fox by Ronald Harwood, whose early experience as an actor in Donald Wolfit's company had led to his backstage hit, *The Dresser*.

Slightly schematic and finally hollow, *Interpreters* nonetheless did have some texture within which Maggie could rehearse her special line in despair and vulnerability as Nadia Ogilvy-Smith, a spinsterish Russian language interpreter known as 'the old maid of Whitehall' who, on the eve of a summit conference between the political leaders of Russia and Great Britain, recalls an old affair in New York with her randy Russian opposite number, Viktor (Edward Fox). Moffatt umpired their tryst as a ramrod-backed Foreign Office official.

For these past ten years, Nadia has kept passion at bay, walled up in a Kensington flat with a ninety-three-year-old grandmother who once danced with the Ballets Russes and knew Tolstoy and Chekhov. When Viktor calls to collect a copy of *Heartbreak House*, Nadia mistakenly believes that his ardour indicates a long-term emotional commitment. The comic climax of their renewed encounter occurs at a diplomatic pow-wow where Maggie plays footsy under the table. She mistakenly manipulates her emboldened leg into the lap of the Soviet president and watches, stunned and alarmed, as Edward Fox calmly gets up and crosses the room.

A lesser actress would have milked this moment for coarse laughter. Maggie did indeed win her laugh, but she made of it something more truthful and complex by immediately immersing us in the pain of her embarrassment. Her transforming powers were evident, too, in the way she could make quite a modest one-liner like 'I don't approve of making love as if it was an oil change' sound, as Benedict Nightingale said, 'simultaneously droll and wan, witty and desolate, and very good indeed'.

Moffatt reports that Maggie was not very happy with this production and that the direction of Peter Yates, better known for his work in the cinema, was virtually non-existent. Maggie also hated the set, which was of a predominantly bilious green colour, with a lurid green carpet to match. Invoking the name of one of the outstanding snooker champions of the day, she would complain to anyone within earshot, 'When I get out on that stage I feel like Hurricane Higgins.'

Just over a year later, Maggie was snared in another Anglo-based Eastern European scenario of misunderstanding and despair, *Coming in to Land* by Stephen Poliakoff at the National Theatre. This was Maggie's first role on the South Bank, the occasion of a long overdue reunion with Peter Hall as her director and, considered in retrospect, one of the last significant British plays to examine the false visions East and West entertained of each other before the extraordinary political upheavals at the end of the decade.

Poliakoff, who in 1980 had written a wonderful television film along similar culture-clash lines, *Caught on a Train*, for Peggy Ashcroft, sent the play to the National as he had promised his next one to Peter Hall. He had thought of Maggie as Halina Rodziewizowna, an unmarried Polish design student who wants custody at British immigration, because of the impression she had made on him in *The Prime of Miss Jean Brodie*, especially in the scene where she pleads with the headmistress Celia Johnson 'and suddenly becomes terribly moving.' When Maggie read it, she accepted the role at once.

Ironically, in a play whose main confrontation is set in an immigration office in Croydon, a bleak and soulless *quartier* of South London, Maggie found herself particularly alienated in real life in the concrete labyrinth of the new National. Poliakoff, whose reputation as a dramatist is rooted in the poetry of urban desolation, retains a vivid image of Maggie inhabiting those bleak corridors like a lost soul unhappily dislocated from her natural West End ambience of plush and gilt.

John Moffatt sent her a poem which she carried close to her heart as she wandered, perpetually lost, between her featureless box dressing room and the unwelcomely wide proscenium of the Lyttelton auditorium: 'Fuck and bloody arsehole, shit bugger damn; I don't know where the fuck I am.'

Poliakoff had always wanted his play to be staged in the smaller Cottesloe Theatre, but knew it would be nonsense to have Maggie confined there with a limited audience. He wanted to kid the audience with a seeming boulevard structure and then lead them into 'something messier'. Because Maggie came from that boulevard background, she took the audience on exactly the journey Poliakoff prescribed:

'Of all my plays, this was the one which has had the best audience reaction. And a lot of that was to do with the great performance of Maggie Smith. She is brilliant at accents, and captured to absolute perfection this thing of Poles who speak wonderful, slightly flowery English, in the tradition of Joseph Conrad, or a comparable Czech example like Tom Stoppard. She has a brilliant ear. And she has a ready-made public. She walks on the stage and can say anything, even if it's just "Have a cup of tea", and people start laughing. This is not true of Judi Dench.'

Her first entrance was indeed remarkable. She had spent twenty-nine years looking after her father, a disgraced Polish politician, and learning English in preparation for her own life. She appeared in a doorway, weighed down with her belongings in two vast plastic bags, wearing oversize boots and juggling a cigarette. Michael Ratcliffe in the *Observer* likened this aggressive manifestation to that of Sybil Thorndike entering in a scuffle of cardigans and bumping into someone expendable in N. C. Hunter's *Waters of the Moon*. It was at once clear that Halina would not go away. She personified and combined, said Ratcliffe, laziness, sensuality, reticence and indestructibility.

There was dispute over the merit of Poliakoff's play: 'a piffling piece of over-produced flim-flam,' said Jack Tinker, possibly because of a battery of television screens designed to fill up the cavernous Lyttelton in the hi-fi emporium where Halina has gained illegal employment; 'thin and disappointing piece,' said Ratcliffe; 'Maggie Smith could not be this good if Stephen Poliakoff had not given her the material to work on,' countered Billington.

There was elegantly silky support from Andrew C. Wadsworth as an oil executive and from Anthony Andrews as a show-business lawyer, both allies to her cause for patriation in England.

But the major sparks were fired in a half-hour scene in the second act between Maggie and Tim Pigott-Smith as a ruthless immigration officer who turns the interrogation screws rather like Dostoevsky's Porfiry in *Crime and Punishment*. Cutting right down to the bone, Maggie, dressed in eye-catching scarlet, tore into the scene with an animal ferocity she had not tapped in London since *Hedda Gabler*, crying to be allowed into the country with, as Billington said, 'the naked desperation of the potentially stateless'.

Between these two contemporary plays she fitted in an appearance at the Lyric, Hammersmith, as Jocasta in Jean Cocteau's high-camp 1934 version of the Oedipus story, *The Infernal Machine*. This was a good example of Maggie being talked into something about which she had nurtured no previous ambition whatsoever.

The person responsible was Simon Callow, who was infatuated with the play and saw in Maggie the Jocasta of his dreams. The role, he felt, was one which could accommodate her full range, demanding a woman who appeared, by turns, skittish, amorous, haunted, tender, stark and suicidal. It was the tragedienne in Maggie that appealed above all to Callow and indeed had inspired him to become an actor in the first place.

Cocteau has rather fallen from fashion in the British theatre, if indeed he had ever fallen into it. The reviewers remained sceptical. Michael Billington branded the play 'poppy Cocteau' (not all that risible a tag as the playwright had conceived of the piece in a haze of opium) and John Peter in the *Sunday Times* thundered about bad art being gloriously sent up. But Callow was sincere in his admiration for the play, which covers Oedipus's return to his mother's womb as her lover, after he has killed his father.

There is a famous scene with the talking Sphinx, and a long bedroom scene in which mother and son, magnetised by sexual attraction, are permanently on the verge of sleep. Cocteau, said Callow, set out 'to write the great nightmare of Western civilisation as a dream play', and by using a brilliantly evolved technique of repetitions, non-sequiturs, unmotivated impulses, quotations and slangy anachronisms, 'he creates a hypnotised world moving imperceptibly from dream to reality and back' in which the characters, all variants of boulevard archetypes, are caught up in the cogs of the infernal machine, i.e. the plot.

One of Callow's other heroes, the Irish actor Micheál MacLiammóir, whom he met while a student at Queen's University, Belfast, had produced the play in Carl Wildman's translation at the Gate in Dublin in 1937. Callow, who was convinced that, in the face of AIDS, nuclear war and starvation, it was harder to dismiss Cocteau's vision of life as a trap devised by a remorseless divinity, provided his own script, even racier than Wildman's and flavoursomely sensitive to the tension, flipness, misery, extravagance and ecstasy of the original.

Callow had long wanted to do the play and he knew that Peter James, the director of the Lyric, Hammersmith, an avowed internationalist with a liking for mad projects (Callow would play the lead in Goethe's *Faust* there a few years later), might be interested. He was. Callow was building up his courage to approach Maggie Smith when he was thrown together with her on the film of *A Room With A View*.

He was paranoically certain that she found him too noisy, but his dread dissolved when they acted together: 'The contact, concentration and responsiveness were thrilling.' Still, he remained tongue-tied on the subject of Cocteau and started to entertain thoughts of Jeanne Moreau. A chance meeting with the French film star in Florence, on a rest day from shooting the Forster film, resulted in a series of telephone calls and messages which finally, however, led to a stalemate.

During *Interpreters*, Callow resumed his hunt for Maggie and was rewarded with a positive response first time. Over supper, he outlined how he would conduct rehearsals. He asked was there any method she particularly disliked? 'Only stopping work at four and going off to the Garrick for drinkies.'

Without quite getting down to brass tacks, Callow arranged another dinner date at which Peter James joined them. Eventually, James made an impassioned speech about the need to take on Cocteau, as the major subsidised companies weren't interested, and the supplementary need to present him as well as possible with someone who would bring in the audience and do justice to the play. 'I need you, or someone like you,' said the intrepid James. Callow froze. 'Someone like me?' said Maggie. 'You,' said James. 'I know what you mean,' said Maggie. 'Well?' said James. 'Well?' said Maggie. 'Will you do it?' A pause. 'I can't see any reason why not.' 'But will you do it?' 'Pourquoi pas?'

And that, recalls Callow, was it. People told him later that Maggie had said to them that she didn't know why she was doing the play, or she was only doing it to spite her agent, or because Edith Evans had never done it. But deep down she had been taken by Callow's enthusiasm and had herself found something worthwhile and compulsive in the drama. It was typical of her that she should disguise her commitment in a battery of airily bemused disavowals.

Having initially tried, and failed, to interest Alec Guinness in the role of Tiresias, Callow had landed a fine alternative: the blind seer was to be played by the late Robert Eddison, one of the great verse speakers in the old style. Oedipus fell to the French film star Lambert Wilson.

The rehearsal period was troubled, to say the least. One of the reasons was that Eddison simply did not get on with

Maggie. Maggie was also highly critical of Bruno Santini's set, which the designer had covered in cellophane. Each time anyone went anywhere near the surface, it crackled and rustled. Maggie took one look and protested: 'I can't . . . d'you . . . I can't . . . I can't . . . it's like a thousand sweets being unwrapped all at the same time.'

The cellophane went. Three previews were cancelled and, at the last dress rehearsal, when the dry-ice machine had turned the stage into a skating rink, Lambert Wilson fell into the orchestra pit.

At the first preview, Maggie was faced with a total disaster but refused to succumb. According to Callow, she just set to and saved the show. And halfway through, she probably realised that the rescue operation was only half necessary. Then she went through what Callow took to be an habitual rigmarole of ringing up and apologising:

'She fears disaster every day. It's her natural reaction. It's as though she is spontaneously on acid. Which is what makes her acting so great. She will take a word and plumb its depth both comically and tragically until it begins to assume as lurid a life for you as it does for her.'

Jocasta was not popular in Thebes: 'My clothes madden them. My mascara maddens them. My joie de vivre maddens them.' Her attention is caught by a handsome young soldier who reminds her of her son. He would be about the same age, nineteen, now. 'Zizi,' Maggie cooed to Tiresias, 'just look at those muscles . . . feel those biceps, they're like steel.' Michael Ratcliffe described how this darkly murmuring witch then sank 'with an opiate lassitude and gloom on to the enormous pile of furs where she will unknowingly consummate marriage to her son'.

In the last scene, Jocasta appeared in black, in a trough of misery. And then – Cocteau's masterstroke, says Callow – she returns as an apparition, dead, all in white, after she has hanged herself and Oedipus has stabbed out his eyes with his mother's brooch. Suffused with maternal spirit and radiance, her effect on an audience was invariably profound. Callow had begged her to remain as simple as possible, and she did remain as simple as possible. Every night. 'She was just astonishing.'

Number one son Chris was working in the West End. After Chichester, he gained a job through the Fox family connection – Edward, who had appeared at Chichester, was presented as Maggie's co-star in *Interpreters* by his younger brother, Robert Fox, whom Chris had met over dinner. Thus Chris came to be 'crewing' on the Harwood play, humping costumes and assisting in the scene changes, where he 'walked on' in his mother's shadow as a Foreign Office security guard.

Chris and Toby then worked together for a season in the tent at Chichester before Toby, who had long since decided to be an actor, enrolled at a minor drama school for about four months, then auditioned for the major ones. He was turned down because he was too young – he had left Seaford without taking his A-Levels – and spent another season crewing at Chichester before he was accepted at the London Academy of Music and Dramatic Art (LAMDA).

Chris, meanwhile, moved on to Andrew Lloyd Webber's *The Phantom of the Opera* (which dropped anchor at Her Majesty's after *The Scarlet Pimpernel*), where he caught the chandelier every night before it hit the deck. There followed stints at the Redgrave Theatre at Farnham, where he gained his stage-manager's card, and the Mercury at Colchester, where he served as deputy stage manager.

Both boys had kept their father's surname, Stephens, but Chris had to trade it in, just as his mother had had to adopt 'Maggie' in 1956, because another 'Christopher Stephens' was registered with Equity. He tried registering under his maternal grandmother's names of Hutton and Little but they, too, were taken. Maggie said that, as he liked the poetry of Philip Larkin, why not use that name?

So Chris Stephens became, and remains, Chris Larkin. He now decided, after all, that he wanted to train as an actor. Chris, cheerful and lanky, followed his younger brother Toby, confident and barrel-chested, into LAMDA. The boys used Queen's Elm Square as their domestic base for the last few years of the 1980s and beyond.

Toby had first seen his mother on stage in *Peter Pan* and had wondered 'what the hell she was doing swinging around on a piano wire.' In Canada, Christopher Downes remembers sitting with Toby, his face alight, at the end of the last performance of *As You Like It* as Maggie, triumphant in the epilogue, took her curtain calls and was showered with bouquets of pink and yellow roses which matched the colours in her dress. Downes knew at this point – Toby was eight – that he wanted to share what his mother was lapping up.

Toby recalls that when he confirmed that he intended to go on the stage, Maggie quizzed him on how many Shakespeare plays he knew, how many speeches by heart. She did on one occasion bawl him out for never going to see anything and not reading enough. It is the one serious row Toby has ever had with his mother. He started to do as she ordered. He learned that if he was to be even half as serious about his career as she was, he had to start watching and reading immediately.

At about this time, Robert, who was playing a bleary-eyed, unforgettably bloated double of King Herod and Pontius Pilate in Bill Bryden's production of *The Mystery Plays* at the National Theatre, drifted back into his sons' lives. They had gone seven or eight years without seeing him and were now old enough to take responsibility themselves for keeping in touch. Both parents are now seen in appreciative context. Neither came from a family with a pre-history in the theatre, and both had to work very hard to achieve a professional status.

As far as Maggie is concerned, Toby acknowledges that her moderately austere lower-middle-class background, so formative an influence on her career and personality, is denied him and Chris. Maggie is hard on other people because she is primarily hard on herself. The boys know they must learn to combat the relative ease with which they can face the world thanks to their mother's efforts.

Maggie was no more relaxed about her work than she had ever been, but her security at home and the friendship of her sons were cause for at least some satisfaction. Although she immediately regretted it, she allowed the American-based *People* magazine to take a look round the Sussex fastness and to encourage her to put her past into perspective: 'The tumultuous period of my life, so much of it is such a winter in my head . . . that's not me; it's Christopher Fry.'

Toby told the magazine that he and Chris had enjoyed a remarkably smooth transition 'from one father to another', while Chris declared that Beverley was the glue that stuck the family together.

Maggie concurred: 'Bev is a rock. He took on a lot: me and these two boys. I'm just remarkably fortunate that it did happen. When you meet again someone you should have married in the first place – it's like a script. The kind of luck that's too good to be true.'

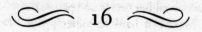

16

A Toast to the
Bard with Lettice

STEPHEN POLIAKOFF and Peter Hall entertained hopes of
Maggie moving to the West End with *Coming in to Land*,
but the Jack Clayton film of *The Lonely Passion of Judith
Hearne* was in the offing and, more to the point, the long-
promised script from Peter Shaffer, *Lettice and Lovage*, was
almost a reality. In his preface to the published text, Shaffer
put the unfashionable view that his purpose as a playwright
was to serve the actor's art:

'Great actors are now a species infinitely more endangered
than White Rhinos and far more important to the health and
happiness of the human race. I am referring to "live" actors,
of course – not their manufactured images on screens large and
small. In our age where most performers have been reduced
to forms of puppetry – neutered by naturalism, made into
miniaturists by television, robbed of their voices by film dub-
bers and their right to structure roles by film editors – the
authentic Great Actor has almost disappeared from the earth.'

Shaffer counted Maggie 'indisputably' great and dedicated
his new play to this Wonder of her Art, 'who incarnates comedy with love'. *Lettice and Lovage* was scheduled for an
autumn 1987 opening in the West End.

The year started well, with Maggie winning the Best

Supporting Actress in the Golden Globe Awards for A *Room With a View*, followed by a nomination in the same category for the Oscars (she did not win). As well as the BAFTA award, she collected a Variety Club award as film actress of the year. Even more unexpected was a curious invitation she received that spring from Bernard Levin.

Levin had given up theatre reviewing, but not his passion for Maggie Smith. He had been asked by his close friend Arianna Stassinopoulos Huffington, the Washington socialite, writer and controversial biographer of Picasso, to arrange a Shakespearean entertainment for the third annual Founders Day dinner at the Folger Shakespeare Library in Washington DC.

This was Mrs Huffington's first chairmanship of a major Washington event and she wanted it, naturally enough, to be a success. The guest list of 170 people, each one paying a thousand dollars for the privilege of attending, included several Roosevelts, Judge Webster, head of the FBI, and many senators from Capitol Hill. A reception in the Great Hall of the library was to be followed by dinner in the Reading Room and whatever appropriate cabaret Levin and Arianna between them might be able to concoct.

Levin had recently published a book, *Enthusiasms*, where, in a chapter on Shakespeare, he had cobbled into one gigantic paragraph all the phrases, first coined in the Bard, which had since assumed the status of common parlance. His script was built around this passage and he sent it off to Maggie, who was intrigued. She agreed with Levin that Alec McCowen would make an ideal partner for such an occasion and all three of them had a splendid meal at Simply Nico's. The actors signed up in exchange for a suite each at the Hay-Adams hotel and a first-class fare.

On arrival in Washington, Levin promptly took his charges out for yet another sumptuous dinner and McCowen half-

remembers returning to the Hay-Adams very much the worse
for wear and quite unable to stand still for long enough to
insert his key in his bedroom door. Maggie descended less
squiffily from her floor and kindly inserted the key for him,
turned down the bed, drew the curtains and put Mr McCowen
safely to sleep within his luxurious sheets.

Levin's account of 'a stupendous triumph' at the Folger on
10 April 1987 is slightly challenged by McCowen's recollection
of 'utter chaos' at the library when they turned up to rehearse,
though it is conceivable that he might have been suffering
from a hangover. Maggie and McCowen insisted on someone
turning off the central heating and the air conditioning, which
made noises similar to those of a lavatory flushing. Americans,
McCowen, reminded his colleagues, simply did not hear such
noises.

The actors wanted Levin to rehearse them, but he protested,
with many a 'good grief' and 'for heaven's sake', that he was
in no position whatsoever to embark on a career in theatre
directing, least of all at this late-ish time of life, and certainly
not, for starters, with the likes of Mr Alec McCowen and, by
the mass, by all the stars in God's firmament, as well as by
untold varieties of heck, the further likes of Miss Maggie
Smith. So he told them just to get up there and do the blessed
thing on their own, which is, after all, what directors usually
say most of the time anyway.

In the afternoon before the event, Levin recalls, Maggie
Smith lost her handbag. She could not move without this
handbag, it had everything in it and so on and so forth, and
a hunt was mounted throughout the hotel. The handbag was
finally found under Miss Smith's bed.

Then Miss Smith lost her spectacles. She was in no position
to read the menu, let alone Bernard Levin's script, without
these glasses, but she did have a prescription about her person.
Probably in the handbag. Levin volunteered to dive into the

Washington maelstrom and find an optician who, for a consideration, made up another pair of glasses on the spot.

Before the dinner and the recital, the artists were bidden to an extremely smart cocktail party at Mrs Huffington's, McCowen in his dinner jacket, Maggie in what she said was her 'only black dress'.

The ride in the limousine was through the rush hour. It took, says McCowen, an hour and a half to travel approximately two kilometres in order to attend a party where he and Maggie knew nobody at all. They stood on the terrace and Maggie looked down the lawn and said rather grumpily, 'Very small pool!' Ten minutes later they piled back into the limo to go to the Folger and Maggie said, 'Well, thank you Bernard, that was a lovely glass of water.'

The library, manned by liveried footmen and populated by Washington's finest, had been transformed into a Midsummer's Eve bower, awash with flowers, moss, ivy, models of little woodland animals, plants and jungle greenery. A large ficus tree sparkled with lights and streamers, and the whole place had been lit solely by candlelight.

'It was magic, absolute magic,' says Levin. 'What I shall never forget was that, as the catalogue unrolled, you could hear the audience stop breathing at this flood of phrases. Of course there were scholars present, but the greater part of the audience did not know that all these phrases came from Shakespeare, nor would most people, on either side of the Atlantic. Maggie and Alec were wonderful, absolutely wonderful. And the cheering. Well, it was unbelievable.'

The actors were more tense. The dinner, according to McCowen, 'went on for hours and hours and of course we both had to have it. I was sitting next to a very obscure Roosevelt. Then there were speeches, then we were given a medal and then it was time for the recital. At which point, as we started, about twenty-eight of the more elderly diners took this as their cue to go to the loo! Anyway, we got through it, and Bernard was overjoyed and very sweet and I had some gin and tonic and Maggie had some champagne and then we both went back to the hotel and behaved disgracefully with room service. It was a very jolly time.'

Maggie endured another, less formal, dinner on 2 June when London Weekend Television, for whom Melvyn Bragg had made a programme about Laurence Olivier, honoured the greatest actor of his day with an eightieth birthday party. Maggie and Beverley joined thirty-two guests – including Joan Plowright, Peggy Ashcroft, Edna O'Brien, Alec Guinness, Frank Finlay, Tom Stoppard and Albert Finney – at the Inn on the Park. Maggie did not, however, take part in the public celebration of Olivier's birthday at the National Theatre gala.

At all stages of her career, Maggie has remained curiously invisible in public. She rarely appears in charity shows, seldom lends her name to committees or educational institutions, and you hardly ever see her on television, or hear her on radio, discussing some forthcoming performance or other.

John Moffatt once confessed to her that he felt he had all the makings of a recluse. And she said, 'Oh, I *am* a recluse. I haven't got any friends.' Although she knows an awful lot of people, she consistently gave the impression during the 1980s, says Moffatt, that the only place she really wanted to be was at home with Beverley and the boys and the dog and the garden and the books.

It is as if she hides away, nursing her gift, and then bursts forth in a new role. She certainly did this as Lettice Douffet, imaginative guide to Fustian Hall and daughter of a theatrical mother who toured the Dordogne with an all-female company, cheerfully swinging her Falstaff padding over her shoulder to play Richard Crookback.

Unusually, Shaffer wrote a great whacking role for a leading actress who had to do all the donkey work of laying down the expository information herself. Several critics felt that these early scenes could be trimmed with little loss to the play apart from Maggie's delightfully pitched variations on the same theme.

John Dexter, who attended the First Night with Riggs O'Hara, was incensed by what he thought was over-indulgence on Shaffer's part. He called him on the telephone and said that the first few scenes should be cut, that the play should open in the office with the secretary and Miss Schoen talking about Lettice's distortions of historical fact and that Maggie should have a big entrance where she removes her black cloak to reveal the red dress and off she goes.

'All that first stuff is ridiculous,' Dexter said. Shaffer admitted that Maggie had been a little bit over the top and Dexter exploded: 'Over the top? You've given her Himalayas of camp to climb!'

But the whole point of Shaffer's play was to expose Maggie's artistry, not win points in a good dramaturgy contest. At the end of the London version of *Lettice and Lovage*, Maggie as Lettice and Margaret Tyzack as the reconciled Miss Schoen, having toasted each other by quaffing a goblet of the Elizabethan home-brewed 'lovage', embark on a course of architectural terrorism. They have formed END, the Eyesore Negation Detachment (as opposed to CND, the Campaign for Nuclear Disarmament), and begin preparing, as the curtain falls, to blow up a select list of modern architectural monstrosities with a petard, a medieval explosive device.

This conclusion, although it uncannily anticipated the conservationist, anti-modernist debate perpetrated in Britain by the Prince of Wales, was generally thought to be unlikely and unconvincing. Shaffer himself wanted to rewrite it, but the actors were reluctant to accept the changes.

It now transpires that they didn't believe in the ending themselves. But Margaret Tyzack says that they didn't mind the preposterousness 'because we were of the mind that we couldn't run a wool shop. The idea that anyone else could believe that we really could get anything together was, to us, astonishing.'

Michael Blakemore, the director, says that Maggie tried to convince him and Shaffer that the rewrite was no good by rehearsing it badly for a couple of weeks but that 'when she did it, and started getting her laughs doing her magic on it, she got to enjoy it a lot.'

The new last (strictly, penultimate) line in New York, after the play had come full circle by Lettice describing her own place, was, 'On behalf of Miss Schoen and myself – a *brimming* goodbye to you!' Shaffer says that Maggie worried and worried about this line not being quite right before inserting the more rhythmically satisfying extra phrase: 'On behalf of Miss Schoen and myself – and all true enemies of the mere – a *brimming* goodbye to you!'

Shaffer acknowledges that there is a school of playwriting which is anti-effective and says to hell with all that sort of thing: 'I do not subscribe to that school. I'm on Maggie's side. You have to honour the musical and the rhythmic side of things, and you have to honour your actress. She wanted to achieve that joyous envoi, to seal her bargain with the audience. I believe she gave one of the great performances of our day.'

Michael Ratcliffe, dismissing the piece as 'a fey heritage comedy', declared that the play's greatest mystery was the failure of Lettice and Lotte to end up in bed together. Margaret Tyzack says that lesbianism, even crypto-lesbianism, was never even discussed by anyone on the production.

The idea would certainly never have crossed Maggie's mind. She was absolutely aghast when Ingmar Bergman had asked her, during rehearsals for *Hedda Gabler*, apropos of her interest in Mrs Elvsted's long hair, if she had ever experienced any physical sensations towards her own sex.

This was Shaffer's first out-and-out comedy since *Black Comedy* in 1964, in which Maggie had also scored a great personal triumph, but as part of a coherent National Theatre ensemble. And Michael Billington pointed out how Shaffer had returned to eccentricity as a subject for the first time since his study of the macaroon-munching private detective (played by Kenneth Williams) in *The Public Eye* on this same Globe stage a quarter of a century before.

Richard Pearson, who hired the detective in that play, was cast as the third act solicitor, Mr Bardolph, in this. D. A. N. Jones in the *Sunday Telegraph* smartly noted that Pearson's unwilling participation in Lettice's charade of the execution of Charles II, for which he mimed the beating of a drum with an absurd 'pam-tititi-pam' vocal improvisation, was a weird echo of the same actor's sinister, savage drum-beating as Stanley at the end of the first act of Pinter's first play, *The Birthday Party*, in 1958.

Shaffer is a magpie writer. The genesis of Lettice Douffet owed something not only to Jean Brodie, but also to E. F. Benson's overbearing heroine, Lucia. In *Mapp and Lucia*, which pivots on a dichotomous female relationship comparable to that of Lettice and Lotte Schoen, we also witness an historic pageant featuring the execution of Mary Queen of Scots, with Lucia's bachelor amigo, Georgie, who plays Drake, approximating to the press-ganged Mr Bardolph. But whereas the impeccably stylish Benson reads like Jane Austen given a going over by Ronald Firbank, Shaffer's more journeyman prose is aimed simply at achieving instant theatrical impact.

The reviews were generally uneasy about the play and divided on Maggie's performance. Irving Wardle tipped his hat to 'an original and hilarious treatment of an important and theatrically neglected subject' but complained that the play kept coming to a stop for memory speeches and that the two characters were of decidedly unequal interest.

And the issue of mannerism was reintroduced with unwonted savagery by Martin Hoyle in the *Financial Times*. There were no two ways about it: Maggie got right up his nose. He bemoaned 'another revue turn' and, having dismissed her Lettice as 'gratingly superficial' and 'a grotesque comic caricature', added insult to injury by complimenting Judi Dench and Peggy Ashcroft on their method of using their own personalities to illuminate character before settling on Alison Steadman as the ideal example of an actress who is unrecognisable from one part to the next.

Even if this were true, which in Miss Steadman's case it surely is not, the assertion that a performance in the theatre should be as unrelated as possible to the fixed personality of the actor is as tendentious as it is impracticable. But it is a common assertion, and one that has been entered as evidence against many great actors, even those who are palpably 'self-transformers', like Olivier. The charge that an actor is always 'the same' seems to me to be self-evidently crass. The sameness of the actor from role to role is the most obvious thing about him, even if he starts each time with the blank neutrality of Alec Guinness.

As Michael Blakemore says, the making of a remarkable actor depends on the extent to which he is an interesting person in the first place. 'And Maggie is a very sharp, very intelligent, witty lady.' Dull actors are the actors whom you never recognise from one part to another, mainly because you can never tell what they are really like.

The additional trouble with Maggie, of course, is the armoury of her technique. The wrist-flapping and whirring of circles in the air were a part of the comic apparatus that had got her into trouble before. But, as Michael Ratcliffe pointed out, following hard on the heels of her 'marvellous performances in plays by Cocteau and Poliakoff . . . we now know she is acting like this because she wants to and not because she can no longer do anything else.'

Maggie certainly felt the play needed cranking up and worked very hard, every performance, to get it going. But the idea that her gestures and inflections were some random selection of uncontrolled whimsicalities was surely wide of the mark. The play needed her gestural aggrandisement, even if, as John Dexter felt, the opening scenes were feebly superfluous.

There was more of a hectic flurry to Lettice Douffet than to Maggie's stiller comic creations for the simple reason that Lettice was habitually putting on an act to disguise the emptiness within. And she was a frustrated thespian. The irritation quotient stems from the frantic pace of the sculptural gesticulation, which in Maggie's case is executed with the style and precision of a speeded-up Kabuki *onnagata*. The character's nerves are always likely to get on ours.

For this reason Maggie can simply fail to strike on your box, but such is the fate of any performer. She struck on Frank Rich's all right. The *New York Times* critic saw the play in London and guaranteed its safe passage across the Atlantic, hailing 'the camp performance of our time . . . she seems to be Mr Shaffer's sexually ambiguous answer to Auntie Mame, or perhaps his sentimental gloss on the Madwoman of Chaillot.'

Bernard Levin wrote a long letter to Maggie after the opening and she told him later that she had cried. 'This was not affectation,' says Levin. 'I think this wonderful brittle façade she puts up is in fact a sort of protection against her doubts about her quality. She shouldn't have any doubts, but she clearly does have them, to my astonishment, to everyone's astonishment, and that's the softer side of her, the vulnerable side. She had cried because I had told her how very good she was. And I was very touched by that side of her.'

The performance became the talk of the town. Fellow professionals wrote fulsome letters, and John Gielgud, who opened next door at the Apollo in February 1988 in Hugh Whitemore's *The Best of Friends* – almost certainly his last stage appearance – asked Maggie to dine with him one evening, if she was not too tired. He thanked her for some flowers she had sent him and, moved by the extraordinary reception he had received on his own First Night, said that 'now we can rejoice in each other's overflow.'

But Maggie did not feel like doing very much in the way of rejoicing. She found the play as draining as anything she had ever done, and she was not well. The thyroid condition which was eventually diagnosed as Graves' disease caused her acute discomfort. And she had been working on two films, both about alcoholics, one for Jack Clayton and one for BBC television, which had been among the most emotionally exhausting of her career. They had not exactly driven her to drink, but they had certainly pushed her as far as she had ever gone in her screen performances.

Entr'acte: Maggie and a Few Not Too Close Friends

P EOPLE around Maggie tend to move in and out of her favour. Michael Blakemore believes that she does organise the world in terms of friends and foes. Her main support system, of course, is Beverley. Most leading actresses denied the sort of calming, solid back-up Beverley offers gain a reputation as either man-eaters or exquisite solitaries.

'I love her, but she's a killer,' says Patricia Millbourn of the Cadogan Club in Kensington, the hairdresser Maggie has used regularly since the late 1950s. Her other clients include the politician Michael Heseltine, the flame-haired novelist Edna O'Brien, and such classily coiffured American visitors to London as Jackie Onassis and Lee Radziwill.

Millbourn bleached Maggie's hair blonde for her first television role, and went backstage in tears after *What Every Woman Knows* at the Old Vic. 'Oh God, you're 'opeless,' Maggie said. She has collected an Oscar with Maggie and been on holiday several times with her to Barbados. Their ideal routine is to swim miles out to sea, swim back, play Scrabble, read and relax, and enjoy a glass or two of bubbly. But the hair is really what keeps them together:

'She does have one of the most wonderful heads of hair as an actress that I've known. It can be so versatile, short or long, off the face, and she has a great profile. She knows instantly what the hair should be for each part. Other actors study the period, read history books. She gets it in one.'

On the First Night of *Mary Mary*, Millbourn sat in front of the *Times* critic, who said to his companion what a marvellous wig Maggie was wearing. It was her own hair. And every night during *Private Lives*, Maggie would affix her eyelashes and put her hair in Carmen rollers to achieve the Marcel-wave style; either she would go to the shop or Millbourn would come into the theatre.

Similar routines have been undertaken on many plays. Maggie always takes advice from Millbourn before going abroad in a play, or unofficially during film shoots. Before Maggie goes off they normally decide on a wig, in order, as Maggie says, to avoid 'funny 'airdressers in Atlanta'.

At which point the wig and make-up specialist, Kenneth Lintott, is invariably contacted. Lintott, who started his career in 'Wig Cremations' (Coral Browne's term for Wig Creations), was for many years associated with the RSC and did not work with Maggie until she needed wigs for the American tour of *Private Lives* in 1974.

Lintott was introduced to Maggie by the designer Anthony Powell. Tall, willowy and ferociously professional himself, he took an instant shine to Maggie having at first been apprehensive. 'I was knocked out by how beautiful she was. She used to wear horrendous make-up in those days and I'd only ever seen her with all that stuff on. It never suited her at all. But she was divine. And everything about her was tiny: tiny hands, tiny feet, tiny head.'

They got on well. And that, Lintott thought, was that. But then he was asked to Stratford, Ontario, by Maggie and Robin Phillips, to work on her wigs and general 'look'. He regards her stay there as 'her cleansing-out period'. Her previous 'look' had been compounded by all the make-up. Now she had some skin removed from her eyelids – she used to call these pouches her 'shopping bags' – and her make-up was simpler, although Lintott wooed her into a false, built-up nose as Titania. There was nothing 'stuck on' for her Rosalind, and the freckles for Ganymede were based on her son's, little Toby's.

Lintott worked on the films *Quartet*, *The Missionary*, *Evil Under the Sun*, and *The Lonely Passion of Judith Hearne*. On the latter, he says that a lot of the crew found her 'in the role' depressions disconcerting. She was given a blue dress to wear one day. She was not pleased. 'I can't wear this. I look like a sofa in Maples,' she said, and it was changed. Lintott thinks she has a thing about blue. Similarly, in Canada, she referred to a dress provided by Daphne Dare for *Antony and Cleopatra* as 'Daphne's revenge'.

Even closer and warmer than Lintott is Anthony Powell, who first worked with Maggie as costume designer on *Travels With My Aunt* and has never lost touch since. Many colleagues declare that they love Maggie. One or two, including Powell, possibly the film director Jack Clayton and certainly the veterans Joe Mankiewicz and George Cukor, were palpably *in* love with her.

Powell even landed her the role of Wendy, aged ninety-two, in *Hook*. The late Peggy Ashcroft had been cast originally and the producer rang Powell when he (Powell) was in New York to see Dustin Hoffman for fittings. He said, not knowing that Powell was a friend of Maggie's, that Ashcroft had withdrawn with illness and back trouble, and that he had always loved Maggie's work. How old was she now, he enquired? 'Ooh, I dunno,' bluffed Powell, 'she must be in her early nineties by now . . . ninety-one – ninety-two . . .' Maggie was cast.

Although she worked only once each with the great film directors Joe Mankiewicz and George Cukor, both men figured as large as anyone in her private life. Maggie and Beverley were ever-welcome house-guests of Mankiewicz and his wife in New York and Florida. Both directors had plans to work with her more often than they did and nearly ignited a project together of putting Maggie and Marlon Brando opposite one another in *Macbeth*.

Maggie was a replacement on *Travels With My Aunt* for Cukor's all-time favourite Katharine Hepburn, but she made a fresh and indelible impression on the director even though the film they came up with in 1973 was hardly one of Cukor's best. He used to travel up to Stratford, Ontario, to see her classical work there in the late 1970s.

Maggie's obsessive attention to detail carries over into the photography sessions. She will not sit for photographs if she does not feel that everything is absolutely right. And if she can choose her snapper, it will usually be Zoë Dominic, who remembers Maggie cancelling a photo-call because she was dissatisfied with her earrings. 'With any other actor,' says Dominic, 'I would have forced the issue. But with Maggie I would never argue.' She finds her a great subject and a great actress, who is primarily physically funny:

'She is the only actress I know who can walk in one direction and be acting with her head in the reverse direction. I've always found that hysterically funny. She has immense physical grace, which is why I like to catch her on the move. On a bad day – and I try not to photograph her if she's unhappy, or not ready – she shrinks, in face and body. But when she feels good, and that's the ideal time to photograph anyone, she positively blossoms. She looks like a wonderful peach. Whether she's conscious of that or not I don't know. I wouldn't dream of discussing it with her. She's tremendously subtle.'

Maggie, says Dominic, commands loyalty, but never demands it. She probably feels a lot closer to some people than she is capable of indicating. During the time of the boys' growing up, she was very close to her brother Alistair and his wife. But she drifted out of touch with the other brother, Ian, when he moved to New York. Letters were exchanged across the Atlantic, but not very many. Ian thinks the difficulty arose because he had not achieved anything as an architect comparable to what she had achieved as an actress. In other words, he is not Robert Venturi or Michael Graves.

It is almost certain that such a thought never occurred to Maggie. But Ian, for years, felt slightly hurt by the distance she maintained between them. He tried to ring every day during *Private Lives* but never got through. During the entire New York run of *Lettice and Lovage*, he saw her once. Not until their father died peacefully in April 1991, and Ian came over to stay with Maggie and Beverley at Fittleworth for ten days, spending more time with her in that week than he had in the previous twenty years, did he realise that his paranoia was only partly justified. He had profoundly misunderstood his own sister.

'I had been very upset all this time, but now I realised I need not have been. What I had been interpreting as a sort of rejection was in fact just this obsessive reclusiveness which had nothing to do with me. I was shocked when she told me that she found it virtually impossible to eat lunch, that to do so would make her physically ill. And of course Beverley is her gatekeeper, screening all the calls. He really does insulate her from the outside world.'

Angela Fox, mother of all the Foxes (Edward, James and Robert), who calls Maggie 'Mrs Prickly' and not *just* because of Maggie's current Lettice-induced addiction to hedgehogs, recalls meeting Beverley for the first time after the First Night of *Snap* in 1974. She walked arm in arm with Maggie to Rules restaurant in Covent Garden for supper, and Maggie simply said, 'There you are, darling, you see I've come full circle. Bev's the right one for me.'

And he undoubtedly is. Maggie's buried inner life only teasingly suggests her great capacity for emotional and sexual love. How much of this is ever expressed only Beverley knows. But he knows above all when to observe the Do Not Trespass signs around the garden, and that is the secret of his success with her.

Maggie has grown closer to her sons as they have grown older. Toby says that she retains a good deal of unnecessary guilt about their childhood, but both he and Chris agree that she certainly set standards in the house. These are the legacy of her own childhood regimens in Ilford and Oxford.

Chris would not describe her in any way as a disciplinarian. 'But she certainly wasn't a freethinker. And she was very hot on articulation. We were not allowed to slur our words. And every Canadian colloquialism was drilled out of us within three months of coming back here. Above all, I remember this very piercing voice from my childhood: "It's pardon, not what!" And she was fairly rigorous about table manners.'

William Gaskill is one of the small handful of people who ever stay in West Sussex. But, as Chris says, when he is there, he and Maggie hardly ever talk at all. 'He goes off and wanders around, they meet, and so on. There's never anything like catching up with this long-lost friend.' Toby feels 'completely unnerved by Bill; whenever I open my mouth I think I sound like a complete cretin.' The reason Maggie is so comfortable with Gaskill is that he is incapable of dispensing sycophancy or false praise. He told her exactly what he thought of *Lettice and Lovage*. He loathed it.

Most of Maggie's friends, with the possible exception of Robin Phillips and Gaskill, are in some way frightened of her. Brian Bedford feels 'the eagle eye' on him all the time. But, like so many people who see her rarely, he misses her deeply.

Bedford first met Maggie in the late 1950s at a London party and remembers her crouching in a corner talking about her prevailing virginity. He has since, she has told him, often featured in her anxiety dreams, 'sometimes wearing a dress while being terribly well organised and saying "Oh, I've got it all together!" I don't know what the hell it means, but I think it's an aspect of her professional insecurity, that she would think I was not only getting something right but also threatening her own position.'

When Maggie was in New York in *Lettice and Lovage*, Bedford was also in town with his one-man show. Finally she agreed to go out to supper with him – 'it was like pulling teeth' – and Bedford said he would pick her up after the performance. He arrived at her stage door and as Maggie came off to her usual tumultuous applause, she swished past him with 'Did you hear them ovating?' 'Yes,' replied Bedford. 'Did it drive you mad?' stabbed Maggie.

They fell laughing into the dressing room, with a bottle of champagne and a table booked for 11.15. Maggie was ready to relax. More bottles were opened, the stage managers and the doorkeeper were brought in.

Bedford recalls suddenly asking someone for the time. It was five to three in the morning: 'We staggered out, Maggie's car's been waiting, and we disappear into another haze of white wine. I woke up late next morning in need of fresh orange juice. I go to a little hole-in-the-wall place on 57th Street and by this time they are serving lunch and I have to sit at the counter. I'm vaguely aware that some woman next to me is ordering black bean soup. This woman grabs me, and it's Maggie.'

She does surprise her friends all the time, but never with any ploys that are calculated or self-conscious. She once met Bedford's brother and his wife in Stratford. Bedford was astonished to learn, some months later, that she had unexpectedly followed up the idle exchange of telephone numbers by ringing his sister-in-law in Yorkshire and asking for her Yorkshire pudding recipe.

Maggie has never been a great letter-writer. But she does write very occasionally to give her friends fleeting encouragement about herself. After her father died, she wrote to Bedford, who had settled into a new Stratford season in a stable domestic relationship:

'I am glad you are enjoying Stratford. You are quite right. If you are happy on the domestic front, as they say, it makes a huge difference. I was so happy when I was there and that was, now I think about it, the main reason. It was terrific having Bev and the boys with me . . . Pissing down as usual in England. It's so cold even the sheep look wrecked.'

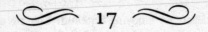

Alone Without God

F OR someone who came from a strict and religious background and who had seriously flirted with the idea of
converting to Roman Catholicism, Maggie's twin portrayal of
ladies disappointed in God, Alan Bennett's Susan in *Bed
Among the Lentils* and Brian Moore's Judith Hearne, drew on
some deep reserves of feeling and confessional anguish. In her
stage and screen work of the 1980s she had demonstrated that
the pathos endemic to her work as a comedienne could be
redistributed as the chief aspect of her acting persona. The
comedy and tears of her earliest revue sketches, tempered by
her years in the classic repertoire, equipped her to play the
modern tragedy of an ordinary woman as well as any other
actress of her day. And she had no qualms about making her
spinsters spinsterish or her married frumps frumpish.

Jack Clayton had wanted to make a film of Brian Moore's
first novel, *The Lonely Passion of Judith Hearne*, for nearly
twenty years. A Catholic himself, Clayton responded profoundly to the novel's portrait of a spinster in conflict with the
sensuality of her own nature, the screen of social desperation
drawn like a mask over the heroine's loneliness and secret
drinking.

He was not the first with aspirations of a dramatic transfer:
in her classic review of Clayton's film, Pauline Kael revealed
that José Quintero had once hoped to stage the story with

Geraldine Page, that John Huston envisaged the screen role for Katharine Hepburn, and that other nearly-Judiths included Rachel Roberts and Deborah Kerr. Nobody had matched the rights and the financing until Clayton, backed by Denis O'Brien of HandMade Films (responsible for *The Missionary* and *A Private Function*), cast Maggie as the impoverished spinster in a skilful and sensible adaptation by Peter Nelson.

Nelson's main innovation was to move the action from Belfast to Dublin, with the consequent loss of one layer of Judith's spiritual alienation in a primarily Protestant community. Like Joyce in Bennett's *A Private Function*, Judith is a part-time piano teacher with hopes of self-improvement. But there is no materialism or dynamism of any sort attached to these hopes. They are merely tickled into something resembling life by the appearance in Judith's boarding house of her landlady's brother, the widower James Madden, played by Bob Hoskins, who has returned to Ireland after thirty years in New York.

This deeply courageous film about escape, dependency and betrayal is possibly the best rebuttal of my own submission that Maggie has often been conservative in her choice of role. There is no hiding place in this portrayal, and no attempt at softening any blows. Maggie's acting is of a complexity and technical perfection unsurpassed by any other British performer of the past twenty years: there is not one single hint of false sentiment, superfluous gesture, inappropriate nasal intonation, swoopingly attenuated diphthongs, wrist acting, brittle evasion or any other of the objections sometimes raised against her.

Another crucial quality, noted by Victoria Mather in the *Daily Telegraph*, is that although Judith Hearne is a withered, drab and nervous figure on the outside, Maggie invests her with 'an inward soul of bright innocence'. Both performance and film are compulsively and irresistibly watchable.

Maggie inspects the characters assembled at the boarding-house breakfast table with more nervousness than when she

beadily contemplated the refined guests in the Florentine pen-
sione in *A Room With A View*. The landlady's son, wonderfully played by the big-bellied RSC actor Ian McNiece, is a
loutish poet, claiming several more years of pampered lodging
at home while he writes his 'masterpiece' and slopes off to
debauch the maid (Rudi Davies) every night.

The agony of eye contact with Bob Hoskins as the returning
prodigal gives way to the most tentative of dimpled smiles
when they make a date to go to church together. Maggie has
to nudge him awake during the sermon and mildly rebukes
him for dressing like a comedian. He has noticed her rings
and, taking them to be a sign of wealth, cruelly arouses Judith's
affection while planning to exploit her as a sponsor for his
hare-brained scheme of starting 'an American eating-place
right in the centre of town'.

He invites her to a movie and a meal. The movie is *Samson
and Delilah* starring Victor Mature, of which Groucho Marx
said, 'No picture can hold my interest when the leading man's
bust is bigger than the leading lady's.'

Judith's world is circumscribed by others' expectations,
notably those of the Church and of Wendy Hiller as a can-
tankerously pious aunt whom she was obliged to nurse after
she suffered a stroke and who continues her mawkish tyranny
over Judith from beyond the grave. Judith has a mobile shrine
of her aunt's photograph and a picture of the Sacred Heart of
Jesus. But the shrine is really a devotional triptych, completed
by the secret bottle.

When she learns that Hoskins's bumptious James Madden
is a fraud with a record of failure and footling menial jobs,
she literally shakes with tears, turns the Sacred Heart to the
wall and sips at her whisky. The camera stays on her
unadorned face of pain for what seems like the time it would
take to say a rosary.

We cut to the physical sweatiness of Hoskins boarding the

landlady's daughter ('just a little fun' is his prelude to a rape) and back again to Maggie clutching her bottle and gibbering a banal song: 'When you're smiling, when you're smiling, the whole world smiles with you.' In the privacy of her room, prayers are followed by alcoholic wipe-out and unconscious reverie on the floor.

Judith begins her descent to the abyss by losing some of her teaching jobs and confessing more than she has dared before to a priest who absolves her, but declines to give her a penance. She embellishes and twists the story of how Madden has proposed to her, clutching a third glass of sherry in a family sitting room, moving just slightly into overdrive, eyes big and absolutely open to the lens and the inquisition of an unseen audience.

With the last of her money, and a bottle in her handbag, she moves into the Shelbourne Hotel. She tells the priest: 'I can't believe any more. I'm all alone . . . I just don't believe God is there any more.' And in the most extraordinary scene of all she runs up the aisle of the church and shouts, 'I hate you' at the tabernacle, repository of the living body of Christ.

In a nursing home, surrounded by white linen and the white habits of Carmelite nuns, Maggie's Judith acquires the mad and powerful radiance of Lady Macbeth sleepwalking, of Lucia di Lammermoor singing her mournful aria and of Mary Tyrone riding high on her sweet powders in the last scene of *Long Day's Journey Into Night*. (Is it possible Maggie might one day play this role on stage, with Robert Stephens as her husband and their two sons as their two sons?) Her hair is plaited on one side of her face, her two holy pictures to hand: 'They always make a new place home.'

Madden pays a visit. He now has a job as a van driver, after a sojourn in Donegal on a little business venture that didn't work out. At last, he proposes marriage to Judith, adding the disastrous rider that she must have some money after all, as he found out that she had stayed in the Shelbourne.

When Judith later leaves the home, she hands a crumpled piece of paper to the taxi driver on which is written Madden's address. The camera once again lingers, searching for clues, anxious to know if, at last, this is to be the really brand-new start she deserves. But Maggie's taut mask, frankly lined with a history of disappointment, is giving nothing away.

The film was shot very quickly, in seven weeks, and Maggie was in almost every shot. Jack Clayton recalls that her concentration was unbelievably intense. She stayed in a different hotel from everyone else in Dublin, not to be awkward, but to concentrate on the loneliness.

There was, however, something temperamentally suited to Maggie about Judith's condition and she submerged herself in the role with relish. Clayton says she hardly took advantage of the dialect coach provided, but her accent is, as usual, spot on and faultlessly maintained.

The same cannot quite be said for Bob Hoskins's blustery Madden; he tackles the role like a rampant rugby player, diving in energetically and not all that convincingly as an Irish American. But his charm and emotional sincerity come through and he much enjoyed working with Maggie for the first time: 'What surprised me is Maggie's so generous. You think a talent of that quality would swamp you a bit. She doesn't.' Hoskins was also convinced that she would win her third Oscar: 'I think [the performance] will put another fellow on Maggie's shelf.'

Although Maggie was honoured with Best Actress awards from BAFTA and the *Evening Standard*, the film was never considered at the Oscars and its distribution was scandalously limited. Why? The matter still rankles with Jack Clayton and points up the dangers inherent in the monopoly system of screen ownership.

Judith Hearne was premièred in New York in December

1987, but did not reach London until exactly one year later. It was held up by a dispute between HandMade and Cannon, the distributors, over debts on another film. The dispute meant that Cannon dropped the film and it therefore found only limited showing in three independent London houses. And in America, a small company handling the distribution failed to provide copies of the film to the Academy membership voting for the Oscars and subsequently went into receivership.

Maggie seemed not to be bothered. As usual, all her concern had been focused on the work itself. Clayton confirms that she is unaware of where the camera is, unlike some of the old Hollywood stars, like Joan Crawford, who knew where every lens and light was stationed, and that she therefore trusts the director to an unusual degree. She never looks at rushes and indeed rarely watches the finished film. She is reluctant to join the publicity circus, as reluctant as the most difficult of donkeys being led to market.

Clayton knows that Maggie's 'difficulty' is not an affectation. 'I've worked with a lot of actors who didn't like doing publicity, but they always did it when asked on behalf of the film. Maggie is the only one who won't. But it's not just that. I've never seen her at a party. I usually have drinks on my sets every Friday and I used to have to really persuade her to come. Once she was there, of course, she enjoyed herself as much as anyone.'

Clayton admits that he admires her as much as any of the great actresses he has directed: Simone Signoret in *Room at the Top*, Deborah Kerr in *The Innocents* or Anne Bancroft in *The Pumpkin Eater*.

'She's not impossible, she's an angel. She needs very little direction except reining her in sometimes. I just love her. She can be very tetchy in the morning and I do know that she ran the wardrobe ladies on *Judith Hearne* a pretty dance. She is pernickety. But she is always right in the demands she makes, which is the difference between Maggie and people who are just awkward for the sake of it. She is unbelievably professional, and unbelievably instinctive. She is top of my list.'

Bed Among the Lentils is a close companion piece to *Judith Hearne*. So close, it nearly overlapped in the shooting. Maggie went straight from one to the other, losing a week's holiday in between because of a slight hold-up on Clayton's film. This meant that she had to learn the new script during the first week of rehearsals.

'She was pretty exhausted,' remembers Alan Bennett, the author who was also the director, 'but that turned out to be no bad thing, really. I didn't have much to do. She did it the first time just as she did straight on the screen. I was bothered that she might slightly camp it up, but she didn't at all. She's got very good taste. There's a bit at the end where she lets her voice break when she's talking about the affair she's had, but she does it without any self-pity. It's just wonderful and I think she did that on the last day of rehearsal, and then she did it on the take, but she fluffed the final line so we had to do it again and I was frightened to tell her, really. But she did it again, and in the end we used the first take anyway and lived with the fluff because the first take was better.'

Maggie's solo was one of six monologues by Bennett, produced by the late Innes Lloyd, which went out under the generic title of 'Talking Heads'. Bennett himself delivered one of them, as a mother-fixated adult bachelor. Other studies in loneliness, compromise and bafflement were entrusted to four superb actresses – Thora Hird, Julie Walters, Stephanie Cole and Patricia Routledge.

Each character was poised between black-outs in a purgatorial state of reflective isolation. And the impulse behind each monologue was a desire to make something of recent events, or at least to explain them to anyone who might listen.

Bennett's style is too idiomatic, inflected and poetically

entranced with the material detail of ordinary life to be totally bleak. But there was something Beckettian about these cries from the genteel suburban wilderness. Life had been tested, ever so quietly, and found to be wanting. Beckett with knitting, place-mats and doilies.

In his introduction to the published texts, Bennett wrote:

'Though much of the church stuff in *Bed Among the Lentils* (including Mr Medlicott the verger) comes from my childhood, the disaffection of Susan, the vicar's wife, I can trace to opening a hymn book in the chapel of Giggleswick School and finding in tiny, timid letters on the fly leaf, "Get lost, Jesus."'

Maggie's Susan was suspended between seething resentment and a sort of bursting sexual anger. She glared and vibrated like a terribly cross stick insect. The first line said it all, but there was plenty more to follow: 'Geoffrey's bad enough, but I'm glad I wasn't married to Jesus.'

With bold, descriptive strokes, and bolstered by Maggie's perfectly pitched, almost sarcastic delivery, the sanctimonious life of a village parish and its boyishly good-looking, ambitious young vicar, Geoffrey, was painted by Bennett in the first few paragraphs.

In this first of five pungent little ten-minute scenes, Maggie's hair is severe, her make-up non-existent, her head tilted slightly into the camera. She is as spare and scrubbed as her own kitchen table. She lets slip that she spends a lot at the off-licence. She is despondently out of kilter with the smug little world she describes and is animated by expatiating on its deadliness.

Next, we see her in the church, on the steps of a side-chapel, wearing a brown coat and polishing a candlestick. She is describing a lunch she and Geoffrey have given to the visiting bishop: 'Disaster strikes as I'm doling out the tinned peaches.' Escape from the suffocation of serving as a wifely appendage is afforded by the regular trip to a little Indian shop behind the infirmary in Leeds. The owner is called Mr Ramesh and he sells everything.

In the third scene, Maggie is at first standing in the kitchen near the Aga and then sitting down and leaning on her elbow, to the left, on a towel rail. Slightly more akimbo, her comic pulse races as she lays into the kind of activity she herself should have pursued as a member of the Women's Institute. Jam-making. And flower-arranging. 'If you think squash is a competitive activity, try flower arrangement.'

She anatomises the show of 'forest murmurs' arranged by Mrs Shrubsole on the altar and recounts how she proves its threat to human well-being by kneeling down and falling over, banging her head on the Communion rail. Later that night she drives into Leeds and Mr Ramesh shuts up shop and takes off his clothes.

It is in a state of reasonable intoxication, on an improvised bed among sacks of lentils, and largely thanks to twenty-six-year-old Mr Ramesh, who has wonderful legs and a child bride waiting for him in India, that Susan, on the second Sunday after Trinity, discovers 'what all the fuss is about'. By this fourth scene in the vestry, Geoffrey's loyal parishioners, 'the fan club', are on red alert: the Communion wine has all gone! Susan is now reduced to knocking back the Benylin and driving more regularly into Leeds for physical consolation with Mr Ramesh.

In the final tableau, Susan has signed up with Alcoholics Anonymous, starchly attired in a suit, blouse and respectable brooch. But 'Geoffrey's chum', the deity, can take credit for this, too. Susan and her plight are brandished as further evidence of Geoffrey's case for ecclesiastical advancement. From being a fly in the ointment, she has graduated to being a feather in his cap. Mr Ramesh has gone home to collect his child bride and is rumoured to be setting up a new shop in

Preston. Although Maggie's eyes are filled with tears, she has all but frozen over with fierce anger and her imprisonment is complete.

It is this glacial surface, rippling with animosity, tension, pain and frustration, that makes the acting so profound and moving in both *Judith Hearne* and *Bed Among the Lentils*. To an extent, these are self-immolating performances just held in control by sheer technique and the sustained effort, over the whole arc of a role, to let us see straight through to the soul of a benighted but resilient human being.

Maggie's full comic armoury serves this purpose, lending sharp edge and clear, high definition to the tragic expression. The characters are never indulged and the actress never wallows. There is nothing random or vague about Judith's or Susan's state of mind. The process Maggie describes is one of truthful, clinical disintegration and the residual but wholly rational manner in which the human spirit rallies to defy the rampant claims of the abyss.

These performances are majestic and beautiful because they celebrate human dignity in conditions of weakness and stress. Maggie had her own share of weakness and stress. After playing at the Globe in *Lettice and Lovage* for a year, she went on holiday with Beverley and Joan Plowright before the planned opening in New York. At Albert Finney's recommendation, they all went to the British Virgin Islands, and the fateful accident occurred on 29 November 1988 when Joan Plowright left early to return to the ailing Lord Olivier in Brighton. Returning from making her farewells on a bicycle, Maggie rounded a bend, came off the road and the bicycle, fell over a smallish escarpment and landed on her shoulder in a prickly bush.

She had splintered the top of her shoulder, and the slow and painful recovery entailed physiotherapy, long daily swims at the Goodwood country club, exercises and a good deal of patience. At the same time, her eyes were causing serious problems – to deal with them, she underwent surgery and a course of radiotherapy.

This period of adjustment was also marked by Olivier's final decline and his death on 11 July 1989. Maggie emerged from her gruesome regimen of recovery, and from deepest Sussex, to attend his memorial in Westminster Abbey on 20 October.

Her eyes were concealed behind great sunglasses and she cut a figure of stylish anonymity in a black and white checked coat, a black skirt and a wide-brimmed black hat. She joined a select band of leading actors associated with Olivier's career who processed slowly up the central aisle carrying mementos and symbols on blue velvet cushions, depositing them on the main altar before resuming their places in the nave.

Douglas Fairbanks carried Olivier's Order of Merit, followed by Michael Caine with an Oscar, Peter O'Toole with the *Hamlet* film script and Ian McKellen with Coriolanus's laurel wreath. Maggie walked slowly alongside Paul Scofield, he bearing a silver model of the new National Theatre and she a similar emblem representing the Chichester Festival Theatre; 'Not the first time she's carried Chichester on her own, dear,' Jack Tinker was heard to remark. Dorothy Tutin bore the crown Olivier wore as King Lear on television, Derek Jacobi the one he had worn on stage as Richard III.

Frank Finlay brought up the rear with Edmund Kean's *Richard III* sword, a gift from Sir John Gielgud to his old sparring partner which more vividly than anything else symbolised the direct succession from Shakespeare, through Garrick and Kean, to Sir Henry Irving and Lord Olivier.

Albert Finney read from Ecclesiastes, Sir John Mills from Corinthians, Dame Peggy Ashcroft the last thirty lines of Milton's *Lycidas* ('At last he rose, and twitched his mantle blue / Tomorrow to fresh woods and pasture new'). And

Gielgud himself, looking frail after recent illness, shook his fist at death in John Donne's 'Holy Sonnet' and Hamlet's 'We defy augury' speech. Sir Alec Guinness gave a twinkling, dispassionate address in which he described the threat of danger that clung to Olivier, both on stage and off: 'There were times when it was wise to be wary of him.'

Maggie was seated between her Sussex neighbour Scofield and her one-time film partner Michael Caine, who had gained the friendship and respect of Maggie on *California Suite* and of Olivier on the filming of Anthony Shaffer's *Sleuth*. An even more unlikely conjunction in Olivier's later career had been formed with Cliff Richard in a West End musical called *Time*, produced by former pop star Dave Clark, in which the great actor took the shape of a disembodied hologram.

This cultural connection was lost on the hapless BBC television commentator, David Dimbleby, whose pointless remark 'And there's Dave Clark, of the Dave Clark Five' struck a note of toe-curling broadcast banality thankfully spared those present in the abbey.

Maggie stood sadly among her peers and colleagues, joining in the singing of 'Jerusalem' at the end. She and Beverley attended the post-ceremonial thrash hosted by Joan Plowright in the upper foyers of the National Theatre. Many actors and backstage people have no recollection of seeing Maggie at this party.

For while old acquaintance was being hectically renewed around her, Maggie sat quietly in a corner talking to a very close and very ill friend of Peter Shaffer. The friend has subsequently died, but Shaffer says that he will never forget the tenderness and sympathy Maggie unfussily evinced during this painful period of his life.

Maggie's own powers of recovery amazed her sons. Toby says that, when his mother went back to see her doctors after a few months of physiotherapy and swimming for two hours every day, 'Their teeth fell out. They couldn't believe it. Most younger people, if they have that injury, just learn to live with the fact that they can't move their shoulders any more. She can now move her shoulder around better than I can. And I've never fallen off my bike.'

She was determined to go to New York with *Lettice and Lovage*. Maggie could face a new start in better health as Dame Maggie Smith: she was secretly delighted, and relieved, to be remembered by the Prime Minister's office one year after Judi Dench had been similarly honoured. On 25 March 1990 she opened in New York at the Ethel Barrymore, the theatre she had first played in *New Faces* in 1956.

In New York, she took up residence in the Wyndham Hotel on the west side of 58th Street. Lettice reduced her to a state of terminal exhaustion and she did not stint on a single performance. The result was that the gradual process of recovery from her other misfortunes – which were further complicated by some root-canal problems with her teeth – was compounded by galloping fatigue. She became more reclusive than Garbo, supping bowls of soup in the hotel suite and only occasionally venturing out of town at weekends to visit Joe Mankiewicz and his wife, and occasionally Hume Cronyn and Jessica Tandy.

Frank Rich hailed 'a spellbinding actress' and drew a distinction between this theatre acting 'of a high and endangered order' and the same actress's 'tightly minimalised film work'.

The Biograph Cinema in New York honoured Maggie with a festival of her films in April, and she and Margaret Tyzack triumphed at the Tonys on the first Sunday in June. Two weeks later, on 18 June, Maggie attended another memorial service, this time for Rex Harrison, at New York's Church of the Transfiguration. The glittering congregation included Douglas Fairbanks, Claudette Colbert, Zoë Caldwell and Kitty Carlisle Hart.

Harrison had been one of the first big stars she had met on

her first trip to New York in 1956, and, although she had only worked with him once, she belonged to the same aristocracy of talent. Maggie's address complemented those of Harrison's two sons and of Brendan Gill.

As one who had successfully battled against being pigeon-holed, Maggie rightly lamented the fact that we never saw Harrison in Molière or Shakespeare, claiming, surely with justification, that 'he would have been wonderful as Tartuffe, Prospero or King Lear.' Unconsciously, she confirmed the kinship of temperament in those who specialise in the rare, demanding skills of light comedy:

'A man of charm, affection and wit . . . but his charm was often not evident offstage [laughter was reported] . . . He was not one to suffer fools gladly, whether it was his director or an overbearing leading lady . . . [He] gave every line, every thought, every movement, a bit of magic.'

She had started her eventful imbroglio with *Lettice and Lovage* just three weeks after finishing work on *Judith Hearne* and *Bed Among the Lentils*. Both roles had left her feeling raw, she told an interviewer in the *Los Angeles Times*. 'I'd got so absorbed, and it doesn't go away from you.'

She took a long time to get the rawness out of her system, and the feeling was one she said she had never known before. She was ready for anything. She told another interviewer: 'I wouldn't want to retire. I am·sure there is something to do, even if it be a wardrobe mistress . . . I take things day by day. You can't plan. You hope.'

Innocence and Experience

A SLIGHTLY alarming development in Maggie's career has been the extent to which she has played old ladies before her time. She stuck out against so doing right at the start, when Leonard Sillman was unwise enough to foist some doddery dowagers on her during the pre-Broadway try-out of *New Faces*. But after the blazing directness of her tragic performances in *The Lonely Passion of Judith Hearne* and *Bed Among the Lentils*, Maggie aged prematurely as the ninety-two-year-old Wendy Angela Darling in Steven Spielberg's Hollywood blockbuster *Hook* and as the seventy-three-year-old but well-tended housekeeper Mrs Mabel Pettigrew in the BBC television adaptation of Muriel Spark's *Memento Mori*.

Hook is the ultimate Spielberg film in that it combines the director's twin obsessions: the glorification of childhood innocence in middle-class Middle America with an application of those homey backyard values to the world of wistful adventure; *ET* meets *Indiana Jones*. Glutinous and often torridly spectacular, the Spielberg films nonetheless amount to a significant strand in the American popular culture at a time when environmental pollution, urban violence and poverty, and the general moral degradation of political and public life demand some sort of compensating reply from art and literature.

The collapse of family life is especially exploited by Spielberg. The tragedy of adulthood, as Spielberg is not the first to observe, is the sacrifice we make of our childishness. In *Hook*, Maggie in the relatively peripheral role of Wendy, her large beseeching eyes daubed on her crinkled face like liquid pools of memory, lays down a single rule in her London house: 'No growing up.'

Peter Pan has forgotten his childhood and, in the shape of the impish Robin Williams as Peter Banning, has matured into a forty-year-old New York mergers and acquisitions lawyer, with a wife, two children, and a cellular phone. The family comes to London – by Pan Am, of course – Williams wrestling with his fear of flying, to see Wendy after a ten-year gap. Peter has married her grand-daughter in a desire for parenthood. But he takes calls during his daughter's school play (a pleasingly gauche performance of *Peter Pan*) and misses his son's key baseball game (he sends along an office colleague with a video camera).

The film opens directly into this contemporary scenario, with no credits and no fanfare. The sense of 'other-worldliness', the familiar Spielberg element of the light on the other side of the window, has an obvious significance in this case. Maggie provides the first shiver when she appears at the top of the stairs, rather like Judith Anderson as Mrs Danvers in *Rebecca*, as Peter and his family arrive: transfigured in the half-light, dignified by age and a walking stick, she intones 'Hello, boy' with the sinister implication of one claiming rights of possession.

When Peter tells her of his busy commercial life in New York, the sadness in Maggie's eyes is briefly enlivened with a twinkling regret: 'So, you've become a pirate.' The tension gathers at a grand dinner in aid of the Great Ormond Street Hospital (the beneficiary of J. M. Barrie's *Peter Pan* royalties) at which Wendy is honoured for her lifetime's work of rehabilitating orphans. One such was Peter, who makes the keynote, moving speech.

This tribute is similar to that afforded Coral Browne as the very old Alice Liddell in Gavin Lambert's *Alice in Wonderland* postscript, *Dreamchild*. Wendy has no chance to reply before the fictional underworld rises frighteningly to reassert its claims on reality. As the ranks of fellow orphans stand emotionally in gratitude to toast their maternal saviour, the windows are flung open in a terrifying blast and the howling rage of the invisible Captain Hook disrupts the self-congratulatory equilibrium. Back at the London house, the children have been snatched and a kidnapper's note is piratically stabbed with a knife to the nursery door.

Wendy now tells Peter that he must return to Neverland and make himself remember. The quest is not just to recapture his children, but to recapture his own childhood. The whole premise of Barrie's play has been turned around. Initially, *Peter Pan* is concerned with a child's defiance of the real world of domestic security in favour of imaginary escapism and the excitement of a brush with the forces of pantomime evil; but even there, Wendy becomes for Peter a potential surrogate mother figure.

Ever since the play's first performance in 1904 the role of Pan was taken by an actress. Maggie herself played it in London in 1973. In America, Eva Le Gallienne and Mary Martin, and latterly Cathy Rigby, are particularly associated with the role. The idea of restoring Peter's masculinity was that of the Royal Shakespeare Company in 1982, when the stage production by Trevor Nunn and John Caird (the middle leg of their great RSC humanist narrative epics, propped either side by *Nicholas Nickleby* and *Les Misérables*) overturned the travesty tradition, the fey schmaltziness, and took on board the post-Barrie Freudian travel baggage.

Spielberg and his writers (Jim V. Hart, Nick Castle and Malia Scotch Marmo) update and appropriate the story for contemporary America while retaining the crucial RSC escapist stage muscularity. Some American critics complained that the Neverland sequences are like a huge musical without numbers, and that, according to Roger Ebert of the *Chicago Sun-Times*, 'the cluttered rag-and-bone shop of art direction' contains 'too many characters, too many props, too many signs, too many costumes, bad traffic direction, and no sense of space or place'.

The fantasy island and the huge dry-docked *Jolly Roger* are the creations of John Napier, who was the RSC designer on all the Nunn/Caird collaborations, including *Peter Pan*. His movie Neverland is indeed a cluttered theme park with skate-board circuits, food-pelting competitions, secret caves, a lagoon populated by seductive mermaids, and a general air of a Duke of Edinburgh Award scheme assault course. Tom Sawyer's island as an outpost Disneyworld. The tribal hair-styles, costumes and smart rap patois – Williams asks if this is a *Lord of the Flies* pre-school – also relate to another influential Nunn/Napier stage production, *Starlight Express*.

This is a way of Spielberg cutting into the youth culture. But it is also a means of taking the make-believe not towards the dreamy, timeless inconsequentiality of Barrie's escapism, but to the tougher, stagebound pantomime conventions of the play itself. Julia Roberts's seven-inch Tinkerbell, a leggy, *gamine* sex object in a ball of light, gives Peter a tough old time, knocking him out, urging him on, before briefly emerging in full womanly dimensions to plant a lascivious kiss on his lips. This pricks the sides of Pan's intent – the Happy Thought which Tinkerbell has bullied him to rekindle is one which ironically defeats her and renders her devotion tragic: Peter wanted to be a father.

His paternity suit is further spruced up by the sight of his son hitting a home run in a baseball game supervised by Hook, who has decided to defer the death sentence in favour of assuming the father role himself. 'That's my boy,' Hook sighs contentedly as the child biffs the ball into the stratosphere. And the staginess of these central episodes is certainly reinforced by Dustin Hoffman's magnificent bravura performance as Hook. Variously likened by the critics to Charles II, Terry-Thomas, William F. Buckley Jr, Basil Rathbone, Captain Morgan on the rum bottle, and every King Louis, Hoffman's gap-toothed, laboriously posh-vowelled rollicking swordsman with a gleaming silver mitt is the ultimate cultural revenge on generations of English actors both flaunting their educated manners in Hollywood and adopting phoney American accents on the stage. Bob Hoskins, delightful as Smee, is Hook's sidekick, waxing his master's twirly moustaches with the contents of his own ear-drums.

The grotesque, Herod-like obscenity of Hook's campaign – Barrie's 1928 re-write included the chilling line 'A holocaust of children, there is something grand in the idea!' – is missing, perhaps, but Hoffman has never been funnier. He may not actually cry out 'Floreat Etona' but he is certainly blooming eaten when time runs out and a concealed crocodile finally swallows him up.

The final, reinforcing message of the film, and a slightly depressing one, is that families are better off staying together because the alternative really is less desirable. More fun, but inadequate to our emotional needs. Wendy's home in London may be cosy and reassuring; but Neverland, threatened by the gruff nastiness of Hook and his crew, is not only dangerous, but depressingly artificial. This may be an unwitting point Spielberg is making, but it amounts to the final overall effect, especially when taken in conjunction with the relentlessly tedious soundtrack devised by John Williams.

Maggie pops up again halfway through in the flashback sequence of Peter's marriage into the family. She is too old to fly herself any more. And she glimmers effectively at the end, taking on the semblance of a softer version of Wendy Hiller, as the family is reunited and Peter Banning throws away his telephone with a sign-off re-write of Pan's most famous line: 'To *live* will be an awfully big adventure.' By living, we now mean spending time with the kids. The frank emotional vulgarity of the film is one of its greatest strengths, and the class of Maggie's acting is an important factor. But you could hardly say she was anything like extended. She is far less strenuously made up than she was for Aunt Augusta in *Travels*. She adopts a slight lisp for the older voice, but otherwise understates the whole process of elderly impersonation, leaving her eyes to do the talking.

In *Memento Mori*, although playing an aged character in Muriel Spark's vigorous and black 1959 mystery comedy of senility and gerontology, Maggie did not have to obliterate herself so much. Mabel Pettigrew is old, but she is less old than most of the other characters dotted around London and tucked up in the Maud Long Medical Ward for female last gaspers. Mabel has a good figure and good legs still, luxuriant and well-cut hair, a well-dressed and confident manner, and the constitution of a horse.

To these attributes Maggie adds a deadly appropriate cutting edge and twinkle as the manipulative blackmailer in a world of ancient and festering liaisons thrown into confusion by the telephone calls of an anonymous agent of mortality. She keeps her own red hair, swept up, and presents Mabel as a woman much nearer her own age, a sexy sixty-year-old, conveying only hints of senescence in the pinching of her mouth, the acquisition of reading spectacles and the sour, grim demeanour of the terminally disappointed. Cut out of a former employer's will when she expected to inherit the lot, she is told there is £50 in her name: '£50? I spent about that much on her sodding wreath!'

Renewing her professional liaison with director Jack Clayton, Maggie leads a magnificent cast – Renée Asherson, Cyril

Cusack, Michael Hordern, Thora Hird, Stephanie Cole, Zoë Wanamaker and John Wood among them – in a buoyant festival of mortality which the BBC had the unexpected wit to broadcast to the nation on Easter Sunday, the Feast of the Resurrection. In fact, Clayton and his fellow screenplay writers, Alan Kelley and Jeanie Sims, perpetrate some crucial adjustments to Spark in the name of narrative coherence, and lead to a point of positive conclusion that is their own. Clayton, no spring chicken himself at seventy, wished to acknowledge what the retired detective inspector Henry Mortimer (John Wood) calls the 'stubborn gallantry' of this extraordinary collection of confused Edwardian relics.

The community of oldsters is rocked by the calls ('Remember you must die') and summons the inspector to investigate. The first, and most spooked, recipient is Dame Lettie Colston (Stephanie Cole) whose brother Godfrey (Michael Hordern) is married to the novelist Charmian (Renée Asherson). Dame Lettie seeks solace and clues from Charmian's old housekeeper, Jean Taylor (Thora Hird), now serenely domiciled in the Maud Long Medical Ward.

The catalyst of anxiety and exploitation is Mabel, who tightens a tyrannical grip on Godfrey not only because she knows about his past affairs but also because she knows that a glimpse of stocking is, in his case, an effective method of subjugation. Clayton's film relishes the black humour of senility – the precarious motorcar driving of Godfrey, the tea-time mayhem caused by Cyril Cusack's enraged and doddery old poet, the amnesia, narcolepsy and general decrepitude – but also celebrates the poetry of survival, the flickering spark of sensual appetite. By overcoming the interference of Mabel, and of Godfrey's sponging second-rate homosexual novelist son Eric (Peter Eyre), and by finally refusing to answer the sinister telephone calls, Charmian and Godfrey are indeed renewed in loving partnership. And the defiance of old age is complete when Jean Taylor comes out of hospital to visit Charmian as a friend, not as a dependent employee.

The brutal murder of Lettie by an unidentified intruder is a stark reminder of the novel's naggingly prescient analysis of the perils of old age in the modern world. But the murder is also pinned by Clayton on a new character, though not one essential to the plot. And Spark's investigative gerontologist, Alec Warner, is obliterated, with elements of his function grafted, quite successfully, on to John Wood's engagingly bemused and inquisitive retired Lancastrian inspector. These are clever and sensible adjustments.

Memento Mori is a richly macabre, stunningly well acted and beautifully crafted film (the lighting, costumes and overall pace are evidence of a governing technical perfection) in which Maggie's Mabel Pettigrew is a captious, lurid villainess, deeply disturbing because her performance goes deliberately against the film's grain of generosity and humour. She epitomises all those who take advantage of the old and weak, perhaps the most despicable of all sinners. Her vowels are mean and common and her campaign one of undiluted viciousness and spite. She fills the house with gas in order to threaten the employment of the cook (Elizabeth Bradley). She fiddles the figures in the housekeeping ledgers. She sighs in impatient exhalations of tetchiness and distaste at each sign of disintegration and decay. She is fighting off her own decline by exploiting and anathematising that of everyone around her. Whereas the old poet's grand-daughter (Zoë Wanamaker) shows Godfrey her stocking tops in a spirit of pity and understanding, Maggie's Mabel traps the old boy like a fly in her web, leading him downstairs with a look of vindictive and petrifying triumph.

It is one of Maggie's tautest and funniest performances, but it thrives especially because of the company it keeps. At the start of her career, Maggie was a comedienne who surprised people by wandering into the murkier tragic waters of Desdemona, Hilde Wangel and Hedda Gabler. In Canada, she had synthesised her comic and tragic elements in a buoyant and idiosyncratic style of high-tension performance flecked with emotional truth and perception. She had matured into a great all-round actress. And she could now play extravagant boulevard comedy and concentrated tragedy with equal fervour and panache.

On the threshold of her fifth decade in showbusiness, Maggie has concentrated of late on the sterner side of her talent, the technically rigorous and reined-in, the mask of optimism, or joy, or kindliness, that screens the inner turmoil. There is another side, the direct, effusive, overspilling buoyancy of her acting which has perhaps been untapped since her sojourn in Canada with Robin Phillips. How to unleash this again? The British theatre is entitled to witness her Arkadina, her Judith Bliss, her Lady Bracknell. These roles bring out her inimitably acidulous nature as a comic performer. The full blast of spiritual magnanimity is something we associate more these days with Vanessa Redgrave. Perhaps, in the next ten years, we might see Christopher Hampton, or Tom Stoppard, or Timberlake Wertenbaker write a role that will stretch her to the limit once again while providing her with lines she can dance and forage among, as in Congreve and Shakespeare. The very worst thing that could happen would be for Maggie to curl up prematurely and disappear inside Lady Wishfort and other old bags of the elderly actress's repertoire. She may never believe in her own physical beauty and intellectual distinction; but that is no reason why the rest of us should be deprived of them.

One of Ilford's other performing sons, Ken Campbell, has extrapolated in his latest monodrama, *Pigspurt*, the two sides of his acting persona in the Jungian sense of conflicting archetypes: the kindly housewife and the spanking squire. Maggie, too, has a soft side and a brutal side, and throughout her career she has brought the one into play against the other. This tension is what characterises her performances in tragedy as much as in comedy. William Gaskill admired her lightness and effervescence, John Dexter her steely backbone; the clown of Oxford revue and *Black Comedy* endured the fire of the classical disciplines, as well as the emotional upheavals of her own private life, to find the sad heartbeat of Judith Hearne and the plaintive resilience of Alan Bennett's alcoholic vicar's wife. She could blaze in glittering merriment as Congreve's Millamant, in fierce splendour as Cocteau's Jocasta, in a cascade of sparkling eccentricity as Shaffer's Lettice Douffet.

John Wood, working with Maggie on *Memento Mori* for the first time since their salad days in the OUDS *Twelfth Night* in an Oxford college garden, said that she had not changed at all. She is recognisably the same talented, funny and attractive girl who broke hearts and burrowed conscientiously into the centre of each role she played. Whatever satisfaction Maggie Smith gains from her acting, the spiritual rewards are transitory and rarely savoured.

The cast and production team of *Memento Mori* gathered at the British Academy of Film and Television Arts in Piccadilly in March 1992 to see the first screening of their work with Jack Clayton and the producer Louis Marks. There were drinks beforehand, drinks afterwards and a high-decibel level of animated conversation, greeting and reunion. The film, a long-cherished project of Jack Clayton, had been an exceptionally happy one for all concerned. Lady Antonia Fraser, the Oxford aristocrat who rode her bicycle while Margaret swept up and made tea in the Playhouse, sat between Sir Michael Hordern and her husband Harold Pinter. Clayton's film-maker best friend Karel Reisz was there, so were most of the actors,

and an impressive array of leading film bigwigs and tech-
nicians.

By not attending the BAFTA screening, Maggie was not
preserving her top-billing status but merely being true to form.
She could not even contemplate the torture of sitting through
the film and her own performance. It was bad enough having
to while away the time between dawn and dusk at home in
West Sussex. As the country prepared for a General Election
and as various leading entertainers ludicrously followed the
American example of declaring their allegiances, Maggie sat
back and disparagingly contemplated the whole sorry spectacle.

Acting, she knew, though she would never say such a thing,
was more interesting and mysterious than the self-deluding
vanities of politicians and their hangers-on. To describe it,
discuss it, or use the reputation won by it to promote a cause
or a politician, is, to her, the biggest betrayal of all. Her personal style, however, though critical, has never been censori-
ous. Her amusement at the follies of others was ever a trick to
compensate for the inflexible standards and recurring sense of
disappointment with which she has been afflicted from the
start.

Where the next work was coming from she was not entirely
sure. But the boys were both well and seemingly poised on the
brink of notable careers of their own. And, most importantly of
all, Beverley was by her side to answer the telephone, reply to
letters, to cheer, encourage and cajole, and to quietly close
the door against all unwanted and potentially embarrassing
intrusions.

Postlude in Earnest

I N the middle of January 1992, in the heart of West Sussex, Maggie was sitting at home and reading. She was well, rested and relaxed for the first time in several years. *Hook* had opened before Christmas in America and its fate was of no particular concern to the actress. She had finished filming on *Sister Act* with Whoopi Goldberg in Los Angeles and Reno, and that was not really worth talking about.

A decision had been taken not to go ahead after all this year with *The Importance of Being Earnest*. The vague plan of producer Robert Fox had been that Terry Hands, the former boss of the RSC, would direct Maggie as Lady Bracknell in the West End and move the show to Broadway in September. Maggie now didn't 'feel right' about it and so the production was not so much shelved, nor even placed on the back burner, as left simmering on 'the middle burner'.

So what next? Maggie must have at least ten, probably fifteen, good working years ahead. She stretches out in her black trousers and top, black boots, copper silk and wool scarf, at ease in her sitting room. The only immediate prospect is of the clear, cold days of this January, and then a three-week February holiday with Beverley in Florida as guests of the ever-hospitable and devoted Joe Mankiewicz and his wife. Not only that: Maggie has given up smoking, for the second time in her life.

Any chance of going back to the National Theatre?

'I just wish the building wasn't such an unfriendly place to work.'

No more Cleopatras?

'Oooh, no. I'm glad I had a go.'

Do you wish someone would write a new play for you?

'Yes, but I never know what to wear in new plays. I spend most of my time on stage and on film, come to that, dressed in costumes. I'm baffled by what to wear in modern dress on stage.'

You have done so many different things in your career.

'That's because people didn't know where to put me. They thought of me in revue, but I did want to *act*. And the age thing was easier then. Nobody minded if you were too old for a part. I'm too old for most things now. I think I'm even too old for Lady Bracknell.'

So, no plans?

'I never know what to do next.'

Are you going to the royal première of *Hook* in April?

'Not unless I really have to. They're just embarrassing, really, premières. I'd quite like to see *Hook*, though. It would be easy to shut my eyes at the bits where I'm on the screen. Hardly have to blink, really.'

Were you nervous at Toby's First Night in *Tartuffe*?

'Very. The whole business is horrendous for actors, and also for everyone in the audience who is nervous for them. You can't stop it, can you?'

Toby comes in to pick up the newspapers. *Tartuffe* closed last Saturday and he and his girlfriend, Jennifer Ehle, who played Elmire, are staying down for a few days. I suspect that Maggie is even more relaxed with her sons around. Chris has gone abroad with the drama school. 'He's on tour,' explains Maggie, 'in Holland.' This sounds funnier than it should.

We are all going for lunch to a nearby pub that serves fish

to general acclaim. It has just won a prize. Beverley, who does not drive, rounds us up and we pile into Maggie's unostentatious Rover. As we leave the farm, we spy a man we take to be acting suspiciously standing by the next field. A mile or so down the road, the general feeling is that we should return.

As we re-enter the drive, the man is still standing by the field, looking at another man who is shooting at birds. 'Won't he think we're a bit odd, going out and coming back straight away?' asks Maggie. Undaunted, Beverley strides manfully over to the potential felon, hands on his hips, putting on his best jolly country manner.

He comes back to the car, appeased. 'Got the password,' he says, relieved and beaming. The two chaps have been given permission by a neighbouring farmer they all know to feel free in the field and take a few pot shots. 'Well, he *definitely* must have thought we were a bit odd,' concludes Maggie, finally.

Off we go again. The pub has an exceptional menu. There are fresh *moules*, scallops, skate, stuffed squid, Dover sole, the lot. Final proof that Maggie is feeling more human is that she admits to being hungry and, when the food comes, she digs in like a trencherman. Clearly it is work, the recurring nightmare of the next performance, that brings on the glooms, the moods, the incipient anorexia.

She asks Toby about Queen's Elm Square. It is being cleared out ready for redecoration. Maggie alleges that Chris hasn't dry-cleaned any of his clothes for several years. Toby stoutly defends his brother. Maggie says she wants a lot of big cardboard boxes and big black plastic bags. She is going up to London tomorrow to 'stay with Joan' and start Operation Clean-Out. And to see the dentist. And to have lunch with Robert Fox. She may not be doing much, but she means business.

Beverley has given up smoking, too, and has started to chew disconsolately on a tooth pick. Another good bottle of Chablis

is ordered, though Maggie is happy with mineral water. Jennifer offers to help out in London, but she has her own flat to
take care of, and she is about to leave London to make a
film in Prague. The table buzzes with domestic arrangements.
Beverley beams and picks up the tab.

Two hours later, driving me back to the station, Maggie
acknowledges for the first time in my hearing that I am writing
the book and thanks me for bothering, as though it had been
the most almighty drudgery and not really worth a year of
anyone's time. I explain that the task has been lightened by
the pleasure that all her friends and colleagues have taken in
talking about her.

Silence. 'I can't imagine what anyone would say. I wouldn't
say anything.'

She drives very fast and very securely. I suddenly remember
that she once berated Simon Callow for not driving. How
could he *not* drive, she wanted to know. Having a car was like
having an extra cupboard. Another place to hide. Just you and
the sky and the music. She is playing a soothing baroque motet
as we speed through the leafy lanes.

We arrive at the station. I say that I won't bother to send
her an invitation to the book launch.

'You never know.'

I kiss her gently on the cheek and take the train back to
London.

Finally, on 9 March 1993, we do have Lady Bracknell. *The
Importance of Being Earnest*, produced by Robert Fox,
directed by Nicholas Hytner and designed by Bob Crowley,
opens at the Aldwych Theatre in London. Quite by chance,
I find myself seated next to Beverley. As the lights dim, I
whisper: 'How is Maggie?' 'On the warpath,' he replies with a
stifled chuckle. The moment she enters I know what he means.
Lady Bracknell may have been lying in wait for Maggie for

years, but she is in no mood to be taken hostage. And she is about to terminate a five-year absence from the London stage with a magnificent thunderclap.

Having already stolen Edith Evans's proprietorial rights on Millamant and Mrs Sullen she sets about scattering to the winds her predecessor's hitherto unviolated claim on Lady Bracknell. Here is no haughty old dowager guarding a bank of magisterial put-downs, but a scheming whirlwind, body askance in dove-grey silk, flyaway hat and perfect coiffure, a figure of frightening elegance who is not to be tampered with. She combines powerhouse presence with a grim but glorious glamour and a blazing eye for the demands of etiquette. And she finds a fresh underbelly to the role in conveying a sense of the arriviste, of one whose right to assume authority on matters of social decorum is deeply suspect and defensively fanatical.

She inspects the young people like a beaky, agitated adjutant on parade, running her eye up and down the hapless Jack, her nephew Algernon's co-conspirator in romantic adventurism, with the alacrity of those zip-fasteners evoked in her disdain for Archer in *The Beaux' Stratagem*. But this is not one of Maggie's frantic, signalling performances; her body language is as tightly corseted as her physical frame. In Act One, she is a silver shark, bustled with fins; in the third act (how we missed her in the second!), she assumes a more dry-land, squirrely appearance, trading grey for brown, a colour more suitable for the country.

And the handbag? That Becher's Brook of a line is no more, for Maggie simply careers straight through it, staggering slightly on the sofa at the accumulation of news concerning Jack's foundling status. The portrayal is fired by the assault on her dignity and the energy with which she defends herself. In ticking off her list of maternal requirements, she is gradually outfoxed by unwanted information ('the line is immaterial' could kill at five paces), gathering laughs as she goes before exploding at the climactic prospect of her daughter marrying into a cloak-room and forming an alliance with a parcel. 'Parcel' is indeed a special delivery, hissed venomously through splayed lips.

Cecily's 'profeel' is applauded in an affected giveaway. For the carapace will crumble. On learning that Cecily has a large income, Dame Maggie turns on her exiting heel to shower the girl with compliments; more surprisingly, when the General's true name is discovered, this final deflation is answered with a weak, girlish admission that she knew what it was all along. It is the most dangerous and delicate moment in Hytner's otherwise mixed production. The amazing designs comprise a louche red and green clubland flat dominated by a stage-high portrait of Algernon; a monumental topiary peacock in the country garden shadowing a tilted model of the Georgian house and a view of five counties; and a creamy morning room, launched on its side like a skew-whiff Heartbreak House, which causes a few traffic jams in the blocking. With Maggie onstage, emphatic and witty angularity is for once superfluous in the design.

This may not be the all-time dream production but it certainly re-establishes Maggie in the forefront. With a vengeance. After the fascinating Bracknell ten years ago of her friend Judi Dench, Maggie restores the monstrous and the gorgonic to the role, while redefining its comedy in the speed and viperishness of her deadly technique. The reviews are ecstatic with one notable exception: Michael Billington in the *Guardian* finds the performance hyperactive, gross and mannered, with no sense of a strongly identified character. Which only goes to show that the critical debate induced by Maggie's high-wire approach to acting will never be conclusively resolved.

The film of *Sister Act* turns out to be much better than

Maggie feared, one of the biggest grossing 'feel good' movies of the summer in America and the winter in Britain and Europe. Maggie's vinegary Mother Superior is a wonderful foil to Whoopi Goldberg's ebullient nun, a disguised nightclub singer in Nevada called Dolores Wilson who has witnessed her married boyfriend (Harvey Keitel) wasting a hoodlum. The police need Dolores as a witness to nail the lover and his gang, and they guarantee protection if she hides out in a San Francisco convent. There, she transforms the choir into a hot-gospelling attraction, much to the initial horror of Maggie's Mother Superior ('I am a relic, and I have misplaced my tambourine,' she irately protests in one of their beautifully played head-on collisions). But Maggie is won round by the part the choir plays in the reanimation of the parish community, whose Irish Monsignor is played by her old friend Joseph Maher. The crooks eventually capture Dolores, and Maggie leads the salvation assault in the Reno casino, bleakly encouraging her squadron of singing nuns to 'try and blend in' as they dash among the blinking fruit machines.

If Maggie in *Sister Act* embodied qualities of English understatement in her expressions of wincing distaste and sour disapproval, she claimed her first major American role as of right in Richard Eyre's BBC film of *Suddenly Last Summer*. Katharine Hepburn, like Edith Evans, is one of the great iconic performers whom Maggie's career both follows and challenges. And Hepburn's over-the-top Mrs Venable in the Gore Vidal 1959 screenplay of *Suddenly* (directed by Maggie's adored Joseph Mankiewicz, who died in early 1993), a juddering compilation of roars and misgivings, is simply out-classed by Maggie's performance. She is stern, bewitching but recognisably human as a still beautiful bereaved mother in her pearls and elegant mauve silks. And, like her Lady Bracknell, this portrait is primarily one of self-justifying defensiveness, the source of its tragic power.

The new film faithfully follows the play's one-act structure and restricts the horror of what befell Mrs Venable's poet son Sebastian – eaten alive by young boys – to the lines, and to the brilliant performance of Natasha Richardson as the infatuated cousin who procured for him. The writing is poised on the disputable border of genuine poetry and gothic self-parody, but assumes a curious new metaphorical resonance in our AIDS-blighted age. Eyre and the *Importance* designer Bob Crowley create a stifling botanical environment in those same Shepperton Studios where Hepburn, Montgomery Clift and Elizabeth Taylor made their freer, more hysterical, version. The thankless Clift role of the prompting doctor who needs money for his research is well taken by Rob Lowe. The tensions finally erupt as Maggie rises in rage and lays about her with a stick, shouting at Lowe that he should cut the hideous story out of the sick girl's brain with nothing less than a full-frontal lobotomy.

It is strange to be reminded that this is Maggie's first American heroine. She not only finds the exact tone of Tennessee Williams's idiosyncratic music, revelling in the careful structure of the sentences just as she revels in the antithetical shape and coloration of Oscar Wilde's prose; she also brings a world of Southern gentility and style to bear on a reading that is as perfectly pitched as it is ornately expressed: 'I was actually the only one in his life. We were a famous couple. Sebastian and Violet are at the Ritz in Venice . . . Sebastian and Violet have taken a house for the season at Biarritz . . . We constructed our days. We would carve out each day of our lives like a piece of sculpture.'

Her son, she believes, was chaste. But instead of suggesting that the shattering of that illusion is a grotesque disaster, as did Hepburn, Maggie invests her playing with the tragic generality of a mother who has, not unreasonably, kept herself warm with the idealised abstraction of the human being she has produced and loved. Her niece offers an alternative biography of sordid sexuality and bleakness, and the whole tale is wrapped up in the consuming imagery of exotic insects, hatching sea-turtles and Venus flytraps. Eyre's production, starting with a slow, portentous dripping in the hothouse, screws the narrative tension so tight that the explosion is all the more terrifying and plausible.

Maggie's status has been confirmed by two more recent acts of recognition: a Fellowship from the British Film Institute and a lifetime achievement award from BAFTA. Exhausted by the filming of *Suddenly* in a swamp-hot studio, she was unable to attend the first ceremony. But at the BAFTA ceremony, a couple of weeks after she had opened in *The Importance of Being Earnest*, she acknowledged her ovation with words that touched on a freshly aroused public debate on sex and violence in the movies: 'If it's possible to be in films without taking your clothes off or killing people with machine-guns, I seem to have managed to do it.'

She is able to call on a deep reservoir of popular affection at such moments. She has direct access to the public through the style, veracity and wit of her acting. That is the rare privilege of a true star. At the Aldwych curtain calls, she seems to melt in the applause, and is revived, shedding Lady Bracknell's severe facial mask and becoming once again the young actress of radiance, beauty and merriment who first flitted across our stages and screens forty years ago. Maggie has delivered the Lady Bracknell she has long promised and we all, to a certain extent, expected: monstrous, withering, funny, snobbish, vulnerable, vocally tremendous and, of course, technically brilliant.

Select Bibliography

(Dates refer to London publication unless otherwise stated)

ANGIER, CAROLE, *Jean Rhys* (André Deutsch 1990)

BERGMAN, INGMAR, *The Magic Lantern* (Hamish Hamilton 1988)

BILLINGTON, MICHAEL, *Stoppard the Playwright* (Methuen 1987)

BROWN, JARED, *The Fabulous Lunts* (Atheneum, New York 1986)

BURTON, HAL (ed.), *Acting in the Sixties* (BBC 1970)

CALLOW, SIMON, *Charles Laughton: A Difficult Actor* (Methuen 1987)

CARPENTER, HUMPHREY, *OUDS: A Centenary History* (Oxford 1985)

DUNSTER, DAVID (ed.), *Edwin Lutyens* (Academy Editions 1986)

FINDLATER, RICHARD (ed.), *At the Royal Court* (Amber Lane Press 1981)

FINDLATER, RICHARD, *The Player Queens* (Weidenfeld & Nicolson 1976)

FORBES, BRYAN, *Ned's Girl: The Life of Edith Evans* (Elm Tree Books 1977)

FREEDLAND, MICHAEL, *Kenneth Williams* (Weidenfeld & Nicolson 1990)

GASKILL, WILLIAM, *A Sense of Direction* (Faber 1988)

HALLIWELL, LESLIE, *Halliwell's Filmgoer's and Video Viewer's Companion* (Paladin 1988)

HAMILTON, IAN, *In Search of J. D. Salinger* (Heinemann 1988)

HAYMAN, RONALD, *Playback 2* (Davis-Poynter 1973)

HIBBERT, CHRISTOPHER (ed.), *The Encyclopaedia of Oxford* (Macmillan 1988)

KAEL, PAULINE, *Hooked* (Marion Boyars 1990)

KERR, WALTER, *Journey to the Center of the Theater* (Knopf, New York 1979)

KNELMAN, MARTIN, *A Stratford Tempest* (McClelland and Stewart, Canada 1982)

LEVIN, BERNARD, *Enthusiasms* (Jonathan Cape 1983)

MCGILLIGAN, PATRICK, *George Cukor: a Double Life* (St Martin's Press, New York 1991)

MEYER, MICHAEL, *Not Prince Hamlet* (Secker & Warburg 1989)

MORLEY, SHERIDAN, *The Great Stage Stars* (Angus & Robertson 1986)

PATTERSON, TOM, AND GOULD, ALLAN, *First Stage: the Making of the Stratford Festival* (McClelland and Stewart, Canada 1987)

PAYN, GRAHAM, AND MORLEY, SHERIDAN (eds.), *The Noël Coward Diaries* (Weidenfeld & Nicolson 1982)

RAINE, KATHLEEN, *Farewell Happy Fields* (Hamish Hamilton 1973)

ROBERTS, PETER, *The Old Vic Story* (W. H. Allen 1976)

SHERRIN, NED, *Ned Sherrin's Book of Theatrical Anecdotes* (Virgin 1991)

SHERRIN, NED, *A Small Thing – Like an Earthquake* (Weidenfeld & Nicolson 1983)

SILLMAN, LEONARD, *Here Lies Leonard Sillman* (Citadel, New York 1959)

STACK, V. E. (ed.), *Oxford High School* (Abbey Press 1963)

SUSKIN, STEVEN, *Opening Night on Broadway* (Schirmer Books, New York 1990)

TYNAN, KENNETH (ed.), *Othello: the National Theatre Production* (Rupert Hart-Davis 1966)

TYNAN, KENNETH, *The Sound of Two Hands Clapping* (Jonathan Cape 1975)

WILLIAMS, KENNETH, *Just Williams* (Dent 1985)

Index